Basic ICD-9-CM Coding Exercises

Third Edition

Lou Ann Schraffenberger, MBA, RHIA, CCS, CCS-P, FAHIMA

AHIMA PRESS

This book includes ICD-9-CM changes announced in the CMS Hospital Inpatient Prospective Payment Systems Proposed Rules, as published in the May 4, 2010 *Federal Register* available online from http://www.access.gpo.gov/su_docs/fedreg/a100504c.html.

Any additional changes to these codes may be obtained at the CMS Web site or in the Final Rule for IPPS in the *Federal Register* when it is available (usually in August).

The final addendum providing complete information on changes to the diagnosis part of ICD-9-CM is posted on CDC's Web site at: http://www.cdc.gov/nchs/icd.htm or http://www.cdc.gov/nchs/icd/icd9cm_addenda_guidelines.htm.

ISBN 978-1-58426-280-0

AHIMA Product No. AC210511

Cynthia Douglas, Developmental Editor
Melanie Endicott, MBA/HCM, RHIA, CCS, CCS-P, Reviewer
Katie Greenock, Editorial and Production Coordinator
Karen Kostick, RHIT, CCS, CCS-P, Reviewer
Tanai S. Nelson, RHIT, CCS, CCS-P, Reviewer
Ashley Sullivan, Assistant Editor
Ken Zielske, Director of Publications

All information contained within this book, including Web sites and regulatory information, was current and valid as of the date of publication. However, Web page addresses and the information on them may change or disappear at any time and for any number of reasons. The user is encouraged to perform his or her own general Web searches to locate any site addresses listed here that are no longer valid.

All products mentioned in this book are either trademarks of the companies referenced in this book, registered trademarks of the companies referenced in this book, or neither.

American Health Information Management Association
233 North Michigan Avenue, 21st Floor
Chicago, Illinois 60601-5809

ahima.org

Contents

About the Author. v

From the Author vii

Preface. ix

Chapter 1   Introduction. 1

Chapter 2   Procedures. 5

Chapter 3   Coding for Prospective Payment:
             Principal Diagnosis, Additional Diagnoses and Procedures. 19

Chapter 4   Infections and Parasitic Diseases 27

Chapter 5   Neoplasms. 35

Chapter 6   Endocrine, Nutritional and Metabolic Diseases,
             and Immunity Disorders 43

Chapter 7   Diseases of the Blood and Blood-Forming Organs. 51

Chapter 8   Mental Disorders. 59

Chapter 9   Diseases of the Nervous System and Sense Organs 67

Chapter 10   Diseases of the Circulatory System. 75

Chapter 11   Diseases of the Respiratory System 83

Chapter 12   Diseases of the Digestive System 91

Chapter 13   Diseases of the Genitourinary System 101

Chapter 14   Complications of Pregnancy, Childbirth, and the Puerperium 109

Chapter 15   Diseases of the Skin and Subcutaneous Tissue 117

Chapter 16   Diseases of the Musculoskeletal System and Connective Tissue 125

Chapter 17   Congenital Anomalies and Certain Conditions Originating
in the Perinatal Period 133

Chapter 18   Symptoms, Signs, and Ill-Defined Conditions 141

Chapter 19   Injuries 149

Chapter 20   Poisoning, Adverse Effects, and Complications 159

Chapter 21   Supplementary Classifications—E Codes 167

Chapter 22   Late Effects 171

Chapter 23   Supplementary Classifications—V Codes 179

Answer Key for Coding Scenarios 187

About the Author

Lou Ann Schraffenberger, MBA, RHIA, CCS, CCS-P, FAHIMA, is employed by Advocate Health Care as the manager of clinical data in their Center for Health Information Services. Advocate Health Care is an integrated healthcare delivery system of ten hospitals and other healthcare entities, based in Oak Brook, Illinois. Her position is dedicated to systemwide health information management (HIM) and clinical data projects, clinical coding education, and coding compliance issues. Prior to her current position, Lou Ann served as director of hospital health record departments, director of the Professional Practice Division of the American Health Information Management Association (AHIMA), and a faculty member at the University of Illinois at Chicago. An experienced seminar leader, Lou Ann continues to serve as part-time faculty and a continuing education instructor in the health information technology and coding certificate program at Moraine Valley Community College. She has also contributed her knowledge and skills as a consultant for clinical coding projects with hospitals, ambulatory care facilities, physicians, and medical group practices. Lou Ann has been active in national, state, and local HIM associations. She has served as chair of the Society for Clinical Coding (2000). She is a former member of the AHIMA Council on Certification and former chair of the Certified Coding Specialist (CCS) Examination Construction Committee (1997–1999). In 1997, Lou Ann was awarded the first AHIMA Volunteer Award. Lou Ann received the Legacy Award from the AHIMA Foundation in 2008 in recognition of her significant contribution to the HIM knowledge base through her authorship of this publication and two other coding books published by AHIMA.

From the Author

The publication, *Clinical Coding Workout: Practice Exercises for Skill Development,* published by AHIMA, would be an excellent follow-up resource, providing beginning to advanced coding opportunities for the student. The case studies in the book help new coders become adept at sorting through detail to prioritize and code diagnoses, skills that will be essential in their coding profession.

Preface

Developing the coding skills necessary to be effective and efficient in coding takes practice. Such additional coding practice is what the student will find in *Basic ICD-9-CM Coding Exercises, Third Edition,* which contains coding exercises related to each chapter of the *Basic ICD-9-CM Coding* textbook, also written by Lou Ann Schraffenberger and published by the American Health Information Management Association. The objective in designing these exercises was to provide the student with further ICD-9-CM coding practice opportunities.

The exercises are short case studies and operative descriptions of real-life patient encounters in healthcare. The case studies provide the student with opportunities to code clinical information, rather than coding one- or two-line diagnostic and procedural statements. Depending on whether the case study describes an inpatient hospital admission or an outpatient visit, the student must determine the appropriate diagnoses and procedure codes to be assigned and in the appropriate sequence. For inpatient hospital admissions, the principal diagnosis is listed first; for outpatient encounters, the main reason for the visit is the first-listed diagnosis code. Students must also decide what information to include as secondary diagnoses according to the clinical information presented and to coding guidelines.

Not every case study will require a secondary diagnosis/diagnoses in addition to a principal or first-listed diagnosis. Not every case study will require a procedure code(s). This is true in real-life as well; the coder must develop strong problem-solving coding skills to correctly decide what clinical information should be coded.

The student must apply the ICD-9-CM Official Guidelines for Coding and Reporting to accurately assign diagnosis and procedure codes for these exercises. The guidelines may be found in the *Basic ICD-9-CM Coding* textbook or at the Web site for the National Center for Health Statistics, Classifications of Diseases, at http://www.cdc.gov/nchs/icd.htm.

The exercises must be used in conjunction with the 2011 edition of ICD-9-CM (code changes effective October 1, 2010). The exercises include the code updates listed in the CMS Hospital Inpatient Prospective Payment Systems Proposed Rules, May 4, 2010 *Federal Register,* available online from http://www.access.gpo.gov/su_docs/fedreg/a100504c.html. Every effort has been made to include the most current coding information.

Students (and teachers) will notice that these scenarios require the student to apply ICD-9-CM procedure codes to both inpatient and outpatient visits. In real-life coding, ICD-9-CM procedure codes are not required for outpatient visits under the Health Insurance Portability and Accountability Act (HIPAA) of 1996. The reason for including the coding of ICD-9-CM procedures for outpatient encounters is simply to allow additional practice and the development of skills.

As of October 2003, the HIPAA Transactions and Code Sets regulations stated that ICD-9-CM procedure codes are the adopted standard code set for hospital inpatient services. *Healthcare Common Procedure Coding System (HCPCS)* with *Current Procedural Terminology, Fourth Edition (CPT-4),* was designated as the code set for reporting procedures performed by physicians and for procedures performed in other healthcare settings, including hospital outpatient departments. Under HIPAA, hospitals may capture the ICD-9-CM procedure codes for internally tracking or monitoring hospital outpatient services; but when conducting standard transactions, hospitals must use HCPCS/CPT codes to report outpatient services at the service-line level and at the claim level on the uniform bill (UB-92) claim form.

Therefore, as the objective for designing the ICD-9-CM exercises was to provide maximum coding practice, students are requested to assign ICD-9-CM procedure codes to both inpatient and outpatient cases.

Comments from students and teachers using the *Basic ICD-9-CM Coding Exercises, Third Edition,* are most welcome. Please send your comments to the publisher (publications@ahima.org) or the author. The book will only improve with your input and feedback.

Chapter 1

Introduction

Basic ICD-9-CM Coding Exercises, Third Edition, is intended to provide additional coding exercises for the beginning coder. The exercises are organized in the same sequence as the *Basic ICD-9-CM Coding* textbook, with case studies for diseases and conditions within each body system. In addition, exercises are provided for the coding of neoplasms, infectious diseases, pregnancy-related conditions, and the like. Chapters are also provided for practicing the assignment of E codes and V codes.

Scenarios are written at an elementary level but provide the reader with the next step in coding proficiency. By moving from one-line diagnosis and procedure statements to short studies of patient care encounters, the student develops the decision-making skills necessary to determine the correct diagnoses or conditions to code, as well as the procedures to code and correct sequence.

Inpatient and Outpatient Encounters

Both inpatient and outpatient encounters are included in the workbook. Inpatient encounters are those in which the patient is formally admitted to the hospital and expected to stay at least overnight, even when the overnight stay is not mandatory. Inpatient settings include acute care short-term general hospitals, acute care long-term hospitals, psychiatric hospitals, and rehabilitation hospitals, as well as psychiatric and rehabilitation inpatient units in acute care hospitals, home health agencies, and nursing homes.

Outpatient visits include healthcare encounters in physician offices, clinics, neighborhood health centers, ambulatory surgery departments or facilities, emergency departments, observation units, therapy departments, and ancillary diagnosis testing departments or facilities. The outpatient facilities may be based in a hospital or within a provider-based office.

Applying the ICD-9-CM Official Guidelines

The coder must apply the ICD-9-CM Official Guidelines for Coding and Reporting to learn to assign and sequence diagnosis and procedure codes for both inpatient and outpatient health encounters.

For inpatient health encounters, the coder must apply Section II, Selection of Principal Diagnosis, and Section III, Reporting Additional Diagnoses, from the ICD-9-CM Official Guidelines for Coding and Reporting.

The definition for *principal diagnosis* is found in the Uniform Hospital Discharge Data Set (UHDDS). The principal diagnosis is the "condition established after study to be chiefly responsible for occasioning the admission of the patient to the hospital for care." In determining the principal diagnosis, the coding conventions in the ICD-9-CM, Volumes I and II, take precedence over these official coding guidelines. The coder must also consider Section I.A., Conventions for the ICD-9-CM, from the ICD-9-CM Official Guidelines for Coding and Reporting.

The UHDDS defines *other diagnoses* as "all conditions that coexist at the time of admission, that develop subsequently, or that affect the treatment received and/or the length of stay. Diagnoses that relate to an earlier episode which have no bearing on the current hospital stay are to be excluded." Other diagnoses also may be referred to as *additional diagnoses* or *secondary diagnoses*.

For reporting purposes, the definition for *other diagnoses* is interpreted as additional conditions that affect patient care in terms of requiring

1. Clinical evaluation

2. Therapeutic treatment

3. Diagnostic procedures

4. Extended length of hospital stay

5. Increased nursing care and/or monitoring

The importance of consistent, complete documentation in the medical record cannot be overemphasized. Without complete documentation, the application of all coding guidelines is a difficult, or even impossible, task.

For all outpatient encounters, the coder must follow the coding guidelines found in Section IV, Diagnostic Coding and Reporting Guidelines for Outpatient Services, from the ICD-9-CM Official Guidelines for Coding and Reporting.

In the outpatient setting, the term *first-listed diagnosis* is used in place of the inpatient terminology of *principal diagnosis*. The term *reason for encounter* may also be used to indicate the intent of what the first-listed diagnosis should be. The coding of outpatient records must also follow the ICD-9-CM coding conventions, including Section I, Conventions for the ICD-9-CM, including general and disease-specific guidelines from the ICD-9-CM Official Guidelines for Coding and Reporting.

The code for the diagnosis, condition, problem, or other reason for the encounter or visit that should be first-listed must also be recorded in the medical records as the reason chiefly responsible for the services provided.

The coder will list other/additional/secondary outpatient diagnosis codes for any coexisting conditions. The conditions to be coded as additional diagnoses must also require or affect patient care treatment or management. History conditions may be used as secondary codes if the historical condition or family history has an impact on the current care or influences treatment.

When a patient presents for outpatient surgery, the coder should assign the ICD-9-CM diagnosis code for the reason for the surgery as the first-listed diagnosis (reason for encounter), even when the surgery is not performed due to a contraindication. For ambulatory surgery, the coder should assign the diagnosis code for the condition for which the surgery was performed. If the postoperative diagnosis is known to be different from the preoperative diagnosis at the time the diagnosis is confirmed, the postoperative diagnosis is assigned as the diagnosis code as it is the most definitive.

When the patient is admitted for observation for a medical condition, the code for the medical condition is assigned as the first-listed diagnosis.

When a patient has had outpatient surgery and develops complications requiring admission to observation, the reason for the surgery should be coded as the first-listed diagnosis followed by codes for the complications as secondary diagnoses.

Principal and Other Significant Procedures

The principal procedure is the one that is performed for definitive treatment rather than for diagnostic or exploratory purposes, or is necessary to resolve a complication. When two procedures appear to meet this definition, the one most related to the principal diagnosis should be selected as the principal procedure. The principal procedure is usually reported as the first procedure.

After selecting the principal procedure, the coder should report other significant procedures. A significant procedure is one that

1. Is surgical in nature

2. Carries a procedural risk

3. Carries an anesthetic risk

4. Requires specialized training

Coding the Scenarios

Each scenario describes the inpatient or outpatient healthcare encounter. The terminology *principal diagnosis* or *first-listed diagnosis* is used as appropriate for each case. The coder must follow the ICD-9-CM coding conventions and policies to accurately and completely code each scenario.

ICD-9-CM, Volume III, procedure classification is used to code hospital inpatient procedures. Hospital inpatient procedures are consistently coded when performed in the range of procedure code categories 00–86. ICD-9-CM, Volume 3, chapter 16, Miscellaneous Diagnostic and Therapeutic Procedures (87–99), may be used selectively, and according to facility-specific coding policies, for inpatient procedure coding.

Hospital outpatient departments and other ambulatory facilities are not required to use ICD-9-CM, Volume III to report procedures performed. Instead, outpatient facilities are required to use CPT and/or HCPCS to report services and procedures.

Because the objective for designing this ICD-9-CM coding workbook is to provide further coding practice, ICD-9-CM, Volume III procedures will be assigned for outpatient scenarios simply to provide more opportunities in the procedural coding assignments. It is understood that ICD-9-CM Volume III codes will never be used in "real life" physician coding situations and may only be used for hospital-based outpatient procedural coding based on institutional coding policies.

If this book is being used in a program designed to prepare physician-based coding professionals, the coding of procedures with ICD-9-CM Volume III can be disregarded since the coder will be using CPT/HCPCS exclusively in the physician practice setting.

Conclusion

Beginning coders will find, as they complete the exercises, they have gained certainty in their mastery of the use of the ICD-9-CM codes. They will be able to apply new decision-making skills based on working knowledge to determine the processes to be coded and the correct sequence for both inpatient and outpatient encounters. The coder will also have applied the ICD-9-CM Official Guidelines for Coding and Reporting and, therefore, will understand how to assign and sequence diagnoses and procedure codes for both inpatient and outpatient settings.

In doing this, the student will understand the distinctions between related terms such as *principal diagnosis* and *first-listed diagnosis,* and *other diagnoses,* and such. The coder then moves on to reinforce principles for the coding of the principal procedures and other significant procedures. All of this will provide the coder with the knowledge base needed to make such decisions every day on the job.

Best wishes for a happy, productive coding career!

Chapter 2

Procedures

Coding Scenarios for *Basic ICD-9-CM Coding*

The following case studies are organized by chapter following the sequence of the *Basic ICD-9-CM Coding* textbook. The objective of the case studies is to provide the student with more detailed clinical information to code, rather than one- or two-line diagnostic and procedure statements. Depending on whether the case study describes an inpatient hospital admission or an outpatient visit, the student is asked to provide the necessary diagnosis and procedure codes in the appropriate sequence—with principal diagnosis code listed first for inpatient admissions and main reason for visit code listed first for outpatient visits.

1

A 65-year-old patient had experienced blood in his stools, or melena, for the past several days. Over the past 12 hours, the bleeding had increased, and the patient felt very weak and dizzy. He was admitted to the hospital by his physician. The patient was known to have diverticulosis, and his physician's first impression was that the bleeding was a result of diverticulitis. The patient was advised to have a colonoscopy and an upper GI endoscopy (EGD), to which he agreed. The colonoscopy was performed and the patient was found to have diverticulosis, but no inflammation was seen. However, an area of erosion, ulceration, and bleeding was seen in the duodenum during the EGD examination. A biopsy of the duodenum was taken during the EGD. The physician's diagnosis was acute duodenal ulceration with hemorrhage; diverticulosis of colon.

Principal Diagnosis: _____

Secondary Diagnoses: _____

Principal Procedure: _____

Secondary Procedures: _____

2

A 59-year-old woman was admitted to the hospital for a scheduled total abdominal hysterectomy (TAH) with a bilateral salpingo-oophorectomy (BSO). The patient also had type II diabetes, which was well controlled by medications. The patient first visited her gynecologist several months ago complaining of postmenopausal vaginal bleeding and abnormal vaginal discharge. An endometrial biopsy was taken in the office and was suggestive of uterine cancer. The TAH-BSO was performed, and the following postoperative diagnoses were recorded by the physician: Stage I endometrial adenocarcinoma (corpus uteri) and bilateral corpus luteum cysts of the ovaries, worse on the right side. The patient continued to receive oral diabetic medications while in the hospital.

Principal Diagnosis: _____

Secondary Diagnoses: _____

Principal Procedure: _____

Secondary Procedures: _____

3

A 65-year-old man was admitted to the hospital through the emergency department with progressive episodes of angina. He had been diagnosed with angina pectoris previously but had refused any diagnostic workup other than an EKG performed in the physician's office. He had been on medication for essential hypertension for more than 15 years. He never had a coronary diagnostic or surgery in the past. The workup in this hospital on this occasion did not find a myocardial infarction. Because of the severity of his symptoms, the patient was advised to have a cardiac catheterization and possible angioplasty to which he consented. The patient was taken to the cardiac catheterization laboratory where he had a left heart catheterization, left ventriculogram, and a coronary arteriography performed using the double catheter technique (Judkins). He was found to have severe three-vessel coronary artery disease. Because of the extent of the patient's disease, angioplasty was not performed, and the patient was transferred to another hospital for possible coronary artery bypass graft surgery.

Principal Diagnosis: _____

Secondary Diagnoses: _____

Principal Procedure: _____

Secondary Procedures: _____

4

HISTORY: The patient is a 38-year-old woman who gave birth 10 weeks ago. This past week she developed abdominal pain and symptoms of a urinary tract infection (UTI), and was admitted to the hospital. She was found to have a left ureteral stone and also small bilateral renal stones, as well as a UTI. It was recommended that the left collecting system be stented because of the hydronephrosis and the infection. Once the infection has been adequately treated, she will undergo ESWL of the ureteral stone.

OPERATIVE FINDINGS: The urethra is normal. The bladder is smooth and without stone or tumor. Orifices are in normal location bilaterally. Right retrograde pyelogram showed no evidence of persistent filling defect; however, there is dilation of the collecting system and very mild hydronephrosis on the right side. One the left side, there was a 1-cm stone over the left SI joint with ureteral dilatation both distal and proximal to this, but especially proximal, and also left hydronephrosis. No other obvious stones were identified.

DESCRIPTION OF PROCEDURE: The patient was taken to the operating area where she underwent IV sedation without problems. Following successful anesthesia, she was placed in the dorsal lithotomy position and prepped and draped in the sterile fashion. A #21 French cystoscopy with lens was introduced into the bladder and thorough inspection of the bladder and urethra was carried out. Following examination, bilateral retrograde pyelograms were obtained and reviewed. Next, under fluoroscopic control, a .035 guidewire was placed up to the left orifice into the renal pelvis. Over this, a 24 cm × 6 F double-J stent was passed without problems, so that the proximal end curled in the left renal pelvis, and the distal end curled in the bladder. The bladder was then evaluated and the cystoscope was withdrawn. The patient was awakened and transported to the recovery room in good condition, tolerating the procedure well. She will be kept on a course of Ampicillin 500 mg 4 times a day for the next week and will then return at that time for ESWL of her left ureteral stone.

Principal Diagnosis: _____

Secondary Diagnoses: _____

Principal Procedure: _____

Secondary Procedures: _____

5

HISTORY: A 55-year-old woman presented to the office with a right breast mass, approximately 2.0 cm × 2.0 cm, in the upper inner quadrant. There was no lymphadenopathy. She has a significant family history of breast cancer being diagnosed in her mother, maternal aunt, and older sister. Three days ago, a fine needle aspiration procedure demonstrated cells suspicious for malignancy. She was admitted to the hospital for definitive surgical treatment with a right breast lumpectomy.

OPERATIVE FINDINGS: A hard 2.0 × 2.0 cm mass in the upper inner quadrant of the right breast with no lymphadenopathy was confirmed. Pathology reports the specimen to be confirmed as carcinoma. The surgical margins on the mass excised were found to be normal. It is felt the entire lesion was removed.

DESCRIPTION OF PROCEDURE: After preoperative counseling, the patient was taken to the operating room and placed in a supine position on the table. The chest, right breast, and shoulder were prepped with Betadine scrub and paint and draped in the usual sterile fashion. The skin around the mass was anesthetized with 1% lidocaine solution. An elliptical incision was made, leaving a 1.5-cm margin around the mass in a circumferential fashion. The mass was sharply excised down to the pectoralis fascia, which was excised and sent with the specimen of the breast. The deep medial aspect of the specimen was marked with a long suture and the deep inferior margin marked with a short suture. The wound was left open until the pathologist returned the call that the margins were negative under frozen section. The wound was copiously irrigated. Hemostasis was achieved with Bovie cauterization and 3-0 Vicryl suture ligatures. The skin was closed with a running subcuticular 4-0 Vicryl, Benzoin, and steri-strips. A sterile dressing was applied. The patient was subsequently transferred to the recovery room in stable condition. She tolerated the procedure well and will be advised of the procedural findings when she is returned to her room.

Principal Diagnosis: _____

Secondary Diagnoses: _____

Principal Procedure: _____

Secondary Procedures: _____

6

HISTORY: This is a 28-year-old man with a recurrent, reducible right inguinal hernia noted on examination. He had undergone surgical repair of a right inguinal hernia 2 years ago, so he was familiar with the symptoms and called this surgeon's office for an appointment. The young man works in a construction job building scaffolds and, therefore, does heavy lifting on a daily basis. Otherwise, he is healthy, well-nourished, and well-built with no other surgical history and no other evident medical problems. Preoperative testing, including a chest x-ray, EKG, and usual laboratory work, were all within normal limits. He is admitted to the hospital for this procedure, as it is a recurrent hernia, and the procedure will require that he have highly limited mobility for the next 36–48 hours. He will also stay in the hospital for a short recovery period. He will then be placed on work-related disability and advised to avoid working for a minimum of 4 weeks.

OPERATIVE FINDINGS: A recurrent, reducible right inguinal hernia, direct and indirect, was found. There was no strangulation or gangrene. A right inguinal hernia repair (Bassini) with high ligation was performed.

DESCRIPTION OF PROCEDURE: The patient was taken to the operating room and placed in a supine position on the table. After satisfactory general anesthesia was administered, the right groin was prepped with Betadine scrub and paint and draped in the usual sterile fashion. The skin overlying the groin was incised through the external inguinal ring, exposing the spermatic cord. The cord was then mobilized and a Penrose drain passed around it at the level of the pubic tubercle. The cord was skeletonized proximally, revealing a very small indirect inguinal hernia sac. The sac was dissected away from the remainder of the cord structure, which was left free of injury. The sac was opened and found to contain no contents. There was also a direct inguinal hernia noted but no femoral hernia noted. The sac was twisted and ligated with 3-0 silk suture ligature. The remainder of the sac was amputated. A floor repair was performed as described by Bassini with interrupted 0 Ethibond sutures between the transversalis fascia and the shelving edge of the inguinal ligament. The internal inguinal ring was left to the size of the tip of an adult finger, and the initial suture medially was from the transversalis fascia into the aponeurosis over the pubic tubercle. Upon completion, hemostasis was adequate, and no relaxing incision was necessary. Spermatic cord was returned to the inguinal canal. The ilioinguinal nerve was blocked prior to this procedure and reblocked again with 0.5% Marcaine and epinephrine solution. The pubic tubercle, inguinal ligament, and subcutaneous tissue were also anesthetized with 0.5% Marcaine and epinephrine solution. The external oblique was then closed with running 3-0 Vicryl. The wound was copiously irrigated and the skin closed with skin clips. A sterile dressing was applied. Gentle traction was placed on the right testicle to fully return it to the scrotum. The patient was transferred to the recovery room in stable condition.

Principal Diagnosis: _____

Secondary Diagnoses: _____

Principal Procedure: _____

Secondary Procedures: _____

7

HISTORY: This is a 65-year-old man who is currently in the hospital under the care of his internal medicine physician for treatment of a duodenal ulcer, GERD, and an enlarged prostate with urinary retention. He has been seen by an urologist and has had a cystoscopic examination. He is medically under control at this time and will be ready for discharge in a day or so. He was referred to orthopedics for the complaint of severe left knee pain that is limiting mobility. He states he has had no particular trauma to the knee but has always felt the left knee to be his "bad knee." The patient wants a knee replacement because his 75-year-old brother had one in the past six months and is back to golfing twice a week. This patient cannot walk the nine holes on the golf course as he was able to do last year. X-ray examination of the left knee is not striking, with some arthritic changes noted but no major pathology suspected. The patient consented to an arthroscopic examination of the knee to determine what treatment can be recommended.

OPERATIVE FINDINGS: An arthroscopic debridement of the left patella was performed. The medial meniscus, lateral meniscus, and ACL were completely normal. Examination of the patellofemoral joints allowed appreciation of the magnitude of the problem with the patella. The entire surface of the patella was involved with chondromalacia with surfaces graded from 3 to mostly 4. He also has a significant degree of prepatellar bursitis of the left knee that likely is also contributing to his pain and stiffness. The pros and cons of a left knee arthroplasty will be discussed with the patient after he recovers from this procedure and determination of pain relief after this debridement is assessed.

DESRIPTION OF PROCEDURE: The patient was provided general endotracheal tube anesthesia and the left lower extremity was prepared and draped in the usual manner for arthroscopic surgery of the left knee. After insufflation of lidocaine and epinephrine, three standard portals, two medial and one lateral, were established in the usual manner. There was difficulty in evaluating the suprapatellar pouch as well as the patellofemoral joint initially because of the extensive chondromalacia and synovial reaction. Prepatellar bursitis was also present. The medial compartment was first able to be evaluated carefully and the medial meniscus was found to be completely normal to observation and to probing, as were the medial femoral condyle and medial tibial plateau. The ACL appeared to be intact. The lateral meniscus and lateral compartment were, in general, completely normal. In order to see the contents of the femoral-tibial joint some debridement of pedunculated synovial tissue was necessary. On returning to the patellofemoral joint, some debridement of synovial tissues was done as well as some of synovial plica material. At this point, the magnitude of the problem on the patella was evident. Essentially the entire surface of the patella was involved with chondromalacia. There was mostly grade-4 chondromalacia over more of the lateral facet but also on the medial facet with grade-3 chondromalacia. This involved a large portion of the main articular surface of the patella. At the conclusion of this procedure, instrumentation was removed, and sterile dressings applied. The patient was awakened and taken to the recovery room in stable condition.

Focusing on this surgical procedure and not the entire hospital stay, identify:

Principal Diagnosis: _____

Secondary Diagnoses: _____

Principal Procedure: _____

Secondary Procedures: _____

8

HISTORY: The patient is a 38-year-old male with a 2-month history of lower back pain radiating down the left leg. The patient reported that he had suffered a work-related injury while acting as a commercial driver and while assisting in the clean-up of the New Orleans hurricane disaster. Because of the severe pain, he was unable to work so he returned home. An MRI of the lumbar spine taken 2 weeks ago shows a large extruded disk herniation on the left side, L5-S1, causing severe nerve impingement. He has failed conservative treatment and is now indicated for nerve root decompression. He reports weakness in the left leg but denies any problems with bowel or bladder control. There is moderate tension in the lower back with flexion to 70 degrees and extension to 10 degrees secondary to lower back pain. He also complains of intermittent pain and numbness in his right hand and fingers that was evaluated during this preoperative episode, and he was diagnosed with right carpal tunnel syndrome. We will consider surgically correcting the carpal tunnel problem after he recovers from this procedure. His past surgical history is a left knee arthroscopy 12 years ago. He has no medical problems other than his back and the carpal tunnel syndrome in his right upper extremity. His preoperative diagnosis is acute left L5-S1 radiculopathy secondary to large L5-S1 disk herniation. He was admitted to the hospital for surgery.

OPERATIVE FINDINGS: The patient had a L5-S1 laminectomy and discectomy. The nerve root was resting freely at the conclusion of the procedures, and there was no dural injury.

DESCRIPTION OF PROCEDURE: After satisfactory induction of general anesthesia, AV boots were applied to both feet. The patient was turned to the prone position on a Kambin frame. Care was taken to make sure that pressure points were well padded. Once the position of the back was judged to be satisfactory, it was prepped and draped in the usual fashion. Epinephrine 1:500,000 solution was injected into the planned surgical incision site in the right lower back. Sharp dissection was carried down to the level of the fascia. The fascia was incised and subperiosteal dissection was carried out along the spinous processes down to the lamina and facet of each vertebral level. Deep retractors were then used to place a marker and intra-operative fluoroscopy confirmed the L5-S1 level. Once oriented to our level, the laminotomy was begun. The ligamentum flavum was débrided. A partial facetectomy of approximately 10% was carried out on the left side. This allowed identification of the nerve root. Upon retracting the nerve root, we could immediately identify extruded disc fragments. We were able to retrieve a moderate size fragment. Further inspection up behind the body of L5 produced a large extruded fragment. Exploration of the annular defect area identified only a tiny amount of loose material, all of which was retrieved. After multiple inspections, we were satisfied that all of the loose fragments of the disc had been removed. The nerve root was resting freely. Satisfactory hemostasis was achieved. There was no dural injury. A dry piece of Gelfoam was placed over the laminotomy defects. The fascial layer was closed with #1 Vicryl. The subcutaneous layer was closed with 2-0 Vicryl, and the skin was closed with 4-0 Monocryl. The patient was turned to the supine position on the hospital bed and awakened in the operating room. The patient was noted to have intact bilateral lower extremity motor function when asked to move both of his legs, which he could do. The patient was extubated in the operating room and taken to recovery in good condition.

Principal Diagnosis: _____

Secondary Diagnoses: _____

Principal Procedure: _____

Secondary Procedures: _____

9

HISTORY: The patient is an 11-year-old boy who was riding his bicycle yesterday in front of his home and fell. Because of severe wrist pain, he was seen in the emergency department. X-rays confirmed displaced right distal radius and ulna fracture. The emergency department physician placed the patient in a splint, and he has returned this morning to be admitted for follow-up care and treatment. He denies any head or neck injury or loss of consciousness. His mother witnessed the fall and confirms he did not appear to hit his head or suffer any other injury except for the right wrist.

OPERATIVE FINDINGS: Examination in the cast room finds both shoulders and elbows to be nontender. The right wrist has a deformity with some expected level of swelling. His fingers are moving, and he is neurovascularly intact. The skin is intact. Contralateral wrist is nontender. Fingertips are pink with good capillary refill. Lower extremities are nontender. X-ray films have been reviewed, which reveal fractures of both the distal radius and distal ulna with 100% displacement. Upon consent of the mother and the patient, closed reduction with fluoroscopy was attempted in the cast room, but his fracture was difficult to reduce without more significant sedation. The supporting splint was put back onto the right wrist, and he was taken, with consent, to the operating room for closed reduction and pinning. Upon completion of the procedure, final films visualized the fractures and the pins to be in good position.

DESCRIPTION OF PROCEDURE: The patient was taken to the operating room and placed supine on the table with all of his extremities adequately padded. The patient was given laryngeal mask anesthesia. The splint was removed from the right upper extremity, and a closed reduction was performed. The fractures were found to reduce. Fluoroscopy was used to view the fractures in multiplanar views. Given the nature of the fracture pattern, it was deemed appropriate to pin the radius to increase stability. Two K wires were then placed percutaneously under direct fluoroscopic guidance across the fracture site. The growth plate was avoided. The fracture and pins were then visualized in multiplanar fluoroscopy, and the fracture and pins were noted to be in good position. The pins were bent and cut. Final films were obtained. Sterile dressings followed by a sugar tong type of splint was then applied. The patient tolerated the procedure well, was awakened in the operating room, and was taken to recovery. There were no complications of this procedure.

Principal Diagnosis: _____

Secondary Diagnoses: _____

Principal Procedure: _____

Secondary Procedures: _____

10

HISTORY: This is a 72-year-old man who presented with a history of epigastric pain for several months. This lasts 3–4 hours each time, and has been occurring every 2–3 days. He has been nauseated, although there was no vomiting. He has had the urge to go to the bathroom for frequent bowel movements after meals. He has tried to avoid greasy food and has been placed on Nexium, but this only helped to some extent. An ultrasound was performed on the gallbladder, and gallstones were found. An upper GI x-ray showed mild esophageal motility problems with a hiatal hernia. He gets a screening PSA every year and has had a colonoscopy, which was normal. He consented to a laparoscopic cholecystectomy and was admitted to the hospital.

OPERATIVE FINDINGS: The laparoscopic examination revealed evidence of inflammation of a chronic nature of the gallbladder along with gallstones. There was also a nodule on the liver on the inferior surface on the right lateral aspect of the gallbladder fossa. The rest of the visualized viscera were unremarkable. After pathologic examination, the postoperative diagnoses are cholelithiasis with chronic cholecystitis with a bile duct adenoma.

DESCRIPTION OF PROCEDURE: The patient was prepared and draped in the usual fashion. An umbilical incision was made. A Veress needle was introduced with a sheath, and pneumoperitoneum was established with the usual precautions. Then an 11-mm port was placed. A laparoscope was introduced. Under direct vision, an operative port in the right upper quadrant and two 5-mm lateral ports were placed. A laparoscopic examination revealed evidence of inflammation of a chronic nature of the gallbladder with gallstones. There was also a nodule in the liver. The rest of the viscera visualized were normal. The cholecystectomy was done by gently grasping the fundus. Adhesions were taken down. The neck was then grasped. The Calot's Triangle was then exposed. The anatomy was carefully defined. The cystic duct and the cystic artery were traced up to the neck of the gallbladder. Herein it was secured with hemoclips, divided, and closed to the neck of the gallbladder. Then it was dissected off of the gallbladder bed and retrieved in an Endopouch and removed. Irrigation was carried out. Excellent hemostasis was ascertained. Following this, an evaluation of the nodule was carried out using a hook cautery. The surrounding borders of this nodule, in the right inferior surface of the lobe of the liver, were cauterized. Then a small wedge biopsy of this tissue was taken. The base was cauterized. This tissue was then sent, with the gallbladder tissue, for histopathological analysis. At this point, having ascertained good hemostasis, all the ports were removed under direct vision. The fascia was closed with 0 Vicryl sutures. Subcutaneous tissue was closed with 0 Vicryl sutures. The skin was closed with 4-0 Monocryl. Marcaine 0.5% with epinephrine was injected to achieve postoperative analgesia. The patient tolerated the procedure well and was stable at the end of the procedure and taken to recovery.

Principal Diagnosis: _____

Secondary Diagnoses: _____

Principal Procedure: _____

Secondary Procedures: _____

11

HISTORY: The patient is an 85-year-old woman who lives independently with her husband in her own home and has been treated for hypothyroidism, hypertension, and dyslipidemia in the past. Medications for these conditions were continued during her hospital stay. Early this morning she awoke with acute onset of right flank pain. Her husband called 911, and she was brought to the emergency department of this hospital. On examination she was found in be in acute pain with a palpable mass in her abdominal area. Radiologic examination found dilated loops of small bowel trapped between the abdominal wall and the ascending colon and cecum. She was taken emergently to the operating room for a suspected small bowel obstruction. The patient was found to have elevated blood pressure, which was proven to be due to her anxiety about her condition and impending surgery.

OPERATIVE FINDINGS: The procedure performed was an exploratory laparotomy and release of acute closed loop small-bowel obstruction due to adhesions by lysis of adhesions. Fortunately the bowel was viable and did not have to be resected.

DESCRIPTION OF PROCEDURE: After routine preparation, the patient was taken to the operating room. A midline incision was made through the scar of previous surgery, which was a hysterectomy. Supraumbilical extension of the scar was performed. Once the adhesions were taken down, the abdominal cavity was entered. One loop of small bowel was going through the defect created between the omentum and ascending colon and was trapped in that space. It was kind of congested but was not ischemic. The omental and intestinal adhesions were transected from the ascending colon. The small bowel obstruction was released. The entire small bowel was mobilized and explored from the ligament of Treitz all the way to the ileocecal valve. The wound was irrigated. Hemostasis was obtained after lysis of adhesions that released the acute small bowel obstruction. Lap count and instrument count were correct. Seprafilm adhesion barrier substance was placed in the peritoneal cavity prior to closure.

The fascia was closed with PDS loop. The skin was closed with skin stapler. A dressing was applied. The patient tolerated the procedure well under general anesthesia and was taken to the post-anesthesia recovery area in good condition.

Principal Diagnosis: _____

Secondary Diagnoses: _____

Principal Procedure: _____

Secondary Procedures: _____

12

HISTORY: The patient is a 65-year-old man with stage IV gastroesophageal junction carcinoma. He developed severe respiratory distress and was brought to the hospital emergency department and admitted. A large left pleural effusion was noted on CT scan and chest x-ray. His condition progressed to acute respiratory failure, and he required intubation and mechanical ventilation for 24 hours. A chest tube insertion was recommended to relieve the patient's respiratory failure caused by the pleural effusion, and the patient consented to the procedure.

DESCRIPTION OF PROCEDURE: The patient was in the supine position in the medical intensive care unit on propofol drip. His left anterior chest was prepped and draped. One percent plain Xylocaine was given, and a small incision was made. Using the hemostat, the chest cavity was entered and fluid was returned. Then, using the trocar, the chest tube was placed in the superior portion of the left upper lobe. There was approximately 1000 mL of fluid returned. The patient tolerated the procedure well, and the chest tube was sewn in place. A follow-up chest x-ray confirmed good positioning of the tube, and a decrease in the amount of pleural effusion was noted.

Principal Diagnosis: _____

Secondary Diagnoses: _____

Principal Procedure: _____

Secondary Procedures: _____

13

HISTORY: The patient is a 62-year-old female who was admitted to the hospital for scheduled surgery to treat her recently diagnosed carcinoma of the rectosigmoid colon. She had noticed a change in her bowel habits about 6–7 months ago but did not seek medical care until two weeks ago when she went to her primary care physician. The patient was immediately scheduled for a colonoscopy, and a 10-cm tumor was found and biopsied with carcinoma diagnosed. She also had an abdominal and pelvic CT scan as an outpatient that identified a tumor. She has a long history of angina and had a PTCA twice in the past 4 years in the right coronary artery. She was cleared for surgery by her cardiologist with the diagnoses of coronary artery disease with stable angina and hypercholesterolemia that continued to be managed with her usual medications while she was in the hospital. The patient was discharged home with home health services following an uneventful postoperative recovery. She has an appointment with her oncologist in 2 weeks to discuss the next treatment options.

OPERATIVE FINDINGS: During an anterior resection of the rectosigmoid colon, the patient was found to have a tumor that extended into the muscular wall but not through the muscular wall of the rectosigmiod colon. No tumor was found outside the rectosigmoid intestine. The pathologist identified the tumor as a primary infiltrating papillary adenocarcinoma of the colon, rectosigmoid junction clinically, that extended focally into the outer muscular wall, and there was no evidence of metastasis to pericolonic lymph nodes. The tumor staging was T2 N0 M0. The colon specimen was a sessile round lesion about 12 cm in length with the tumor measuring 3cm × 2.5 cm. The tumor was elevated about 0.8 cm above the surrounding mucosal surface.

DESCRIPTION OF PROCEDURE: The patient consented to an anterior resection of the sigmoid colon. Under endotracheal anesthesia, the abdomen was prepped and draped in the usual surgical manner. It was opened through a lower abdominal midline incision extending to the left of the umbilicus using a hot knife. Exploration of the abdominal cavity revealed a normal-feeling stomach. Both right and left lobes of the liver felt normal. The gallbladder felt normal. The large and small bowel felt normal. The aorta and iliac vessels had some atheromatous plaque. Both kidneys felt normal. The Bookwalter retractor was used. The sigmoid colon was freed from its attachment in the pelvic on the right and left side by sharp dissection. The ureters were both identified and avoided. The blood supply of the rectosigmoid area was serially clamped, divided, and tied with 2-3 Ethibond. The tumor was palpated just below the peritoneal reflection. The colon was freed below the peritoneal reflection. Again the blood supply was serially clamped, divided, and tied with 2-0 Ethibond. Proximally, a portion of the sigmoid colon mesentery was serially clamped, divided, and tied as well. Satinsky clamps were placed proximally and distally, and the colon and specimen were removed. An end-to-end anastomosis was performed in a single layer with interrupted 3-0 silks. The wound was inspected for bleeding, and it was dry. A Penrose drain was placed down near the anastomosis from the stab wound in the left lower quadrant. The first sponge and needle count was correct. The peritoneum was closed with continuous 2-0 Vicryl, fascia with interrupted 2-0 Ethibond, subcutaneous with Vicryl, and the skin with skin clips. The drain was sutured in place. All sponge and needle counts were correct. The patient tolerated the procedure well and left the operating room in satisfactory condition.

Principal Diagnosis: _____

Secondary Diagnoses: _____

Principal Procedure: _____

Secondary Procedures: _____

14

HISTORY: The patient is a 79-year-old retired woman in generally good health, who was brought to the emergency department with the complaint of pain in her right hip. The patient is on vacation, visiting Nashville from Iowa. She was on a bus trip to the Grand Ole Opry with a senior citizens' group. She fell in the parking lot walking back to the bus after the group stopped at a restaurant en route. She was able to be helped up and got back on the bus and rode on to Nashville. Someone got a wheelchair from the hotel where the group was staying, and she was able to be pushed around, including to the show at the Ryman Auditorium. After the show, she told her companion that she thought she should go to the emergency room because the hip was hurting more than earlier in the day. Radiographs in the ER revealed a subcapital impacted right hip fracture. Emergent orthopedic consultation was obtained, and the patient was admitted. The patient's physician in Iowa was contacted, and he provided her medical history including the type of medication she received for her essential hypertension, which was her only medical problem. The day after admission, the patient was taken to the operating room, where a 3-pin fixation utilizing cannulated screws to the right hip was performed without difficulty. A day after surgery, physical therapy was started and by discharge on day 5, the patient was able to ambulate with a walker. Her son and daughter came to Nashville with a rented motor home to transport the patient back to Iowa. Records and radiographic films were given to the patient so that her orthopedic surgeon at home could continue her care.

DESCRIPTION OF PROCEDURE: The patient was taken to the operating room, placed in the supine position on the fracture table. Once adequate anesthesia was obtained, the right hip girdle was sterilely prepped and draped. The hip was well aligned, and no traction was required. Image intensification was brought into appropriate position, and the AP and lateral projections were obtained. This showed the fracture to be well reduced on its own. A 3-cm incision was then made just distal to the greater trochanter and carried down to the level of the subcutaneous tissues. Small bleeders were cauterized along the way. Great care was taken to insure that no harm came to any significant neurovascular structures. The iliotibial band was identified, incised in line with its fibers, and gently retracted. Access was gained to the lateral femoral cortex. A guide pin was placed without difficulty into the femoral head and neck. AP and lateral projections revealed adequate guide pin placement. Then an appropriately sized 16-mm thread 7.0 cannulated screw was placed over the guide pin. Image intensification revealed adequate screw placement. Two additional screws were then passed in a parallel fashion into the inferior and posterior portion of the femoral head and neck. Once the 3-pin fixation was completed, AP and lateral projections revealed adequate fracture stabilization and hardware placement. The wound was irrigated with copious amounts of normal saline solution. The iliotibial band was reapproximated with 0-Vicryl suture in an interrupted fashion. Subcutaneous tissues were closed with 2-0 Vicryl sutures, the skin was closed with clips, and a sterile dressing was applied. The patient was taken to the Recovery Room by the anesthesiologist and nursing staff in stable condition.

Principal Diagnosis: _____

Secondary Diagnoses: _____

Principal Procedure: _____

Secondary Procedures: _____

15

HISTORY: The patient is a 50-year-old female who was transferred to this academic medical center from a community hospital after she was admitted there for a coronary angiogram. The angiogram findings were noted with an ejection fraction of 30–35% with global dyskinesia. The echocardiogram revealed severe aortic valve stenosis and moderate mitral valve regurgitation. The patient is also known to have hypertensive kidney disease with end-stage kidney disease and requires dialysis. She also has anemia of chronic disease and dyslipidemia. The patient also has a history of hepatitis C. Because the aortic stenosis and mitral regurgitation has caused significant chronic diastolic heart failure and congestive heart failure, the patient has agreed to open heart surgery. The procedures performed are aortic valve replacement with 19-mm tissue valve, mitral valve annuloplasty with 3-mm annuloplasty ring, left radial artery cutdown for arterial line insertion, Swan-Ganz catheter insertion, and cardiopulmonary bypass.

DESCRIPTION OF PROCEDURE: After detailed and informed consent was signed, the patient was brought to the operating room and placed supine on the operating table. General anesthesia was initiated and endotracheal intubation performed. Left radial artery cutdown was performed. She was prepped and draped in the usual sterile fashion. A Swan-Ganz catheter was placed via the left subclavian vein. A sternotomy was performed. The patient was heparinized. A standard cannulation was performed with arterial cannula in the ascending aorta and a single dual-stage venous cannula via the right atrial appendage. Antegrade cardioplegia catheter was inserted. Aortic cross clamp was applied, she was placed on the bypass pump, and the heart arrested. The aorta was opened. The patient had a calcified tricuspid valve. The leaflets were excised and passed off the field. We then opened the left atrium. The echo had shown a central jet. The mitral valve sized to a 30-mm ring, and a 30-mm CG annuloplasty ring was sewn in place. The area was closed with running 4-0 Prolene. We then sized the aorta (valve) annulus to 19 mm and a Magna tissue graft valve was sewn in with interrupted simple sutures. Once the valve was in, the aortotomy was closed with running 2 layers of 4-0 Prolene. De-airing was performed through this aortotomy. The aortic cross clamp was removed. Once the patient was warmed, ventricular pacing wires were placed. Ventilation was begun and the patient was weaned from bypass. Protamine was administered. All cannulae were removed and hemostasis ensured. Two 32-French chest tubes were placed. The sternum was closed with four figure-of-8 sternal wires, and the soft tissue was closed in 3 layers. The patient was taken to the adult cardiovascular intensive care unit in stable condition.

Principal Diagnosis: _____

Secondary Diagnoses: _____

Principal Procedure: _____

Secondary Procedures: _____

Chapter 3

Coding for Prospective Payment: Principal Diagnosis, Additional Diagnoses and Procedures

Coding Scenarios for *Basic ICD-9-CM Coding*

The following case studies are organized by chapter following the sequence of the *Basic ICD-9-CM Coding* textbook. The objective of the case studies is to provide the student with more detailed clinical information to code, rather than one- or two-line diagnostic and procedure statements. Depending on whether the case study describes an inpatient hospital admission or an outpatient visit, the student is asked to provide the necessary diagnosis and procedure codes in the appropriate sequence—with principal diagnosis code listed first for inpatient admissions and main reason for visit code listed first for outpatient visits.

1

A 78-year-old man was admitted through the emergency department with severe heart failure after complaining of fatigue and increasing difficulty in breathing. He also had Type II diabetes mellitus that had been controlled by oral medications. During his stay, he was given insulin to control his blood sugar during this severe illness. He also had hypertension, which was monitored and treated with oral medications. The physician described the type of heart failure this patient has as "acute on chronic systolic heart failure."

Principal Diagnosis: _____

Secondary Diagnoses: _____

Principal Procedure: _____

Secondary Procedures: _____

2

A 52-year-old man, a former professional athlete, was admitted to the hospital for hip replacement surgery to treat localized osteoarthritis that involved both hips. His left hip is considerably worse than his right hip. Otherwise, the patient is in good health. His past medical history included pneumonia 3 years ago and a hernia repair at age 35 years. A successful total hip replacement was performed using a ceramic-on-ceramic hip replacement bearing surface prosthesis. The patient was discharged 3 days later to receive physical therapy at home. He will be scheduled for the right hip replacement in 6 to 8 months.

Principal Diagnosis: _____

Secondary Diagnoses: _____

Principal Procedure: _____

Secondary Procedures: _____

3

A 20-year-old college student was brought to the emergency department complaining of a sudden onset headache, fever, and stiffness with pain in the neck. He had been treated in the college health service center for an ear infection in the past week. After admission, the patient also complained of chest pain, fatigue, cough, and nausea. A lumbar puncture was performed and the findings were positive for meningitis. A chest x-ray revealed pneumonia. Sputum and spinal fluid cultures grew the pneumococcus organism (Streptococcus pneumoniae.) The physical examination also confirmed the presence of acute otitis media. The patient was treated with intravenous antibiotics for the infections. The discharge diagnoses written by the physician were pneumococcal meningitis with pneumococcal pneumonia and acute suppurative otitis media.

Principal Diagnosis: _____

Secondary Diagnoses: _____

Principal Procedure: _____

Secondary Procedures: _____

4

A 60-year-old male patient was admitted to the hospital with stable angina, which was continued under treatment. He underwent a combined right and left heart cardiac catheterization with coronary angiography, Judkins technique, and was determined to have significant atherosclerotic heart disease. Triple coronary artery bypass surgery was recommended for the 80 to 90% occlusion found in three native coronary vessels. The patient was also treated for Type II diabetes that has been well controlled. With counseling and upon consent, the patient was scheduled for open heart surgery. A triple coronary artery bypass graft, using saphenous veins from the leg, was performed on the left anterior descending, the circumflex, and the diagonal arteries. This was done using extracorporeal circulation.

Principal Diagnosis: _____

Secondary Diagnoses: _____

Principal Procedure: _____

Secondary Procedures: _____

5

A 75-year-old woman was admitted to the hospital 4 weeks ago for treatment of a fractured left wrist she suffered as the result of a fall. At that time, the patient underwent a closed reduction with application of an external fixator device. The patient is now admitted for an open reduction and bone grafting as part of her traumatic fracture aftercare. She was found to have severe bone loss as a result of senile osteoporosis, and the physician fears the fracture area will collapse at the time the external fixator is removed. She was taken to surgery to remove the external fixator device with an open reduction of the distal radius with bone grafting to the radius performed. Human bone tissue from a bone bank was used. The patient was placed in a well padded secure wrist splint.

Principal Diagnosis: _____

Secondary Diagnoses: _____

Principal Procedure: _____

Secondary Procedures: _____

6

A 5-year-old girl was admitted for dehydration due to gastroenteritis. The patient had been seen in the pediatrician's office and was treated for the gastroenteritis, but the patient's family brought her to the emergency department when she became increasingly lethargic and weak. Intravenous fluids were administered for rehydration, and the patient was admitted for treatment of the dehydration. During the 2-day hospital stay, the patient's gastroenteritis was also treated, but the focus of her treatment was to correct her dehydrated status. The pediatrician noted that the patient would not have been admitted for treatment of the noninfectious gastroenteritis alone.

Principal Diagnosis: _____

Secondary Diagnoses: _____

Principal Procedure: _____

Secondary Procedures: _____

7

A 59-year-old man was brought to the emergency department by a fire department ambulance with his family, who reported that he was found unconscious on his front porch. The patient was admitted. The family and later the patient confirmed that the man suffered from chronic continuous alcoholism. The diagnostic work also found evidence of alcoholic liver cirrhosis. The immediate concern was the life-threatening hepatic encephalopathy, which required intensive treatment. The physician was unable to determine what triggered the encephalopathy and possible infection, but it was suspected that a recent heavy dose of alcohol consumption was probably the cause. The liver cirrhosis was evaluated and treated but will remain a continuing problem for the patient. He recovered from his extreme condition, however, and was able to be discharged. He was strongly advised to stop drinking, and he agreed to return to Alcoholics Anonymous meetings, as he realized the seriousness of his alcoholism.

Principal Diagnosis: _____

Secondary Diagnoses: _____

Principal Procedure: _____

Secondary Procedures: _____

8

This 70-year-old woman was brought to the emergency department by her family because of right-sided temporary blindness that lasted only a few minutes on one day but then occurred two more times on different days. The patient was admitted with a diagnosis of transient monocular blindness. The physician described her condition as a unilateral temporary blindness, also known as amaurosis fugax. After study, the physician documented that the underlying cause of the amaurosis fugax was carotid artery stenosis. As documented in the record, the physician explained to the patient that transient ischemia resulting from carotid artery disease affects the optic nerve and the retina and causes blindness. This may be seen as a warning of internal carotid disease. Carotid arteriography confirmed the presence of carotid artery stenosis as well. The patient consented to carotid endarterectomy and was discharged in good condition.

Principal Diagnosis: _____

Secondary Diagnoses: _____

Principal Procedure: _____

Secondary Procedures: _____

9

The patient was a 55-year-old man who was admitted to the hospital by his private physician after vomiting bright red blood during a visit in the office the same day. A consultation with a gastroenterologist was requested. After radiological studies, it was determined that the patient had an acute duodenal ulcer that was hemorrhaging. The patient consented to an upper gastrointestinal endoscopy. During the esophagogastroduodenoscopy, the physician located several bleeding points in the duodenum and proceeded to control the bleeding through the endoscope. It was also noted that the patient had a sliding hiatal hernia. The patient recovered from the procedure well, suffered no further episodes of vomiting or bleeding, and was discharged with medications. Follow-up appointments with his physicians were scheduled.

Principal Diagnosis: _____

Secondary Diagnoses: _____

Principal Procedure: _____

Secondary Procedures: _____

10

A 40-year-old man was brought to the emergency department by a fire department ambulance that was called by police to a building where suspected drug sales and use were occurring. The patient was found unresponsive on the floor in the apartment where other individuals were arrested for solicitation and possession of narcotics, including cocaine, crack, and heroin. The patient was later identified by his sister and known to be a chronic drug addict. Upon admission to the emergency department, the patient was found to be in acute respiratory failure. He required immediate intubation and was placed on continuous mechanical ventilation and admitted to ICU. The drug toxicology screening test later returned the finding of a high level of cocaine, known to be a central nervous system stimulant. The patient's respiratory function continued to worsen. He developed acute renal failure and became unresponsive to treatment. The patient expired within 48 hours of admission. The physician's final diagnosis was "Acute respiratory failure as a result of a crack overdose."

Principal Diagnosis: _____

Secondary Diagnoses: _____

Principal Procedure: _____

Secondary Procedures: _____

11

The patient is a 60-year-old woman who came to the emergency room with many medical problems. She complained of rectal pain, diarrhea, swelling of her face, especially around her eyes, weakness, and fatigue. Given the variety of her problems and her extensive medical history, the patient was admitted to the hospital with the admitting diagnosis of "multiple medical problems."

The patient is known to have multiple malignancies. She has carcinoma of the kidney with metastasis to the intra-abdominal lymph nodes, non-small-cell carcinoma of the lung with metastasis to the mediastinum, and a past history of carcinoma of the anal canal. She also has hypertension and hyperthyroidism that was treated. She has had diarrhea for 2 days and was found to be dehydrated. She has been at home receiving antibiotic therapy through a PICC line for a staph aureus septicemia infection from an implanted chemotherapy port that was removed. She has significant swelling of her face and neck with prominent periorbital swelling. Upon further investigation, it was thought that she actually had angioneurotic edema, which is the result of an allergy—probably to one of the many medications she is currently receiving—as well as cellulitis of the face and orbital areas. She received her ongoing antibiotic therapy for the septicemia, her chemotherapy, intravenous therapy for her dehydration, topical treatments for the anal ulcer, and medications for the diarrhea, hypertension, and hyperthyroidism. Repeat CT and MRI scans were taken to examine the progression of her renal and pulmonary malignancies and metastases. The patient was relieved of some of her distressing symptoms and allowed to go home to continue receiving antibiotic therapy through her PICC line. The patient inquired about hospice care and was given information but decided she was not interested at this time. Home health nurses and infusion nurses will follow the patient at home.

Principal Diagnosis: _____

Secondary Diagnoses: _____

Principal Procedure: _____

Secondary Procedures: _____

12

A 75-year-old male was admitted to the hospital because of refractory temperature elevation, probable urinary sepsis that did not respond to outpatient antibiotics. He became more acutely ill the day before admission. He lives alone but was coherent enough to call a neighbor to ask for help. His fever was 104.5 at home the day of admission. He had been on Ciprofloxacin for approximately 12 hours prior to admission with no change in his fever. He has a history of urinary tract infections and was hospitalized 6 months ago for life-threatening septic shock. He is known to have an enlarged prostate with lower urinary tract symptoms. His only other medical problem is hypertension, which is treated with medications that continued in the hospital. A consultation with a urologist resulted in a nonsurgical workup. After appropriate cultures were drawn, he was started on IV antibiotics and vigorous IV hydration. His blood cultures were returned as negative. His urine culture demonstrated large amounts of a mixed growth that was suggestive of a possible contaminant. This was not unexpected, with the source of his infection considered to be his prostate. He responded dramatically to the IV antibiotics, but it took several days before he became close to afebrile. After 4 days in the hospital he was well enough to be taken off all IV support and was transferred to a skilled (swing) bed for 2 more days of observation on oral antibiotics to be sure it is safe to discharge him to home care. His discharge diagnoses were urinary sepsis/UTI due to chronic prostatitis with possible acute prostatitis, BPH, hypertension, history of UTIs. He will have a cystoscopy performed as an outpatient within the next month.

Principal Diagnosis: _____

Secondary Diagnoses: _____

Principal Procedure: _____

Secondary Procedures: _____

13

The patient was transferred to this hospital from another hospital's emergency department because his HMO physician is on staff at this hospital. The patient is a 42-year-old male with end-stage renal disease due to chronic glomerulonephritis. He has been dialyzed through an arteriovenous (AV) fistula in his left arm for 2 years, most recently 2 days ago. His kidney disease is the result of his long-standing hypertension. When he went for his dialysis treatment this morning it was noted that the access was clotted, and he was taken to an emergency room and then transferred to this hospital. Because of his urgent need for dialysis, a central venous (Quinton) catheter was placed in the left internal jugular vein, and dialysis was accomplished. He was placed on antibiotics and taken to surgery on day 3 for an arteriotomy of the right AV fistula and thrombectomy of the graft. Findings were that of an obstructive arterial graft with obstructed outflow and inflow, and the thrombo-embolus was noted. The AV graft did not have to be revised, only opened, and a thrombectomy performed. The patient had no complications from the procedure or during his 6-day hospital stay. The Quinton catheter that was used for his dialysis access while in the hospital was left in place for the doctor at the renal dialysis center to evaluate at his next dialysis appointment to determine whether it can be removed and whether the AV fistula will be available for access for dialysis. His discharge diagnoses were written by the physician as (1) end-stage renal disease, (2) chronic glomerulonephritis, (3) hypertension, (4) clotted obstructive AV fistula graft. The procedures performed were dialysis, insertion of the left internal jugular vein catheter and arteriotomy of the right AV fistula with thrombectomy.

Principal Diagnosis: _____

Secondary Diagnoses: _____

Principal Procedure: _____

Secondary Procedures: _____

14

An 80-year-old man who has been a long-term nursing home resident with chronic obstructive pulmonary disease was admitted to the hospital by his primary care physician with shortness of breath, elevated white blood count, and bibasilar infiltrates. A pulmonary disease consultant agreed with the attending physician that the patient had aspiration pneumonia and acute respiratory failure, both present on admission. In addition, the pulmonologist describes the man's COPD as obstructive chronic bronchitis with exacerbation. Intravenous antibiotics were administered with oxygen therapy also provided. Fortunately, appropriate treatment was able to control the conditions quickly, and the patient was taken to a skilled nursing facility for extended recovery from the pneumonia and respiratory failure. Given the fact that the patient had symptoms of three conditions (chronic lung disease, pneumonia, and respiratory failure) all present on admission, and any could have been the reason after study for the admission to the hospital, the coder asked the attending physician what was the principal diagnosis determined by the circumstances of admission, the diagnostic workup, and/or therapy provided. The physician chose the aspiration pneumonia as this man's principal diagnosis, as it was one of the main reasons for the admission and got the most treatment while the patient was in the hospital. According to the doctor, the respiratory failure was suspected to have resulted from either the pneumonia or the worsening chronic lung disease affected by the pneumonia. But in this patient, the respiratory failure was quickly managed and did not require ventilation.

Principal Diagnosis: _____

Secondary Diagnoses: _____

Principal Procedure: _____

Secondary Procedures: _____

15

The patient is a 40-year-old female who is admitted for prophylactic robotic-assisted laparoscopic total abdominal hysterectomy and bilateral laparoscopic salpingo-oophorectomy. She is having this elective removal of her uterus, tubes, and ovaries because she has a strong history of ovarian cancer in her family, including her grandmother, aunt, sister, and cousin. The surgery was performed without complications, and the patient had an uneventful postoperative period. After surgery, the gynecologic oncologist who performed the surgery informed the patient that a malignancy, Stage 1 ovarian carcinoma, was found in the right ovary in a very minute tumor. The doctor was encouraging that the patient's decision to have this surgery was the right decision. The patient was discharged for recovery at home with the assistance of a home health agency and will return to her oncologist office in two weeks to discuss further treatment.

Principal Diagnosis: _____

Secondary Diagnoses: _____

Principal Procedure: _____

Secondary Procedures: _____

Chapter 4

Infections and Parasitic Diseases

Coding Scenarios for *Basic ICD-9-CM Coding*

The following case studies are organized by chapter following the sequence of the *Basic ICD-9-CM Coding* textbook. The objective of the case studies is to provide the student with more detailed clinical information to code, rather than one- or two-line diagnostic and procedure statements. Depending on whether the case study describes an inpatient hospital admission or an outpatient visit, the student is asked to provide the necessary diagnosis and procedure codes in the appropriate sequence—with principal diagnosis code listed first for inpatient admissions and main reason for visit code listed first for outpatient visits.

1

A 22-year-old woman presented to the Family Practice Clinic after being told she should see her physician because her partner had recently been treated for nongonococcal urethritis. The woman did not have any complaints other than some vague pelvic discomfort and vaginal discharge that she did not consider serious. A physical examination, pelvic examination, and Pap smear were performed. Based on her history and physical findings, the patient was diagnosed with acute chlamydial cervicitis and given a prescription for 2 weeks of antibiotic oral medications and an appointment for a follow-up examination in 3 weeks.

First-Listed Diagnosis: _____

Secondary Diagnoses: _____

First-Listed Procedure: _____

Secondary Procedures: _____

2

A male patient, known to have AIDS, was admitted with a fever, shortness of breath, and a dry cough. The symptoms had been increasing in severity over the past several days. A chest x-ray showed extensive pulmonary infiltrates. A sputum culture was obtained, and the diagnosis of pneumocystic pneumonia was made based on the microscopic examination. The patient was told that his pneumonia was a result of having AIDS. During his hospital stay, he developed oral candidiasis, which was treated along with the pneumonia with a combination of medications administered intravenously and orally. The patient was discharged, with an arrangement to have follow-up care by a home health care agency.

Principal Diagnosis: _____

Secondary Diagnoses: _____

Principal Procedure: _____

Secondary Procedures: _____

3

A 40-year-old man with known chronic viral hepatitis resulting from hepatitis B is seen in the outpatient infectious disease clinic to be evaluated for therapy. The patient also has cirrhosis of the liver with suspected early stages of liver failure. This continues to be monitored. The patient is a known heroin addict in remission and faithfully has been taking methadone on a long-term basis through a program at this university medical center. All of these factors were considered when a combination of antiviral agent interferon-alpha plus lamivudine treatment was chosen and will be initiated at his next visit, scheduled in 1 week.

First-Listed Diagnosis: _____

Secondary Diagnoses: _____

First-Listed Procedure: _____

Secondary Procedures: _____

4

A 70-year-old woman who lived alone was found in her bed semi-conscious during a well-being check. She was able to tell her first-responders that she had been sick for a week with a fast heart beat, fever, chills, and difficulty breathing. She had been in bed for 3 days and was unable to get out of bed to answer the phone or the door. When she was taken to the emergency department, her vital signs were markedly abnormal with a fever of over 39 degrees C, a heart rate of 100, and a respiratory rate of 22/min. She was admitted to the ICU, with an admitting diagnosis of "sepsis" and was treated with antibiotics administered intravenously. Within 1 day of admission, the infectious disease physician described her condition as severe sepsis with resulting respiratory failure. Despite aggressive measures, the patient required endotracheal intubation and mechanical ventilation for 36 hours to treat acute respiratory failure. The physicians sought to identify the underlying source of infection as well as to provide hemodynamic and respiratory support and were successful in avoiding septic shock in this patient. The patient's physician provided the diagnoses of severe gram negative sepsis with acute respiratory failure.

Principal Diagnosis: _____

Secondary Diagnoses: _____

Principal Procedure: _____

Secondary Procedures: _____

5

A 60-year-old woman came to her primary care physician's office complaining of the abrupt onset of a fiery-red swelling of her face. The physician's physical examination found that the swelling covered nearly all of the right side of the woman's face with well demarcated raised borders. Her face was erythematous and edematous on the right side and the patient had a slightly elevated temperature. The patient stated that her face felt hot but only described feeling mildly ill. An infectious disease physician's office was next door to this physician and he came to see this patient, as her primary care physician had never seen this type of facial swelling. The infectious disease physician recognized the condition immediately as a superficial dermal and subcutaneous infection, usually caused by group A beta-hemolytic Streptococcus. He called the condition "acute erysipelas cellulitis" or "acute facial erysipelas" and advised immediate hospital admission for intravenous antibiotics. The patient was transferred to the hospital by her family in a private car.

First-Listed Diagnosis: _____

Secondary Diagnoses: _____

First-Listed Procedure: _____

Secondary Procedures: _____

6

An 18-year-old woman, who attends a state university about 90 miles away from home, is brought to her family physician's office after her parents brought her home because of a mumps epidemic at the college. During the office visit, the patient complained of fever, malaise, myalgia, and anorexia. She also had an earache and, due to the swelling of her jaw, reported that it was difficult to chew and swallow. A physical examination found the classic findings of mumps. Both sides of the woman's face were swollen consistent with bilateral acute parotitis. Given her recent exposure to other students diagnosed with mumps, the family physician concluded that the patient had mumps but could not find evidence of any complications in other body systems. The patient was sent home and was advised to avoid contact with people outside her family. The treatment included analgesics and warm compresses to the parotid area to relieve swelling and reduce symptoms. No medications are known to be effective in treating this viral infection.

First-Listed Diagnosis: _____

Secondary Diagnoses: _____

First-Listed Procedure: _____

Secondary Procedures: _____

7

A 20-year-old student came to the college health service center at this state university with complaints of urethral discharge, frequent urination, blood in the urine, and a stinging sensation during urination. The man, who admitted to several sexual partners, stated that these symptoms had become obvious in the past week. A physical examination confirmed the presence of a urethral discharge and swollen glands in the groin region. A urinalysis and urine culture was ordered. The patient noted that his symptoms were similar to a previous episode when he was told he had an acute gonococcal infection. An oral antibiotic was prescribed and the patient was advised to stop all sexual activity until the treatment was completed. The patient was given an appointment to return in 14 days. The college health service physician wrote acute gonococcal urethritis and acute gonococcal cystitis on the outpatient encounter form.

First-Listed Diagnosis: _____

Secondary Diagnoses: _____

First-Listed Procedure: _____

Secondary Procedures: _____

8

A 50-year-old Filipino man came to his primary care physician's office with the following complaints: coughing, chest pain, shortness of breath, fatigue, fever, sweating at night, and a poor appetite. He recently returned from a 1-month vacation in the Philippines where one of the relatives he visited was recently diagnosed with pulmonary tuberculosis. The patient, who works as an accountant in a hospital, previously had tuberculin skin tests that were negative. The physician ordered a chest x-ray and a tuberculin skin test was administered. Sputum was obtained and submitted for culture. The physician made the diagnosis of pulmonary tuberculosis based on the patient's symptoms and recent exposure to the disease. The patient was given a prescription for an oral medication, isoniazid, which would probably be required for 6 months to 1 year. The patient is also known to have essential hypertension and is status post percutaneous coronary angioplasty for coronary artery disease 1 year ago. His cardiovascular status was also accessed and prescriptions were renewed. A follow-up visit with the patient was scheduled for 2 weeks.

First-Listed Diagnosis: _____

Secondary Diagnoses: _____

First-Listed Procedure: _____

Secondary Procedures: _____

9

A 60-year-old female patient came to the neurologist's office on the advice of her physician because of a new onset of weakness, fatigue, and pain in her left leg that had been affected by the acute poliomyelitis she had 50 years ago. She had atrophy of the muscles of the left leg since having polio as a child. She walks with a limp because of the weakened, slightly shortened leg. On this occasion, following examination, the neurologist concluded that her symptoms reflect postpolio syndrome, which includes a progressive dysfunction and loss of motor neurons that had been compensating for the neurons lost during the original infection. The patient did not have a new onset of the polio infection. The consultant's diagnosis was atrophied leg muscles due to postpolio syndrome.

First-Listed Diagnosis: _____

Secondary Diagnoses: _____

First-Listed Procedure: _____

Secondary Procedures: _____

10

A 12-year-old boy was brought to the emergency department by his parents who stated that the child had an acute onset of fever, chills, headache, neck stiffness, photophobia, and pain in his eyes. He also had some nausea and vomiting. Upon physical examination, the emergency department physician found meningismus—a constellation of signs and symptoms—suggestive of meningitis. The child was admitted to an isolation room as an inpatient, and a spinal tap was performed. The examination of the cerebral spinal fluid and results of other tests led the physician to conclude the patient had aseptic meningitis, specifically coxsackie-virus meningitis. Because this is a viral illness, medical treatments are limited and are directed at relieving symptoms. The patient had an uncomplicated recovery and was discharged home for continued rest.

Principal Diagnosis: _____

Secondary Diagnoses: _____

Principal Procedure: _____

Secondary Procedures: _____

11

The patient is a 67-year-old female admitted to the hospital from the emergency room. She reported that she had nausea and vomiting and a fever for the last 2 days. She had been eating poorly for at least 3 days and within the last 12 hours started having chills, some shortness of breath, noticed a strong odor and dark color in her urine, and felt her heart beat was racing. The complete blood count on admission had a result of 24,000 white cells with a shift to the left. Other laboratory tests confirmed she was dehydrated. The urinalysis showed too many white blood cells to count and many bacteria present. She was admitted for intravenous antibiotics and rehydration fluids. The patient had been undergoing chemotherapy for metastatic carcinoma in her axillary lymph nodes that was recently discovered. The patient had breast cancer diagnosed and treated 5 years ago with surgery and chemotherapy. Her diagnosis on admission was acute sepsis with a suspected urinary infection as the cause. A urine culture was positive for Klebsiella organism and the two blood cultures were positive for Klebsiella as well. After the initiation of the IV fluids and antibiotics, the patient improved and was able to eat more and ambulate. She had no vomiting or diarrhea. The repeat urinalysis and blood counts showed values that were approaching a normal range. The oncologist examined the patient in the hospital and determined her next chemotherapy session would be delayed by two weeks to allow the patient to recover from this infection and regain her strength. Both the attending physician and the oncologist agreed that the patient's final diagnosis was sepsis due to urosepsis, Klebsiella organism, with dehydration as well as history of breast cancer with metastatic disease in the axillary lymph nodes. The patient was discharged home with home care nurses to visit the next day.

Principal Diagnosis: _____

Secondary Diagnoses: _____

Principal Procedure: _____

Secondary Procedures: _____

12

The mother of a 3-year-old female brought the child to the emergency room because of fast breathing, a fast heartbeat, and a generalized erythematous rash. The mother stated the child had been refusing food and drink and had not urinated much during the past 12 hours. The ER physician found the child to be dehydrated, febrile, lethargic, and clinging to her mother. The child was started on an IV for rehydration and respiratory treatments of Albuterol to improve her respiratory rate. Multiple chicken pox lesions were noted over the child's face, trunk, and legs, but the majority were crusted and nonvesiculating. The mother reported that her 6-year-old son had chicken pox recently. The physician also noted the child's abdomen to be distended. Examination of the ears showed a right otitis media with the left ear tympanic membrane normal. The chest exam demonstrated expiratory and inspiratory rhonchi with expiratory wheezes at the bases that were consistent with pneumonia. The child was placed into the pediatric observation unit. An x-ray of the abdomen taken while the child was in the emergency room showed significant ileus present. Over the next 12 hours, a repeat x-ray of the abdomen showed the ileus to be improved, the rash disappeared, the patient heart and respiratory rates decreased, and Amoxicillin medication was started for the ears. The child became more alert, smiling and happy, but still clinging to her mother. The mother was allowed to take the child home 28 hours after arriving in the emergency room with pediatric home care follow-up ordered. Discharge instructions included the patient continuing to receive Albuterol suspension and Amoxicillin. Discharge diagnoses included chicken pox complicated by pneumonia, dehydration, gastrointestinal ileus, and right otitis media.

First-Listed Diagnosis: _____

Secondary Diagnoses: _____

First-Listed Procedure: _____

Secondary Procedures: _____

13

A 21-year-old male made an appointment with his optometrist because he thought he had a problem with his new contact lens. The patient complained of increasingly severe eye pain. When the optometrist questioned the patient on how he took care of his contacts, the patient described rinsing the lens in tap water at work (a sports/exercise facility) during the day and not always using the contact solution prescribed to store the lens at night, again using tap water. The optometrist examined the patient and documented the patient had a mild to moderately severe case of acanthamoeba keratitis. The patient was told to throw out his current contacts, wear his glasses until his next doctor's appointment in one week, only use contact solution for rinsing and storage, and take nonsteroidal anti-inflammatory drugs to ease the eye pain.

First-Listed Diagnosis: _____

Secondary Diagnoses: _____

First-Listed Procedure: _____

Secondary Procedures: _____

14

The patient is a 50-year-old female who is being seen today in the Transplant Clinic of the University Medical Center as part of her evaluation for a possible liver transplant. The patient is known to have chronic hepatitis C and autoimmune hepatitis. Her autoimmune hepatitis was diagnosed recently by antibody tests and a liver biopsy. The patient's symptoms from her disease have been significant, including fatigue, aching joints, jaundice, enlarged liver, and ascites. The patient's father and brother have died from "liver failure," and this patient's physician suspects there is a genetic factor in the family that leads to autoimmune hepatitis in which the patient' liver is attacked by the patient's immune system. The patient is on the liver transplant list and waiting for an orthotopic transplant to occur. The patient or her husband carries her transplant beeper at all times. The patient's diagnosis listed on the encounter form for this visit is (1) chronic hepatitis C, and (2) autoimmune hepatitis.

First-Listed Diagnosis: _____

Secondary Diagnoses: _____

First-Listed Procedure: _____

Secondary Procedures: _____

15

On Monday evening, the parents of a 15-year-old female brought her to the Emergency Room and stated she had abdominal cramps, headache, muscle aches, chills, diarrhea, nausea, and vomiting for the past 12 hours. The family had been at a family picnic on Sunday with food served throughout the day, and the weather was hot. The teenager ate mostly raw foods and salads at the event. Today the mother learned that other members of her extended family had similar symptoms, but her daughter appeared to be the most acutely ill. The patient was very lethargic and continued to have diarrhea and vomiting in the Emergency Room after she arrived. Immediate laboratory testing found her to be dehydrated, and intravenous fluids were prompted started. Based on her symptoms and history, the physician concluded the patient had acute gastroenteritis caused by salmonella food poisoning and complicated by dehydration. The patient remained in the Emergency Room for 6 hours and was discharged to her parents care for rest at home with a clear liquid diet to be served and acetaminophen for discomfort.

First-Listed Diagnosis: _____

Secondary Diagnoses: _____

First-Listed Procedure: _____

Secondary Procedures: _____

Chapter 5

Neoplasms

Coding Scenarios for *Basic ICD-9-CM Coding*

The following case studies are organized by chapter following the sequence of the *Basic ICD-9-CM Coding* textbook. The objective of the case studies is to provide the student with more detailed clinical information to code, rather than one- or two-line diagnostic and procedure statements. Depending on whether the case study describes an inpatient hospital admission or an outpatient visit, the student is asked to provide the necessary diagnosis and procedure codes in the appropriate sequence—with principal diagnosis code listed first for inpatient admissions and main reason for visit code listed first for outpatient visits.

1

A 75-year-old male patient, known to have emphysema, was advised by his physician to be admitted to the hospital to evaluate and treat his worsening lung condition. The patient complained that his coughing and wheezing had become worse and his sputum was streaked with blood. A chest x-ray done on an outpatient basis the previous week showed a mass in the main bronchus. A fiberoptic bronchoscopy and needle biopsy of the bronchial mass was performed. The pathologic diagnosis of the biopsy examination was small cell type bronchogenic carcinoma located in the main bronchus. A nuclear medicine bone scan found areas of suspicious lesions that were determined to be bone metastasis. The diagnoses provided by the physician at discharge were bronchogenic, small cell carcinoma of the main bronchus, with metastatic disease in the bones, and emphysema.

Principal Diagnosis: _____

Secondary Diagnoses: _____

Principal Procedure: _____

Secondary Procedures: _____

2

A 65-year-old man with a diagnosis of acute myeloid leukemia is admitted for the first scheduled chemotherapy infusion, which will last several days. The patient is given intravenous chemotherapy through the multilumen right atrial catheter that had been placed during a previous hospital stay.

Principal Diagnosis: _____

Secondary Diagnoses: _____

Principal Procedure: _____

Secondary Procedures: _____

3

A patient, with terminal carcinoma of the large intestine/colon with metastases to the liver, was admitted to the hospital with dehydration. The patient's dehydration was the focus of the treatment with intravenous therapy, and the patient felt relief from his symptoms. Chemotherapy had been recently discontinued after discussions with the patient about its ineffectiveness in curing his disease and how sick the treatment made the patient feel. During the hospital stay, the patient and his family were offered the services of hospice care, which they discussed with hospice staff and accepted. The patient was discharged home to begin receiving the benefits of the hospice care and support given for the cancer conditions.

Principal Diagnosis: _____

Secondary Diagnoses: _____

Principal Procedure: _____

Secondary Procedures: _____

4

A 90-year-old man was brought to the emergency department after falling at home with minor injuries sustained to his face and hands. The man, who was very alert and oriented for his age, stated that he was feeling increasingly tired with each day, causing him to sleep 10 to 12 hours a day. He also stated he had lost his appetite and felt slightly nauseated all the time. He described symptoms of dehydration, which were proven by examination and laboratory findings, and intravenous hydration was started. Other laboratory tests showed evidence of chronic kidney disease, stage 4, and liver enzymes were markedly abnormal. The patient was admitted with the diagnosis of dehydration. Further workup revealed a mass at the head of the pancreas and a lesion in the liver. Because the patient did not want surgery or aggressive chemotherapy or other treatments, he received supportive and comfort care only. The patient and his family consented to hospice care at home and the patient was discharged. The physician's final diagnoses included the statement "probable carcinoma of the pancreas and liver metastasis based on radiologic studies and patient's symptomatology, not a candidate for surgical or aggressive treatment."

Principal Diagnosis: _____

Secondary Diagnoses: _____

Principal Procedure: _____

Secondary Procedures: _____

5

A 40-year-old woman with known cervical dysplasia had been seen in the outpatient surgery department the previous week for a colposcopy and biopsy. Pathologic exam of that tissue suggested the possibility of a malignancy in the cervix. Today the patient returns for a conization of the cervix by loop electrosurgical excision (LEEP) to determine the underlying cause of the dysplasia. The specimen was submitted for histopathologic examination with the findings returned as carcinoma in situ of the uterine cervix. The patient will follow-up in the office.

First-Listed Diagnosis: _____

Secondary Diagnoses: _____

First-Listed Procedure: _____

Secondary Procedures: _____

6

This is a 65-year-old woman who has biopsy-proven malignant melanoma of the right calf. The pathology diagnosis was superficial spreading of malignant melanoma. The patient is brought to the hospital outpatient department for excision of the 2.5 × 1.5 cm lesion. She will be seen in the office for suture removal and a discussion on what further treatment might be indicated.

First-Listed Diagnosis: _____

Secondary Diagnoses: _____

First-Listed Procedure: _____

Secondary Procedures: _____

7

This is a 65-year-old woman who had biopsy-proven malignant melanoma and excision of the lesion on the right calf. Since the last visit the patient learned that her brother and possibly her father (who is now deceased) had lesions and moles removed that were skin cancer and, in her father's case, probably a melanoma. All three people shared the same history of extensive sun exposure as this patient. Her brother and father worked many hours in the sun on the farm where they lived. On this occasion, she is brought back to the hospital outpatient department 2 weeks later for a "wide excision" of the same location on the leg where the lesion had previously been removed, 4 × 3 cm in area at the site of the original excision. The reason for the second excision was stated as "further excision as margins of initial excision showed evidence of remaining malignancy" The physician said this procedure was to "finish" the original excision to make certain the "margins are clean" and no malignant tissue remains. The pathology report states "normal tissues, margin clean, no evidence of remaining malignant melanoma." The patient will be seen in the office for suture removal and further treatment options are to be discussed.

First-Listed Diagnosis: _____

Secondary Diagnoses: _____

First-Listed Procedure: _____

Secondary Procedures: _____

8

A 70-year-old male patient was admitted to the hospital with the diagnosis of ureteral obstruction. Known to have a primary malignancy of the stomach that was surgically resected 6 months earlier, the patient was still receiving chemotherapy for the gastric malignancy. Outpatient testing showed evidence of ureteral obstruction, and the patient was admitted for evaluation and possible surgical treatment to relieve the obstruction and abate the symptoms it produced. A surgical consultation was obtained from a urologist, and the patient consented to surgery. The urologist performed a nephrostomy to relieve the obstruction that was caused by ureteral metastatic disease. Evidence of intra-abdominal metastasis was also found. The patient did not want further aggressive therapy and was discharged home to consider using hospice services.

Principal Diagnosis: _____

Secondary Diagnoses: _____

Principal Procedure: _____

Secondary Procedures: _____

9

The patient is a 40-year-old woman with breast cancer, metastatic to the bone and brain, all diagnosed in the past 6 months with continued management. The patient is seen in the hospital's outpatient oncology clinic for her next cycle of Aredia. She is receiving Aredia as palliative treatment for bone metastases and does not receive treatment for the malignancy.

First-Listed Diagnosis: _____

Secondary Diagnoses: _____

First-Listed Procedure: _____

Secondary Procedures: _____

10

A 64-year-old man was seen in his physician's office with a variety of gastrointestinal complaints, including vague abdominal pain, diarrhea, urinary frequency and flushing across his face, neck and chest. Laboratory and radiology tests were inconclusive, but based on his continuing symptoms, the physician suspected the patient might have a chronic form of appendicitis. An outpatient laparoscopic appendectomy was performed in the hospital ambulatory surgery department. A frozen section was requested during the procedure and the findings returned were "suspected carcinoid tumor of the appendix awaiting final histopathological exam." Upon recovery from the anesthesia, the patient agreed to be admitted the same day. Further pathology studies confirmed the diagnosis of malignant carcinoid tumor of the appendix. Other testing found that the patient was experiencing a "carcinoid syndrome" because of this tumor, which explained many of his vague symptoms, including the flushing. The appendectomy is considered curative treatment for the appendiceal tumor. Upon discharge, the patient will be seen in the oncologist's office for further recommendations, especially to treat the carcinoid syndrome.

Principal Diagnosis: _____

Secondary Diagnoses: _____

Principal Procedure: _____

Secondary Procedures: _____

11

The patient is a 60-year-old woman who is readmitted to the hospital for her next cycle of chemotherapy, which requires close monitoring because of the nature of the drugs used. The patient is known to have metastatic serous papillary carcinoma, and the chemotherapy is directed to controlling the effects of the primary tumor as well as the metastases. The patient was discharged on day 2.

Principal Diagnosis: _____

Secondary Diagnoses: _____

Principal Procedure: _____

Secondary Procedures: _____

12

The patient is a 42-year-old man who was recently diagnosed with a seminoma and underwent an inguinal orchiectomy. The patient is admitted at this time for retroperitoneal radiation therapy and is seen in consultation by the radiation oncologist who planned and delivered the initial radiation treatments. Additional testing was performed to determine the possible spread of the disease but none was found. Final diagnosis was stage I seminoma treated with retroperitoneal radiation therapy, course 1.

Principal Diagnosis: _____

Secondary Diagnoses: _____

Principal Procedure: _____

Secondary Procedures: _____

13

The patient is a 52-year-old painter who was washing windows at his home with his wife one day prior to admission when he developed what he called the "mother of all headaches" or the worst headache of his life. He had nausea but no vomiting. He later noticed visual disturbances and dizziness. Thinking the headache would go away, he went to bed but was unable to sleep all night because of the intensity of the headache pain, which was not relieved by Tylenol. He called his physician the next morning and was advised to go to the Emergency Department, where he was admitted. CT and MRI scans of the head and chest were abnormal. The MRI of the head found a three ring-enhancing lesion located in the parietal area associated with a large amount of edema extending into the occipital and temporal regions. The CT of the chest found pulmonary lesions that seem to be cavitating in right lower lobe. The patient had smoked for the past 40 years. The patient consented to and had performed the following two procedures: (1) closed biopsy of the brain through a burr hole approach; and (2) broncho-scopic transbronchial lung biopsy. Based on the pathological findings, the physician concluded the patient had a glioblastoma multiforme of the parietal region with metastases to the lung. In addition to these diagnoses, the physician gave other final diagnoses of pre-diabetes and smoker. The patient was discharged home as he wished to seek a second opinion at a major university medical center. Copies of his records and radiology films were given to the patient for this purpose.

Principal Diagnosis: _____

Secondary Diagnoses: _____

Principal Procedure: _____

Secondary Procedures: _____

14

The patient is a 69-year-old gravida 3, para 2, AB 1, female whose last menstrual period was in 1985. She originally came to the gynecologist's office complaining of postmenopausal bleeding. As an outpatient, she had an endometrial biopsy that revealed poorly differentiated adenocarcinoma with clear-cell features of the endometrium. Her pap smear was consistent with adenocarcinoma of endometrial origin. Today the patient was admitted to the hospital for a hysterectomy and related surgery. Her medical history includes ongoing treatment for hypertension, anxiety disorder, hyperlipidemia, and type 2 diabetes. She also has a history of breast cancer that was treated in 1989 with no recurrence. The surgery performed was a radical abdominal hysterectomy, bilateral salpingo-oophorectomy, and regional pelvic lymph node dissection. There was no evidence of metastasis into other pelvic organs. A consultation with an oncologist was performed. The patient had an uneventful recovery from the surgery and was discharged on day 3 to follow up with her gynecologist and oncologist in the next two weeks.

Principal Diagnosis: _____

Secondary Diagnoses: _____

Principal Procedure: _____

Secondary Procedures: _____

15

The patient is a 45-year-old female who was diagnosed with breast cancer 2 years ago. Her chemotherapy and radiation therapy treatments ended 6 months ago. She has had follow-up CT imaging, and there is no evidence of residual disease. The patient is in the doctor's office today to receive her first intravenous infusion of Herceptin (trastuzumab), which she will receive on a weekly schedule for the next 5 years. The doctor reminds the patient that the drug is not an antineoplastic chemotherapy drug. It is a monoclonal antibody that attaches itself to cancer cells and signals the body's immune system to destroy them. The drug decreases the risk of the cancer recurring in a patient like her with HER2 positive type breast cancer. The drug is considered long-term therapy for consolidative treatment of her breast cancer.

First-Listed Diagnosis: _____

Secondary Diagnoses: _____

First-Listed Procedure: _____

Secondary Procedures: _____

Chapter 6

Endocrine, Nutritional and Metabolic Diseases, and Immunity Disorders

Coding Scenarios for *Basic ICD-9-CM Coding*

The following case studies are organized by chapter following the sequence of the *Basic ICD-9-CM Coding* textbook. The objective of the case studies is to provide the student with more detailed clinical information to code, rather than one- or two-line diagnostic and procedure statements. Depending on whether the case study describes an inpatient hospital admission or an outpatient visit, the student is asked to provide the necessary diagnosis and procedure codes in the appropriate sequence—with principal diagnosis code listed first for inpatient admissions and main reason for visit code listed first for outpatient visits.

1

An elderly woman who lives alone was brought to the hospital emergency department by fire department ambulance after being discovered by neighbors in a semi-conscious state. She was known to have type I diabetes. The doctors described her diabetes as very brittle with fluctuating blood sugar measurements during her hospital stay. A type and dosage of insulin was finally established. During her hospital stay the patient complained of vision problems. She was examined by an ophthalmologist and found to have mild nonproliferative diabetic retinopathy. The patient was able to be discharged home to be followed up in her doctors' offices, as well as by home health nurses. The discharge diagnosis was uncontrolled type I diabetes on insulin with mild nonproliferative retinopathy.

Principal Diagnosis: _____

Secondary Diagnoses: _____

Principal Procedure: _____

Secondary Procedures: _____

2

A 48-year-old female patient was sent to the hospital outpatient laboratory department by her physician with a written order for a blood glucose test. The patient has known type II diabetes mellitus with nephropathy, and this was documented on the order as the reason for the blood test.

First-Listed Diagnosis: _____

Secondary Diagnoses: _____

First-Listed Procedure: _____

Secondary Procedures: _____

3

A 22-year-old female patient who has had type I diabetes for 10 years was admitted with ketoacidosis. She recently had an abscessed tooth, which was determined to be responsible in part for the ketoacidosis. The patient's diabetes had been poorly controlled but with this episode of care was clearly uncontrolled with the ketoacidosis present. With intravenous hydration and insulin drip, the patient's ketones cleared quickly. Antibiotics were also continued for the abscessed tooth.

Principal Diagnosis: _____

Secondary Diagnoses: _____

Principal Procedure: _____

Secondary Procedures: _____

4

A 45-year-old man is seen in his doctor's office for ongoing management of type II diabetes mellitus. As of this time, no obvious manifestations of diabetes are affecting any other body system. The patient takes insulin daily and has received a renewed prescription for insulin and needles. The patient noted that he was very satisfied with the new glucose monitoring device he was advised to use during his last visit. A follow-up appointment was made for 60 days following this visit.

First-Listed Diagnosis: _____

Secondary Diagnoses: _____

First-Listed Procedure: _____

Secondary Procedures: _____

5

A 60-year-old woman was seen in her physician's office as a follow-up visit. Results for laboratory tests ordered during the previous visit revealed elevated calcium in the bloodstream. A second laboratory test found an excessive amount of parathyroid hormone in the bloodstream. Follow-up imaging studies confirmed the presence of a benign parathyroid adenoma. The patient is presently complaining of muscle weakness, fatigue and some nausea and intermittent vomiting. Based on these findings, the doctor concludes that the patient is demonstrating primary hyperparathyroidism. The physician explains to the patient that the parathyroidism can only be cured by surgical excision of the parathyroid adenoma. The patient refuses surgery. The physician agrees the need for surgery is not urgent at this time and orders a bone density radiologic examination to be done next week. The patient will have a follow-up appointment in 1 month and measurement of calcium levels and renal functions in 6 months. Symptoms of the primary hyperparathyroidism were treated at this time.

First-Listed Diagnosis: _____

Secondary Diagnoses: _____

First-Listed Procedure: _____

Secondary Procedures: _____

6

A 52-year-old woman had been seen in her physician's office because of increasingly irritating symptomatology, including nervousness, irritability, increased perspiration, shakiness, and increased appetite with unexplained weight loss, increased heart rate, palpitations, sleeping difficulties, and other problems. The patient is returning to the office today for test results. The physician advised the patient of the following findings: The blood test for thyroid stimulating hormone had an elevated measurement, and a nuclear medicine scan of the thyroid found hyperactivity in the entire gland. Based on these findings, the diagnosis of hyperthyroidism in the absence of a goiter (rule out Graves disease) was made. The physician had eliminated a thyroid adenoma or a multi-nodular goiter as the cause of the hyperthyroidism. The patient was placed on an oral anti-thyroid medication to lower the level of thyroid hormones in the blood. Additional tests were ordered, and the patient was scheduled to return to the office in 10 days. Because the patient's heart palpitations were more pronounced than seen in other patients with hyperthyroidism, arrangements were made for her to have a consultation with a cardiologist tomorrow.

First-Listed Diagnosis: _____

Secondary Diagnoses: _____

First-Listed Procedure: _____

Secondary Procedures: _____

7

The parents of a 15-year-old boy accompanied him to the hospital for admission for the insertion of a totally implantable insulin pump with venous catheterization and injection of insulin. The patient has had type I diabetes since the age of 11 years. The insertion of the pump was successful. The patient's diabetes had been uncontrolled with various types of insulin. The patient was discharged but will return to the hospital in 1 week for insulin pump titration and training. For the next week the pump will run with saline.

Principal Diagnosis: _____

Secondary Diagnoses: _____

Principal Procedure: _____

Secondary Procedures: _____

8

The patient is a 33-year-old woman who is admitted for bariatric surgery for morbid obesity. The patient, who has been obese since childhood, currently weighs 150 lbs over her ideal body weight. The patient's BMI is 48.4. In the past 15 years, she has been treated for essential hypertension, hyperlipidemia, sleep apnea, cholelithiasis, insulin resistance, oligomenorrhea, and osteoarthritis of back, hips, and knees. She has had repeated failures of other therapeutic approaches to losing weight and has been cleared by a psychiatrist who could find no psychopathology that would make her ineligible for this procedure. Her group health insurance has approved payment for the surgery. The patient underwent a Roux-en-Y gastric bypass (gastroenterostomy) procedure, had an uneventful postoperative recovery in the hospital, and was discharged for follow-up in the office. During this hospital stay, hypertension, hyperlipidemia, insulin resistance, and osteoarthritis of the spine and multiple joints were also treated.

Principal Diagnosis: _____

Secondary Diagnoses: _____

Principal Procedure: _____

Secondary Procedures: _____

9

The patient is a 27-year-old man who is admitted for laparoscopic bariatric surgery for morbid obesity. The patient currently weighs 200 lbs over his ideal body weight with a body mass index of 54. In the past 10 years he has lost and gained back more than 100 lbs, but now suffers from several major health conditions that require more aggressive management of his obesity. He has a strong family history of morbid obesity. It occurs in his parents, two sisters and one brother. In the past 10 years, he has been treated for essential hypertension, dyslipidemia, obstructive sleep apnea, gallstone pancreatitis, type II diabetes, and osteoarthritis localized to his knees. He has had repeated failures of other therapeutic approaches to losing weight and has been cleared by a psychiatrist who could find no psychopathology that would make him ineligible for this procedure. His HMO has approved payment for the surgery. The patient underwent a laparoscopic gastric restrictive procedure with an adjustable gastric band and port insertion. The patient had an uneventful postoperative recovery in the hospital and was discharged for follow-up in the office. During this hospital stay, the conditions of hypertension, dyslipidemia, type II diabetes, and osteoarthritis localized to the knees were also treated.

Principal Diagnosis: _____

Secondary Diagnoses: _____

Principal Procedure: _____

Secondary Procedures: _____

10

A 50-year-old man is seen in his doctor's office for follow-up and ongoing management of his familial hypercholesterolemia, low density lipoid type. He has been taking the HMG-CoA reductase inhibitor drug, lovastatin (Mevacor), as directed. He has no identifiable adverse effects from the medication. He recently quit smoking and was counseled to maintain his smoke-free status. Recent laboratory tests show a slight reduction in his cholesterol levels. A follow-up appointment is made for a repeat visit in 3 months.

First-Listed Diagnosis: _____

Secondary Diagnoses: _____

First-Listed Procedure: _____

Secondary Procedures: _____

11

The patient is a 67-year-old man who was seen in the office for a regular follow-up appointment for the management of his Type II diabetes and his insulin dosage. The Accucheck performed in the office showed a result of 315. The patient stated his glucose is usually over 300 when he checks it at home. He reported feeling fairly well with a little more fatigue than usual. The patient is a retired truck driver and is fairly active, including helping his neighbors with yard work and snow shoveling. The patient is also known to have hypertension and chronic renal insufficiency that is fairly well controlled on medication. The patient was admitted to the hospital for control of his uncontrolled Type II diabetes. The patient is also obese with a body mass index of 37. The patient's 70/30 insulin was discontinued as well as the glyburide and Prandin. He was given Lantus insulin once a day with Novolog with every meal. The patient was directed to monitor his glucose with every meal. No other complications of his diabetes were found. His renal function was examined, and he was continued on his hypertensive medications. The patient also complained of pain in his right ankle that he said he sprained when he slipped on ice while cleaning the snow off his car while preparing to go to the physician's office. An x-ray revealed a nondisplaced fracture of the lateral malleolus. An orthopedic consultation was obtained, and the patient was placed in a cast. No fracture reduction was required. Acquired spondylolisthesis of the ankle was also diagnosed. The patient will be seen in the primary care physician's office in 1 week and in the orthopedic surgeon's office in 4 weeks.

Principal Diagnosis: _____

Secondary Diagnoses: _____

Principal Procedure: _____

Secondary Procedures: _____

12

The patient was admitted to the hospital after being seen in his physician's office 1 day prior to admission and was found to have a potassium level of 6.3 with a repeat value of 6 on the day of admission with elevated creatinine. For these reasons he was admitted to the hospital. A nephrology consultation was obtained to evaluate his hyperkalemia. His Aldactone medication was stopped, and he was given Kayexalate. His potassium levels improved. The consultant's report suggested that two issues may be contributing to his high potassium. He was taking spironolactone as well as furosemide. He did not avoid high potassium foods, and the combination of meds and food may have resulted in the inadvertent potassium intake excess. He is also on high dose of Toprol, and significant beta blocker may contribute to the elevated potassium level. The attending physician and consultant took the opportunity of this hospital stay to evaluate the patient's many chronic conditions and encourage compliance with his medications and dietary restrictions. In addition to hyperkalemia, the physician included the following conditions in the discharge summary dictated for the patient: hypertension with chronic renal insufficiency, gout, coronary artery disease, status post coronary artery bypass surgery, hypercholesterolemia, benign prostatic hypertrophy, sickle cell trait, atrial fibrillation, diabetes type II uncontrolled, obesity, and noncompliance with medications, diet, and physician followup. The patient was encouraged to return to the physician's office in 2 weeks.

Principal Diagnosis: _____

Secondary Diagnoses: _____

Principal Procedure: _____

Secondary Procedures: _____

13

The patient is a 68-year-old female who was a former office employee of her primary care physician. She had called the doctor's office 3 days prior to admission complaining of general weakness and nausea and was apparently not able to get around her house very well. Doctor advised her to come to the office, and she agreed but did not show up. The patient had often been noncompliant with medications and treatments recommended. When the doctor's office called her, she said she did not feel well enough to drive but her niece would drive her to the doctor's office the next day. The patient did not show up the next day either. On the third day, the doctor's office called her again. When she sounded less responsive on the telephone,

one of the doctor's office staff members was given permission to go to the house to check on the patient. When the office worker got to the home, she found the front door unlocked and the patient in bed very lethargic and not responding clearly to questions. An ambulance was called, and the patient was brought to the emergency room. The patient was known to have type I diabetes with several body systems affected. She was also known to have alcoholism. Initial laboratory work showed a glucose level of 245, urinalysis with 3+ bacteria and greater than 150 white cells with 10-20 RBCs, a positive blood alcohol level, and metabolic acidosis or ketoacidosis. The patient had not had ketoacidosis in the past but had uncontrolled diabetes at this time. She did have a history of repeated urinary tract infections. A subsequent urine culture grew E. coli bacteria. She was started on IV antibiotics. She improved steadily and described herself as feeling the best she had felt in a long time. She was watched closely for signs of alcohol withdrawal, but nothing obvious was noted. During her hospital stay, the following conditions were treated: diabetes mellitus, type I, with ketoacidosis uncontrolled; diabetes mellitus with worsening nephropathy; diabetic severe nonproliferative retinopathy with worsening vision; E. coli urinary tract infection; history of UTIs; alcoholism; and non-compliance with medical care. A social work consultation was requested, and the patient was given information about assisted living centers to help the patient live safely with some medical supervision. However, the patient flatly refused to consider the option and was discharged home with home health services requested for medical management.

Principal Diagnosis: _____

Secondary Diagnoses: _____

Principal Procedure: _____

Secondary Procedures: _____

14

The patient is a 10-month-old female infant who was discharged from the hospital 48 hours ago after treatment for a community-acquired pneumonia and gastroenteritis. The child received IV antibiotics in the hospital. The fever and the diarrhea abated, and the child was discharged to her parents' care. However, early this morning the child's father called the doctor and said she appeared less well, with increasing lethargy and refusing to take fluids or food. The child was re-admitted to the hospital for dehydration and hyperkalemia. Both were treated with IV fluids and medications. Within 24 hours the child was afebrile with no diarrhea and a good appetite. The potassium level dropped from 5.3 on admission to 4.7 the next day. Electrolyte values were back in the normal ranges. The baby also had a diaper rash that was treated in the hospital with medication that was also given to the parents to take home. The patient was discharged to her parents' care with prescriptions given and a follow-up appointment made for 5 days later. The diagnoses listed by the physician in the discharge summary were (1) dehydration, (2) hyperkalemia, (3) resolving pneumonia, community-acquired, (4) gastroenteritis, and (5) diaper rash.

Principal Diagnosis: _____

Secondary Diagnoses: _____

Principal Procedure: _____

Secondary Procedures: _____

15

A 30-month-old male child was admitted to the university hospital for investigation of a complex group of symptoms. The child and parents live 4 hours away from the hospital so the child was admitted so that the majority of the testing could be done at one time without repeated long trips back and forth to the hospital. The mother reported she noticed changes in the child's facial appearance starting about 6 months ago. She also noted a loss of previously acquired skills, including language and observed new aggressive behavior. Upon examination, the doctor noted an enlarge liver and spleen with a distended abdomen and suspected there were cardiovascular complications as well. A series of laboratory tests were performed and an extensive medical history was taken from both parents. The physicians concluded the patient had a type of inherited metabolic disorder called mucopolysaccharidosis (MPS), specifically type MPS IIA, also known as Hunter's Syndrome. The patient's problem is his body's inability to produce specific enzymes to carry out essential functions. The parents were told there is no cure for Hunter's Syndrome at this time and treatment focuses on managing signs and symptoms of the disease to provide relief to the child as the disease progresses. Known life-threatening complications include cardiovascular, respiratory, brain, and nervous system, in addition to skeletal and connective tissue problems. Because this condition is known to be an X-linked recessive disease, the mother of the child was tested for the mutated gene known to cause Hunter's Syndrome. It was determined the mother was a carrier of this disease because she had the X-linked recessive disorder with the mutated gene located on one of her X chromosomes and the normal gene on the other. The mother is unaffected by the disease but can pass it on to children, most often to a son. The parents were told that enzyme replacement therapy and other emerging therapies may off their son more help in the future. The family was given a follow-up appointment to return in three months for possible hematopoietic stem cell transplant planning. The family was also made aware of the National MPS Society that provides support for families and research support.

Principal Diagnosis: _____

Secondary Diagnoses: _____

Principal Procedure: _____

Secondary Procedures: _____

Chapter 7

Diseases of the Blood and Blood-Forming Organs

Coding Scenarios for *Basic ICD-9-CM Coding*

The following case studies are organized by chapter following the sequence of the *Basic ICD-9-CM Coding* textbook. The objective of the case studies is to provide the student with more detailed clinical information to code, rather than one- or two-line diagnostic and procedure statements. Depending on whether the case study describes an inpatient hospital admission or an outpatient visit, the student is asked to provide the necessary diagnosis and procedure codes in the appropriate sequence—with principal diagnosis code listed first for inpatient admissions and main reason for visit code listed first for outpatient visits.

1

A 20-year-old African American man is admitted to the hospital from the emergency department with acute vaso-occlusive pain and pulmonary symptoms including shortness of breath, chills, and cough. He was known to have Hb-S sickle-cell disease. A chest x-ray showed new pulmonary infiltrates. Treatment was focused on reducing the chest pain to improve breathing and treat the respiratory infection. The physician's discharge diagnosis was acute chest syndrome due to the sickle-cell crisis.

Principal Diagnosis: _____

Secondary Diagnoses: _____

Principal Procedure: _____

Secondary Procedures: _____

2

A severely anemic 75-year-old male patient with known inoperable carcinoma of the pancreas is admitted to the hospital for blood transfusions, which were given. The discharge diagnosis was anemia of chronic disease due to inoperable carcinoma of the pancreas.

Principal Diagnosis: _____

Secondary Diagnoses: _____

Principal Procedure: _____

Secondary Procedures: _____

3

A 60-year-old woman was referred to the outpatient procedure department with a diagnosis of anemia. A bone marrow aspiration biopsy through the sternum was performed. Pathological analysis of the specimen concluded the patient had "hypercellular marrow with diminished iron consistent with iron deficiency anemia." The attending physician agreed with the pathologist's conclusion.

First-Listed Diagnosis: _____

Secondary Diagnoses: _____

First-Listed Procedure: _____

Secondary Procedures: _____

4

An 80-year-old woman was seen by her family practice physician for symptoms of fatigue, palpitations, and weakness. She had recently moved from her home of 50 years to an assisted living center. Although she likes the new residence, she feels the move has caused her to become ill. She has no appetite and was distressed over all she had to do prior to the move. Laboratory tests were ordered, including a CBC, a comprehensive metabolic profile, and an EKG and chest x-ray. Her hemoglobin and hematocrit were abnormal and, given her history, especially the lack of adequate nutrition, the diagnosis of nutritional anemia was made. The patient was encouraged to take advantage of the assisted living center's on-site dietitian to review her nutritional needs. The patient was scheduled to return to the physician in 2 weeks. If the blood count does not improve by then, the option of administering packed cells via transfusion will be discussed. The only other finding of her diagnostic studies was known COPD that is under treatment and a past myocardial infarction that is currently asymptomatic.

First-Listed Diagnosis: _____

Secondary Diagnoses: _____

First-Listed Procedure: _____

Secondary Procedures: _____

5

The patient, a 40-year-old man, was diagnosed with acquired hemolytic anemia, autoimmune type with warm-reactive (IgG) antibodies, and had been treated with glucocorticoids (prednisone.) The patient failed to respond to this medication. The patient is also under treatment for systemic lupus erythematosus. Given the aggressive nature of his anemia, he was advised to be admitted to the hospital and have a splenectomy to eliminate the body's further destruction of red blood cells. The splenectomy was performed without complications, and the patient was discharged to be followed in the physician's and surgeon's offices.

Principal Diagnosis: _____

Secondary Diagnoses: _____

Principal Procedure: _____

Secondary Procedures: _____

6

A 70-year-old man was referred to the outpatient diagnostic testing center by his family physician for outpatient tests. His physician requested an upper GI series, x-ray, and CBC. The diagnoses written by the physician on the order were blood loss anemia and chronic gastric ulcer with recent hemorrhage.

First-Listed Diagnosis: _____

Secondary Diagnoses: _____

First-Listed Procedure: _____

Secondary Procedures: _____

7

A 60-year-old woman was seen for a follow-up visit at the hematologist's office for recently diagnosed pernicious anemia. The patient is also known to have agammaglobulinemia that is frequently found in patients with pernicious anemia. The patient is also being treated for chronic atrophic gastritis that is a consequence of her pernicious anemia. The patient is treated with medications to replace the cobalamin deficiency or pernicious anemia.

First-Listed Diagnosis: _____

Secondary Diagnoses: _____

First-Listed Procedure: _____

Secondary Procedures: _____

8

A 50-year-old woman is seen in her hematologist-oncologist's office for a follow-up visit concerning her acquired aplastic anemia that the physician also refers to as "pancytopenia with hypocellular bone marrow." The patient has been undergoing aggressive cytotoxic chemotherapy for ovarian carcinoma. Despite all of her serious conditions, the woman looks and feels remarkably well, even though drastically reduced blood counts were reported on recent laboratory tests. A recent bone marrow aspiration also confirmed the aplastic anemia diagnosis. The patient is scheduled to report to the hospital outpatient transfusion center tomorrow for two units of red blood cells to be infused for the aplastic anemia, an adverse effect of her chemotherapy.

First-Listed Diagnosis: _____

Secondary Diagnoses: _____

First-Listed Procedure: _____

Secondary Procedures: _____

9

The patient is a 20-year-old man who was born with factor VIII deficiency and diagnosed with hemophilia, type A. He has been receiving factor VIII replacement therapy with some response to treatment. The patient is admitted to the hospital on this occasion for his first course of extracorporeal immunoadsorption. The procedure is performed by drawing blood from an antecubital vein through a needle and returning it to another vein in the other arm. The access vein is connected to a primed blood processor. Blood is drawn into a cell separator. The plasma is passed to a monitor that controls continuous plasma flow through one of two ECI protein A columns. One column absorbs antibodies, and the other treats the remaining plasma. The treated plasma is returned to the blood processor, mixed with the patient's red blood cells, and reinfused back to the patient. This treatment took 4 hours 10 minutes. The patient was kept in the hospital overnight to observe for any possible complications. The patient is known to have "hemophilic arthritis" of the knees as a result of bleeding into these joints. This arthropathy caused by his hemophilia was evaluated by an orthopedic physician during his hospital stay. No complications of his immunoadsorption treatment were detected, and the patient was discharged, accompanied by his parents, for a follow-up visit in 1 week in the physician's office.

Principal Diagnosis: _____

Secondary Diagnoses: _____

Principal Procedure: _____

Secondary Procedures: _____

10

The patient is a 55-year-old woman with known chronic idiopathic thrombocytopenic purpura. The patient has been treated for this autoimmune disorder for approximately 1 year. Today, however, the patient is in the office of her internal medicine specialist to discuss an elective splenectomy. The patient has failed to maintain a normal platelet count after a course of prednisone therapy. She also had major side effect reactions to the prednisone medication. After hearing of the risks and benefits of the splenectomy versus another course of steroid therapy, the patient consents to the surgery. A surgeon, also a member of the group practice with the internal medical specialist, will see the patient tomorrow and schedule the surgery.

First-Listed Diagnosis: _____

Secondary Diagnoses: _____

First-Listed Procedure: _____

Secondary Procedures: _____

11

A 68-year-old woman was admitted to the hospital from a local nursing home because of anemia with altered mental status. She has two large pressure ulcers on her sacrum and hip that appear to be oozing blood. The patient received blood transfusions for her acute blood-loss anemia. The wound care physician and nurses treated her massive sacral pressure ulcer and the smaller pressure ulcer on her right hip. Both ulcers were described as stage III pressure ulcers. The patient was also treated for her diabetes and hypertension. The patient also has chronic pain from spinal osteoarthritis. Given the size of the pressure ulcers, the intensive care necessary to manage the ulcers, her chronic back pain, and subsequent immobility, a surgical consultation was obtained to consider creating a diverting colostomy to alleviate the fecal incontinence that she recently has acquired and the potential damage that fecal matter could do to her skin ulcers. This surgical intervention will be considered again when the blood loss anemia is corrected. The patient was transferred back to the nursing home for continued wound care and treatment.

Principal Diagnosis: _____

Secondary Diagnoses: _____

Principal Procedure: _____

Secondary Procedures: _____

12

A 70-year-old female patient with metastatic bone carcinoma from carcinoma of the breast, still under treatment, is diagnosed by her physician during an outpatient visit as having anemia caused by her chemotherapy based on the lab work done prior to the office visit. The patient will begin receiving Epoetin Alfa injections as an outpatient next week.

First-Listed Diagnosis: _____

Secondary Diagnoses: _____

First-Listed Procedure: _____

Secondary Procedures: _____

13

A 55-year-old male patient with chronic kidney disease requiring dialysis is seen in his nephrologist's office for an evaluation of his known anemia due to chronic kidney disease. Up until now, the anemia was not severe. However, based on the patient's hemoglobin, transferrin saturation, and serum ferritin laboratory values, the physician concludes the patient will need to receive Epogen to treat the anemia. The medication will be given intravenously 3 times a week at the dialysis center with the drug's dosage based on the patient's hemoglobin values and iron status. The patient will be monitored by the dialysis center physician and return to his nephrologist's office in 1 month.

First-Listed Diagnosis: _____

Secondary Diagnoses: _____

First-Listed Procedure: _____

Secondary Procedures: _____

14

The patient is a 28-year-old female who returns to her physician's office for a discussion of recent testing to determine her sickle-cell genetic status. The patient is married to a 29-year-old man who is known to carry the sickle cell trait. The patient is informed she also is a carrier of the sickle cell trait. The patient and her husband are anxious to begin a family. The physician informs the patient that the gene that causes sickle cell anemia must be inherited from both parents to cause full-blown sickle cell anemia in a child. With both the father and mother carrying the sickle-cell trait, the couple has a 25 percent chance of having a child with the disease and a 50 percent chance of having a child who is a carrier. Otherwise, neither of the parents with the sickle cell trait require treatment for the trait.

First-Listed Diagnosis: _____

Secondary Diagnoses: _____

First-Listed Procedure: _____

Secondary Procedures: _____

15

A 40-year-old man of Mediterranean descent is seen in the hospital outpatient hematology clinic for his scheduled transfusion of packed red blood cells. The patient has beta thalassemia major and requires blood transfusions every 3 to 4 weeks. Prior to the infusion, the patient is evaluated by his physician for the status of his splenomegaly, which is unchanged. This sign, as well as the patient's reported fatigue and reduced appetite, are classic symptoms of this hereditary hemolytic anemia. The patient will return to the clinic in 3 weeks to evaluate the need for another transfusion.

First-Listed Diagnosis: _____

Secondary Diagnoses: _____

First-Listed Procedure: _____

Secondary Procedures: _____

Chapter 8

Mental Disorders

Coding Scenarios for *Basic ICD-9-CM Coding*

The following case studies are organized by chapter following the sequence of the *Basic ICD-9-CM Coding* textbook. The objective of the case studies is to provide the student with more detailed clinical information to code, rather than one- or two-line diagnostic and procedure statements. Depending on whether the case study describes an inpatient hospital admission or an outpatient visit, the student is asked to provide the necessary diagnosis and procedure codes in the appropriate sequence—with principal diagnosis code listed first for inpatient admissions and main reason for visit code listed first for outpatient visits.

1

A 30-year-old man was brought to the emergency department by police who found him walking down the middle of a highway. The patient was obviously intoxicated and initially uncooperative but went to sleep in the emergency department. Based on the physical examination and laboratory work, with information later provided by the patient, the physician concluded the patient's diagnosis was acute and chronic alcoholism of a continuous nature. The patient was noted to have a "black eye," facial contusions, and multiple small lacerations on the fingers of his right hand, which he said was the result of a fight he had been in with another man earlier the night of this visit. The lacerations did not require suturing, but the wounds were cleaned and dressed. His vision appeared to be normal, but he was advised to seek treatment if he noticed visual problems developing. The patient was released with family members to go home with referral information for substance abuse treatment facilities in the area.

First-Listed Diagnosis: _____

Secondary Diagnoses: _____

First-Listed Procedure: _____

Secondary Procedures: _____

2

A 35-year-old woman was seen by the psychiatrist in the community mental health center for group therapy to deal with her anxiety depression. The patient also has agoraphobia with some panic disorder symptoms, so coming to the group meetings is often difficult for her. Following the group therapy, an individual therapy session was held with the patient today to help her manage her disease.

First-Listed Diagnosis: _____

Secondary Diagnoses: _____

First-Listed Procedure: _____

Secondary Procedures: _____

3

After numerous drug possession arrests, a 40-year-old man was mandated to the substance abuse treatment facility for admission to undergo detoxification and rehabilitation for his continuous cocaine addiction. The procedure of detoxification occurred over the first 3 days of stay at the residential center, with rehabilitation therapy following for the next 25 days.

Principal Diagnosis: _____

Secondary Diagnoses: _____

Principal Procedure: _____

Secondary Procedures: _____

4

A patient with bipolar disorder, type II, most recently in a depressed state, was admitted to the hospital with side effects due to the prescription lithium carbonate she had been taking. According to her caregivers, the drug had been administered correctly, and there was no possibility of a drug overdose. The patient had been sleeping 20 hours a day and was diagnosed with a drug-induced hypersomnia as a result of lithium toxicity. A therapeutic drug level for the lithium carbonate was found to be increased. The dosage was adjusted, and the patient received supportive verbal psychotherapy for the bipolar disorder while in the hospital. The patient was able to be discharged to the residential living center where she resided.

Principal Diagnosis: _____

Secondary Diagnoses: _____

Principal Procedure: _____

Secondary Procedures: _____

5

A 48-year-old male was brought to the emergency department after suffering an episode of syncope at a family picnic. The patient had been involved in a heated argument with several family members when he suddenly grabbed his chest and neck and collapsed to the ground. He awoke prior to the arrival of emergency medical personnel but was weak, diaphoretic, and confused, and brought to the hospital emergency department. Once in the emergency department, cardiovascular studies including an EKG and serial cardiac enzymes were performed, but no cardiovascular disease was immediately evident. There was no history of alcohol or substance abuse, and the patient had not consumed a large amount of alcohol at the party. After admission, the patient's private physician performed a comprehensive history and a physical examination. The patient admitted to a similar episode during a past business meeting, but this episode of syncope was more profound and disturbing to the patient. Upon questioning, it was learned that his mother had suffered similar attacks when the patient was a child, but he knew nothing of their causes and did not think she was ever treated by a physician for the attacks. Other diagnostic tests failed to reveal any cardiovascular or pulmonary pathology to account for the syncope or feelings of panic. A psychiatric consultation was obtained, and the patient was started on antidepressant medication and recommended to begin psychotherapeutic interventions with the psychiatrist in his office. The patient agreed and was discharged in improved condition on day 3. The patient was much relieved that his problem was taken seriously and committed to ongoing treatment and management. The family physician agreed with the psychiatrist's conclusion of panic disorder without agoraphobia and added the secondary diagnosis of chest pain, resolved.

Principal Diagnosis: _____

Secondary Diagnoses: _____

Principal Procedure: _____

Secondary Procedures: _____

6

A 30-year-old woman is referred to the psychiatrist for continued management of her somatization disorder. The patient has a history of many physical complaints over the past 10 to 12 years and has suffered significant impairment in social, occupational, and other areas of normal functioning. The patient is receiving an antidepressant medication and this seems to be helping her. The medication is also helping with her obsessive ruminations that were identified through psychotherapeutic interventions. After each investigation of her complaints, there has been no known medical condition to explain them. On one occasion, when an episode of acute gastritis was discovered based on her complaints, her physical symptoms were far in excess of what is normal in a person with a mild form of gastritis. Her treatment of choice by this psychiatrist is behavior modification therapy as an attempt to control her access to other physicians for repeated physical investigations and to give her support that her psychological condition is treatable. The patient will return for follow-up visits three times per week.

First-Listed Diagnosis: _____

Secondary Diagnoses: _____

First-Listed Procedure: _____

Secondary Procedures: _____

7

A 38-year-old man was admitted to the drug treatment unit of the local hospital for detoxification from heroin, a drug he has been dependent on for several years. The addiction medicine physician describes his dependence as "continuous." In anticipation of expected withdrawal symptoms, the patient is managed medically, pharmacologically, and psychologically over the next 5 days. The patient suffers multiple symptoms of withdrawal but copes with the process appropriately. By day 6, the patient is actively engaged in individual and group therapy to reach his goal of an "opioid-free lifestyle" within his drug rehabilitation therapy. He has undergone drug detoxification in the past but appears much more committed during this hospital stay. The patient is discharged from the hospital on day 8 to immediately enter a 21-day residential program at a local residential treatment facility. Long-term plans include a future stay at a drug-free recovery center and job training to enable the patient to improve his chances of recovery.

Principal Diagnosis: _____

Secondary Diagnoses: _____

Principal Procedure: _____

Secondary Procedures: _____

8

The patient is seen in his psychologist's office for individual psychotherapy as part of his long-term treatment for borderline personality disorder. The psychologist describes his condition as a "cluster B personality disorder." The patient has been faithfully taking his monoamine oxidase inhibitor (MAOI) medication and reports he feels it has helped him manage his impulsive, overly emotional, and erratic behavior. The patient is also a recovering cocaine addict whom the therapist describes as being "in remission." The patient attends Narcotic Anonymous (NA) meetings twice a week and enjoys the interactions with other recovering individuals. The patient will return next week for his scheduled appointment.

First-Listed Diagnosis: _____

Secondary Diagnoses: _____

First-Listed Procedure: _____

Secondary Procedures: _____

9

The patient was brought to the emergency department by city police after exhibiting extremely erratic behavior in jail after being arrested for a fight with the owner of a local restaurant in which he frequently dines. The business owner reports the man can be very nice and reasonable one day and completely "crazy" the next time he is in the restaurant. Today the patient got into a fight with another person in the restaurant, and the police were called. His family members arrived at the emergency department and informed the emergency department physician on duty that the patient is known to have paranoid-type schizophrenia and is under treatment by a physician at the VA Medical Center. The family also suspected the patient had not been taking his medication and had exhibited more paranoia recently. The emergency department physician contacted the VA physician and arranged for an immediate transfer to the psychiatric unit at the VA Medical Center. Ambulance transfer was also approved. The emergency department physician used the diagnosis provided to him by the VA psychiatrist as chronic paranoid schizophrenia in acute exacerbation.

First-Listed Diagnosis: _____

Secondary Diagnoses: _____

First-Listed Procedure: _____

Secondary Procedures: _____

10

A 17-year-old girl is admitted to the eating disorders/psychiatric unit of the University Hospital for anorexia nervosa. The patient's current weight is less than 80% of her expected weight for height and age, and her body mass index (BMI) is 18.2. A thorough history, physical, and psychological examination is performed. It is determined the patient has a "restricting" subtype of anorexia nervosa, because she loses weight by use of caloric restriction accompanied by excessive exercise. The patient is also known to "fast" 2 days a week to "cleanse her system of food toxins." The patient is extremely reluctant to gain even a small amount of weight. Intensive medical and psychological support was given to the patient. Weight restoration to 90% of her predicted weight was her primary treatment goal. After admission, laboratory tests revealed a serious electrolyte imbalance, which was treated. Along with medical and psychological support, the patient established a positive relationship with a young female dietitian who gained the patient's trust and respect, and this was extremely positive in helping the patient regain control of her disease. The patient was discharged on day 8 with a small weight gain recorded. The patient was transferred to a residential treatment facility with a successful eating disorders management program for further care.

Principal Diagnosis: _____

Secondary Diagnoses: _____

Principal Procedure: _____

Secondary Procedures: _____

11

A 25-year-old man was brought to the hospital emergency department by fire department ambulance after being found by his father hanging from a rope in an attached garage at home. The father cut the rope, and the patient fell to the ground. When paramedics arrived on the scene, the patient was unconscious but became responsive after being administered oxygen. The patient complained of a sore neck and a "cold." The patient's past medical history includes methadone for heroin dependence, continuous basis, and chronic pain syndrome as the result of an old back strain. The patient was taking the following medications: Xanax, lithium, methadone, Seroquel and norco. The patient was first admitted to the medical floor for "depression" and then consented to be transferred to the inpatient psychiatric unit for treatment. His psychiatric diagnosis was major depressive disorder, moderate. He admitted to the suicide attempt and said it was impulsive after an argument with his parents and not planned ahead of time. He admits to depressive symptoms for the past 1–2 months, if not longer. While in the hospital he was diagnosed with pneumonitis and treated with antibiotics. The orthopedic surgeon evaluated his neck and diagnosed an acute cervical strain. The pain management physician, who knew the patient, evaluated the patient and agreed with the present medical management. The patient was discharged from inpatient status on day 10 and was scheduled to begin outpatient therapy through the partial psychiatric hospitalization program the next day.

Principal Diagnosis: _____

Secondary Diagnoses: _____

Principal Procedure: _____

Secondary Procedures: _____

12

The male patient was brought to the emergency department by fire department ambulance after being found unresponsive lying under a bench at a bus stop. People in the area told the paramedics they saw the man sitting on the bench then have a "seizure" and fall under the bench. When they checked on him, they thought he had stopped breathing and died, and they called 911. When paramedics arrived, they found the patient breathing very shallowly and placed him on oxygen. The patient was not able to be aroused but reacted to painful stimuli. Blood and urine was obtained for laboratory testing, and the patient was placed on a cardiac monitor, which showed a slow but regular heart rhythm. The lab results returned with a very high blood alcohol level. Based on the information in his wallet, his identity was determined, and his brother was called. The brother stated the patient had long suffered from chronic alcoholism but had been living independently and working part-time as a custodian cleaning office buildings at night. The brother promised to come to the hospital and pick up the patient when he got off work in about 8 hours. The patient slept in the ER for several hours and then awoke. He was pleasant, cooperative, appreciative of the attention, and hungry. He was fed dinner and, later, a snack. His brother arrived to drive him home. The patient was given information about alcohol treatment programs and encouraged to consider. The patient knew all about such programs and told the staff he would call his "sponsor" when he got home and return to Alcoholics

Anonymous meetings to resume his recovery. His final diagnosis was acute alcoholic intoxication in a patient with chronic alcoholism.

First-Listed Diagnosis: _____

Secondary Diagnoses: _____

First-Listed Procedure: _____

Secondary Procedures: _____

13

The patient is a 15-year-old male who was recently released from a long stay in an adolescent psychiatric therapeutic hospital and has entered a 5-day-week day program to continue the management of his challenging behavioral health conditions. The young man has been followed by his psychiatrist and psychiatric social worker for 2 years prior to the recent hospital stay. For many years he has had difficulties in school, having been dismissed from 2 traditional schools and more recently threatened to be discharged from an alternative school, which, along with major family conflicts and an encounter with the police, led to his recent hospitalization. He has been arrested on multiple occasions for battery but never convicted of the charges. He was first thought to be suffering from a conduct disorder and attention deficit hyperactivity disorder, and these have been confirmed. As time passed it became evident that the patient's main disability was chronic schizophrenia of a schizophreniform type. Also, since the age of 4, the patient has been attracted to matches, lighters, and fires, and a diagnosis of pyromania was also established. The patient was raised in a chaotic household. His father has a long history of psychiatric disorders, and an older brother left home 4 years ago and had no contact with the family until recently, when the family learned he was incarcerated in another state's psychiatric prison. During the patient's recent hospital stay, his physicians were able to determine which medications were most beneficial to him. Since joining the day program, the patient has reported that his home life is more peaceful, he has not had a fight with anyone, has not set anything on fire, has enjoyed cooking meals with his mother, and has written several letters to his brother in prison. He has been able to comply with his behavioral contract and reports that he has not had any flare-up of his auditory hallucinations and feels more in control of his hyperactivity disorder. The patient attributes his "success" to the medications, which he initially resisted because he didn't want to become an "addict" but realizes he must take the rest of his life. He also recognizes the importance of continuing his behavioral therapy, family therapy, and other group therapy, along with his psychiatric drug therapy. His current Axis I diagnoses are (1) schizophreniform schizophrenia, chronic type, (2) conduct disorder, socialized, aggressive type, (3) attention deficit hyperactivity disorder. Axis II diagnosis is (1) learning disabilities. There are no Axis III disorders. His Axis IV is moderate to severe. Axis V is a GAF score of 40 upon discharge from the hospital.

First-Listed Diagnosis: _____

Secondary Diagnoses: _____

First-Listed Procedure: _____

Secondary Procedures: _____

14

The patient is a 32-year-old male admitted to the hospital for medical detoxification for his cocaine and cannabis dependency. The patient has been free-basing and snorting cocaine sporadically with increasing frequency over the past 10 years. He is now considered to have a continuous cocaine addiction. He has also been using marijuana on an almost daily basis for 14 years, which is also considered a continuous dependence. He has been totally unable to quit using either drug on his own and now agrees to enter a residential treatment program for his drug addictions with the full support of his family and employer in order to save his marriage and his job. Prior to entering the residential program, the patient must complete at least a 48-hour detoxification program, and this is the reason he is admitted at this time. The patient was treated with Chlorazepate for withdrawal and agitation. He received Phenobarbital for insomnia. He was also treated with Thiamine hydrochloride and Allbee with vitamin C capsules. His admission drug screen was positive for marijuana and cocaine. For his persistent insomnia, he received L-tryptophan. His very controlling personality in detoxification gradually subsided over the next 72 hours, and he became very cooperative and interested in becoming fully invested in the chemical dependency rehabilitation program he was about to enter. He was discharged on day 4 after a difficult detoxification experience to enter the predicted month or longer residential program. If successful, this stay is to be followed with transition to a very strong outpatient day hospital rehabilitation program and later phase into a full 2-year aftercare program and lifelong Narcotics Anonymous meetings.

Principal Diagnosis: _____

Secondary Diagnoses: _____

Principal Procedure: _____

Secondary Procedures: _____

15

The patient is a 28-year-old male veteran of the Iraq war who served two tours of duty. He was referred to a Veterans Affairs Medical Center for evaluation. He experienced combat and survived two improvised-explosive-device (IED) explosions while riding in military vehicles. Four fellow soldier friends were killed in the two vehicle explosions. After returning from Iraq two years ago, the patient began experiencing anxiety-like symptoms, including a pounding heart, sweating, and trouble breathing on occasions. He also reported bad dreams of his war experiences. He had difficulty falling and staying asleep. He also reported trouble getting along with his family members and co-workers in his civilian job because of his angry outbursts over relatively minor things. He describes himself as "emotionally numb" and admits to having thoughts of and plans for suicide. The patient is diagnosed with chronic posttraumatic stress disorder with suicide ideation. To fully evaluate the patient and begin therapy, the patient is admitted to an inpatient unit. Over the next 5 days, the patient is treated with psychotherapy, pharmacotherapy (psychiatric drug therapy), and cognitive-behavior therapy. At the time of discharge, the patient reported feeling better and is scheduled to continue receiving outpatient cognitive-behavior therapy.

Principal Diagnosis: _____

Secondary Diagnoses: _____

Principal Procedure: _____

Secondary Procedures: _____

Chapter 9

Diseases of the Nervous System and Sense Organs

Coding Scenarios for *Basic ICD-9-CM Coding*

The following case studies are organized by chapter following the sequence of the *Basic ICD-9-CM Coding* textbook. The objective of the case studies is to provide the student with more detailed clinical information to code, rather than one- or two-line diagnostic and procedure statements. Depending on whether the case study describes an inpatient hospital admission or an outpatient visit, the student is asked to provide the necessary diagnosis and procedure codes in the appropriate sequence—with the principal diagnosis code listed first for inpatient admissions and main reason for visit code listed first for outpatient visits.

1

An 85-year-old woman was brought to the family physician's office by her family. She has severe dementia due to Alzheimer's disease. She is becoming increasingly difficult to manage at home. At times, she becomes aggressive and attempts to strike family members with household objects. She also has repeatedly wandered away from the home's backyard and has had to be located by calling police to assist in the search. The family members have refused to admit the patient to a long-term care facility. The family members will continue to care for the woman in their home. The physician's diagnosis is Alzheimer's dementia with behavioral disturbances such as aggression and wandering.

First-Listed Diagnosis: _____

Secondary Diagnoses: _____

First-Listed Procedure: _____

Secondary Procedures: _____

2

A 50-year-old man, who has had type II diabetes for more than 10 years, complains of vision problems, worse on the left side. He is seen in the ophthalmologist's office upon the recommendation of his family physician. The patient's diabetes is treated with oral medications and diet. After examining the patient, the physician concludes that the patient has moderate nonproliferative diabetic retinopathy, as a result of his type II diabetes.

First-Listed Diagnosis: _____

Secondary Diagnoses: _____

First-Listed Procedure: _____

Secondary Procedures: _____

3

A patient is seen in the eye clinic at the University Medical Center. After taking a thorough history and conducting an extensive physical eye examination, the physician orders several tests to be done over the next week. At the conclusion of the visit, the physician writes the diagnosis of "suspect glaucoma."

First-Listed Diagnosis: _____

Secondary Diagnoses: _____

First-Listed Procedure: _____

Secondary Procedures: _____

4

An 8-year-old boy was seen in the pediatric neurologist's office for his absence attack or petit mal epilepsy. The mother reports two episodes of motor seizures over the past month that consisted of localized twitching of his right arm and leg. The patient has an older brother (age 18 years) who had the same type of epilepsy during childhood but has been seizure-free for 4 years. The young patient is treated with mild antiseizure medications and is scheduled for a repeat EEG in 2 weeks.

First-Listed Diagnosis: _____

Secondary Diagnoses: _____

First-Listed Procedure: _____

Secondary Procedures: _____

5

The patient is an 88-year-old woman who was remarkably alert and cogent for her age. She lives alone in her own home and has no relatives in the area. The type of procedure planned for the patient could usually be performed on an outpatient basis but because of her lack of support, the patient's procedure is scheduled as an inpatient procedure. The patient was diagnosed with retinal macular hole, right eye, with localized retinal detachment, single defect. The patient has vision of 20/400 in the right eye. She is status post cataract extraction in the left eye. The procedure performed was a pars plana vitrectomy, gas/fluid exchange with autologous serum injection, C#3/F#8 gas injection, which are components of the procedure of cryoretinopexy of the right eye, which was performed to repair the detached retina. The procedure performed was done with intravenous moderate sedation. At the conclusion of the procedure, injections of dexamethasone and gentamicin were given subconjunctivally. The patient was kept in the hospital 2 days until Friday when a neighbor was able to pick up the patient and care for her over the weekend.

Principal Diagnosis: _____

Secondary Diagnoses: _____

Principal Procedure: _____

Secondary Procedures: _____

6

A 40-year-old woman came to the ophthalmologist's office last week complaining of a fleshy fold of tissue that appeared in the corner of her eye near her nose and started growing toward the center of her eye. She reported that it had begun to obstruct her vision. Upon examination, the physician found a progressive peripheral pterygium that starts in the conjunctiva and attaches to the cornea as it grows. Today the physician performed an excision of the pterygium with a corneal graft. No problems were encountered during the procedure, and the patient will be seen in the office next week for a surgical follow-up examination.

First-Listed Diagnosis: _____

Secondary Diagnoses: _____

First-Listed Procedure: _____

Secondary Procedures: _____

7

A 3-year-old female was admitted to the hospital for strabismus surgery. The physician states her condition is concomitant convergent strabismus or early acquired esotropia, monocular. The physician described the deviation as 25 prism diopters and stable. The child was otherwise healthy and able to receive general anesthesia. Surgery was recommended to reestablish binocular vision. The extraocular muscle surgery performed was a unilateral 6-mm lateral rectus muscle resection on the affected eye. The child was discharged in the care of her parents on the day after surgery.

Principal Diagnosis: _____

Secondary Diagnoses: _____

Principal Procedure: _____

Secondary Procedures: _____

8

A 4-year-old boy was brought to the emergency department by his mother, who stated the child had become ill very rapidly over the course of 1 day. He had been treated for an ear infection at the pediatric clinic last week. Upon physical examination, the emergency department physician noted a high fever, drowsiness, and stiffness in the neck. The mother reported the child had said his head hurt and also reported that he had vomited at home. The physician noted slight rash on the child's upper trunk and axilla bilaterally. Suspicious for meningitis, a pediatric consult was requested and obtained. The emergency department physician and pediatrician obtained consent for a spinal tap and the child was admitted to the pediatric unit.

Over the next couple of days, the pediatrician made the diagnosis of bacterial meningitis with the causative organism of haemophilus influenzae (H. influenzae) based on the physical findings and the examination of the cerebrospinal fluid obtained by the spinal tap. The child is treated with intravenous antibiotics and other medications as well as supportive care. The pediatrician found the acute suppurative otitis media still needed treatment. The child made a full recovery but will be followed closely as an outpatient to determine whether any effects of the meningitis, such as hearing loss, occur later. The child was discharged to the care of his mother.

Principal Diagnosis: _____

Secondary Diagnoses: _____

Principal Procedure: _____

Secondary Procedures: _____

9

A 2-year-old girl was brought to the emergency department by her mother, who stated the child had a cold, runny nose, congestion, and a mild fever. The patient then developed a dry, hacking cough that progressed to prolonged coughing spasms. Overnight the child became very ill. Upon physical examination, the emergency department physician noted a high fever and stiffness in the neck, and the child was very difficult to arouse. The mother reported the child had said that she vomited at home. The child was admitted to the pediatric service. Infectious disease and pulmonary medicine specialists consulted with the attending pediatrician to make the diagnosis of whooping cough with complicating meningitis. The child was treated with intravenous antibiotics. A 4-year-old brother at home was brought to the pediatric clinic for examination because this condition is so contagious, and he was found to have a mild form of pertussis which was treated. The girl recovered from the bacterial illness and was discharged to the care of her mother with Home Health Agency nursing follow-up.

Principal Diagnosis: _____

Secondary Diagnoses: _____

Principal Procedure: _____

Secondary Procedures: _____

10

A 30-year-old man who is a member of a well-known musical band is seen in the "Performing Arts Clinic" at the university medical center. The musician complained of ringing, buzzing, and clicking in his ears and hearing loss, especially on the right side. The musician said he was told by other musicians that he had "rock and roll deafness." Upon examination and audiometric testing, the physician diagnosed the patient as having sensorineural hearing loss and subjective tinnitus as a result of acoustic trauma from performing loud music over the past 12 years. The patient was advised to return for further evaluation and possible hearing aid fitting as this type of sensorineural deafness is likely to be permanent.

First-Listed Diagnosis: _____

Secondary Diagnoses: _____

First-Listed Procedure: _____

Secondary Procedures: _____

11

The patient is a 35-year-old female who was in an auto accident four months ago. She was treated in the emergency room of a local hospital and in this doctor's office following the accident and had been diagnosed with an intracranial head injury. The patient reported to her doctor during this visit that she has had headaches almost every day since the accident. She stated that over-the-counter pain medication helps relieve the pain but she is concerned that the headaches are still present. The doctor examines the patient and makes the diagnosis of "post-traumatic headaches due to old intracranial injury from a previous auto accident." The patient is referred to a neurologist for a consultation and will return to this doctor's office in 2 weeks to determine the next course of treatment if necessary.

First-Listed Diagnosis: _____

Secondary Diagnoses: _____

First-Listed Procedure: _____

Secondary Procedures: _____

12

The patient is a 78-year-old man who was admitted to the hospital today for the implantation of a dual-chamber permanent pacemaker device. The patient had a several-month history of syncope that was investigated on a couple of encounters. Finally it was determined that the patient's neurocardiogenic syncope was caused by carotid sinus syndrome, which another physician referred to as carotid sinus hypersensitivity. The dual-chamber cardiac pacemaker was implanted to treat the carotid sinus syndrome, and the patient had no complications from the procedure and was discharged home with an appointment with his cardiologist in 10 days.

Principal Diagnosis: _____

Secondary Diagnoses: _____

Principal Procedure: _____

Secondary Procedures: _____

13

A 45-year-old man was admitted to the hospital for a decompressive laminectomy to treat his long-standing lumbar spinal stenosis. The back pain from the spinal stenosis has not been relieved by pain management treatment or physical therapy. The man has been off work for 3 months due to the chronic back pain and agreed to the spinal surgery as his last option to relieve the pain and support his family. The patient is healthy and has no other medical problems. The surgery was performed on the day of admission. During the surgery, a dural tear was noted as the result of an unintended durotomy. The tear was immediately repaired during the same procedure. The patient was informed of the unintended durotomy and the necessary repair. Otherwise the patient had no complications of the procedure and recovered well enough to go home in three days. The patient will be seen in his surgeon's office in one week.

Principal Diagnosis: _____

Secondary Diagnoses: _____

Principal Procedure: _____

Secondary Procedures: _____

14

The patient is a 60-year-old male farmer who was treated a month ago for the apparent toxic effects of herbicide chemicals that he was applying to his crops. Since that time the patient has had severe vertigo, headaches, nausea, and loss of sensations in his hands and feet. The patient was admitted to evaluate the relationship between his past toxic exposure and his current symptoms. Toxicology studies indicated a moderate level of herbicides in the blood but less than one month ago when initially tested. The physician documented the final diagnosis as toxic neuropathy as a late effect of the herbicide toxicity. In other parts of the record, the physician describes the condition as toxic polyneuropathy. Medications were prescribed to manage the symptoms the patient continued to experience, and the patient will return to the physician's office for additional blood tests in one month. In the interval, the patient is advised not to operate machinery or drive a car.

Principal Diagnosis: _____

Secondary Diagnoses: _____

Principal Procedure: _____

Secondary Procedures: _____

15

A 35-year-old male was admitted to the hospital. The admitting diagnosis documented on the history and physical examination report was "chronic pain syndrome and chronic lower back pain with exacerbation of lower back pain and lower extremity pain." Also included in the patient's history is the fact that the patient was injured in a serious automobile accident three years ago and has had back pain ever since that injury. However, the patient's pain has increased over the past three months and has become excruciating over the past week. The patient was admitted to the hospital specifically for pain management. The patient received intravenous and intramuscular pain medications as well as physical and occupation therapy to manage his pain, which he reported as much improved at the time of discharge. The final diagnosis written by the physician was acute exacerbation of chronic pain syndrome, chronic lower back pain, and lower extremity pain. The physician also wrote that the pain was likely the consequence of lumbar nerve root damage from the injuries sustained in the automobile accident.

Principal Diagnosis: _____

Secondary Diagnoses: _____

Principal Procedure: _____

Secondary Procedures: _____

Chapter 10

Diseases of the Circulatory System

Coding Scenarios for *Basic ICD-9-CM Coding*

The following case studies are organized by chapter following the sequence of the *Basic ICD-9-CM Coding* textbook. The objective of the case studies is to provide the student with more detailed clinical information to code, rather than one- or two-line diagnostic and procedure statements. Depending on whether the case study describes an inpatient hospital admission or an outpatient visit, the student is asked to provide the necessary diagnosis and procedure codes in the appropriate sequence—with principal diagnosis code listed first for inpatient admissions and main reason for visit code listed first for outpatient visits.

1

A 50-year-old man was admitted to the hospital complaining of chest pain that was determined to be a result of an acute inferior wall myocardial infarction (MI). The patient was treated for the acute MI. In addition, a right and left heart catheterization was performed with a Judkins coronary angiography and a right and left angiocardiography. The patient was found to have coronary arteriosclerosis due to lipid rich plaque. The patient was also treated for pre-existing atrial fibrillation and discharged on day 5 in stable condition.

Principal Diagnosis: _____

Secondary Diagnoses: _____

Principal Procedure: _____

Secondary Procedures: _____

2

A 59-year-old male patient with coronary artery disease of the native arteries was admitted to the hospital for scheduled coronary artery bypass grafts using saphenous vein grafts of four vessels performed under cardiopulmonary bypass. Postoperatively, the patient developed pulmonary emboli that were treated successfully with no catastrophic consequences. After 3 days in the surgical ICU, the patient was transferred to a surgical floor and monitored closely. Phase I of cardiac rehabilitation was started on day 4, and the patient was able to be discharged on day 7. The patient will be seen in the surgeon's office 7 days later and is scheduled to begin Phase II cardiac rehabilitation within the next month.

Principal Diagnosis: _____

Secondary Diagnoses: _____

Principal Procedure: _____

Secondary Procedures: _____

3

An 80-year-old woman was seen in her physician's office as a follow-up visit. Six months previously she had a cerebrovascular accident (CVA) for which she was admitted to the hospital at that time. As a consequence of her CVA, she has right-side (dominant) hemiparesis and dysphasia. She has been receiving outpatient physical therapy and has made good progress. She also is being treated for essential benign hypertension and atrial fibrillation. The patient's prescription medications were renewed, and she will be seen in the office in 6 months. She was advised to call her physician if she does not feel well or if new problems develop.

First-Listed Diagnosis: _____

Secondary Diagnoses: _____

First-Listed Procedure: _____

Secondary Procedures: _____

4

The patient, a 75-year-old man, collapsed at home and was brought to the emergency department by fire department ambulance and admitted to the hospital. A computed tomography scan showed an acute cerebral embolus with cerebral infarction. Dysphagia and left hemiparesis were present on admission. The patient is right-handed. The patient is also under treatment for hypertension. At the time of discharge, the dysphagia had cleared, but the hemiparesis was still present. The patient was transferred to a rehabilitation facility.

Principal Diagnosis: _____

Secondary Diagnoses: _____

Principal Procedure: _____

Secondary Procedures: _____

5

A 65-year-old man collapsed in his garage after shoveling heavy wet snow from his driveway. Fire department ambulance brought the man to the nearest hospital in full cardiac arrest. Family members stated the patient had cardiomegaly and had been on prescription medication for hypertensive heart disease in the past but had not seen a doctor for over one year. Cardiopulmonary resuscitation was initiated but was unsuccessful, and the man was pronounced dead 50 minutes after arriving at the hospital. The patient was never admitted to the hospital with all of his medical care received in the emergency department. The emergency department physician's conclusion in the emergency department record was "Cardiac arrest, probably due to acute myocardial infarction triggered by strenuous exertion. Hypertensive heart disease."

First-Listed Diagnosis: _____

Secondary Diagnoses: _____

First-Listed Procedure: _____

Secondary Procedures: _____

6

A 70-year-old woman was seen in her physician's office for ongoing management of several medical conditions. The patient has congestive heart failure, as a result of hypertension, chronic kidney disease, stage 2, and longstanding type II diabetes with polyneuropathy. Her main reason for being at the doctor's office today is to renew medication for her heart failure.

First-Listed Diagnosis: _____

Secondary Diagnoses: _____

First-Listed Procedure: _____

Secondary Procedures: _____

7

The patient is a 70-year-old man who was admitted by his cardiologist with the diagnosis of acute coronary syndrome. The patient had not had coronary angioplasty or coronary bypass surgery in the past. The patient consented to and underwent a diagnostic left heart cardiac catheterization and coronary arteriography by Judkin's technique, which showed extensive arteriosclerotic coronary occlusion of the left anterior descending (LAD). Other vessels also had minor coronary artery disease. Prior to the procedure, the patient understood there was the possibility that he would require a coronary stent placement to which he also consented. Following completion of the diagnostic catheterization, the physician performed a coronary angioplasty of the LAD with the insertion of one nondrug-eluting coronary stent into the LAD. A platelet inhibitor drug (Integrilin) was also infused intravenously. The physician's final diagnosis was "acute coronary syndrome due to arteriosclerotic coronary artery disease." The patient was discharged for follow-up evaluation and possible cardiac rehabilitation therapy.

Principal Diagnosis: _____

Secondary Diagnoses: _____

Principal Procedure: _____

Secondary Procedures: _____

8

A 72-year-old retired family practice physician called an ambulance from his home to take him to the hospital in which he had practiced medicine for 40 years. En route to the hospital, he asked the paramedics to call the interventional radiologist at the hospital to meet him in the emergency department. The radiologist was waiting for the physician-patient when the ambulance arrived in the driveway. The physician-patient described his symptoms to the emergency department physician and radiologist and said "I'm certain I have an abdominal aortic aneurysm." The symptoms he experienced—abdominal pulsatile mass, abdominal pain and tenderness, rigidity, lower back pain, rapid pulse, paleness, nausea, clammy skin, sweating—were classic symptoms of what physicians call a "triple A." The physician-patient was taken immediately to the interventional radiology suite. Based on a quick physical examination and ultrasound of the abdominal aorta, an aneurysm was found. The physician-patient consented to a repair by the interventional radiologist and within 1 hour of arrival, the following procedure was started: Endovascular implantation of a graft into the abdominal aorta. After the procedure, the physician-patient was taken to the ICU for postoperative monitoring. The patient was also treated for long-standing essential hypertension, as well as for gouty arthritis that was current. The patient had an uneventful recovery and was able to leave the hospital within 1 week for further recovery at home.

Principal Diagnosis: _____

Secondary Diagnoses: _____

Principal Procedure: _____

Secondary Procedures: _____

9

The patient, a-68-year-old woman known to have congestive heart failure currently controlled by medication, is admitted to the hospital by her physician because of posterior calf pain with warmth and swelling of the proximal right lower leg. A duplex venous ultrasonography with pulse-wave Doppler detected a thrombus by direct visualization. Anticoagulant therapy was started to prevent pulmonary embolism or further venous embolization. The patient was stabilized and was able to be discharged home. Home health nurse services were arranged to take blood samples for ongoing prothrombin time (PT) laboratory tests to assure the therapeutic level of the anticoagulant therapy in the blood. The patient was also treated for her compensated congestive heart failure while in the hospital.

Principal Diagnosis: _____

Secondary Diagnoses: _____

Principal Procedure: _____

Secondary Procedures: _____

10

The same patient described in Question 9, a 68-year-old woman known to have congestive heart failure, was readmitted to the hospital with fatigue, shortness of breath, and swelling of the legs. Upon questioning, the patient admitted to excess foods that were not on her low-fat, low-salt diet over the past week, and her symptoms returned. Intravenous medications, including diuretic and cardiotonic drugs, were started and the patient's heart function improved. The patient was still receiving maintenance warfarin sodium (Coumadin) to prevent recurrence of the deep vein thrombosis she experienced 3 months previously. Doctor described this condition in the progress notes as DVT and history of DVT. A duplex venous ultrasonography with pulse-wave Doppler did not detect a recurrent thrombus. The patient was stabilized and was able to be discharged home. Home health nurses were arranged to take blood samples for ongoing prothrombin time (PT) laboratory tests to assure the therapeutic level of the anticoagulant therapy in the blood. The patient was also treated for compensated congestive heart failure while in the hospital.

Principal Diagnosis: _____

Secondary Diagnoses: _____

Principal Procedure: _____

Secondary Procedures: _____

11

The patient is a 100-year-old woman who was admitted to the hospital for further management of her congestive heart failure. The patient, who lives with her 82-year-old son, has been remarkably well in spite of her advanced age. Six months ago she was admitted to the hospital, was found to be in congestive heart failure with chronic respiratory failure, and became oxygen dependent. The heart failure was described as chronic combined systolic and diastolic type. These conditions continue to be present. Her son states that the patient has been sleeping more and has less energy. A couple of days ago she fell while getting up from the commode but insisted she was fine. Her son noticed her left wrist was slightly swollen and bruised. The patient has been treated for hypertension for many years and has a history of urinary tract infections. During this admission, she was found to have another urinary tract infection and was treated for it. She was continued on oxygen, and her hypertension and congestive heart failure medications were adjusted. An x-ray of the wrist showed a minimally angulated fracture involving the left distal radius. The wrist was placed in a splint for support. On day 2 of the hospital stay, the patient was noticeably weaker, in mild respiratory distress, and sleeping almost continually. Whenever she was attended to by the nurses, doctors, or her son, she asked them to "just let me be." The patient and her son were offered the services of hospice care and accepted. Within 48 hours of receiving supportive and comfort care, the patient died peacefully in her sleep.

Principal Diagnosis: _____

Secondary Diagnoses: _____

Principal Procedure: _____

Secondary Procedures: _____

12

The patient is a 35-year-old man who drove himself to the Emergency Room early in the morning because he had chest pain. The patient had been gambling in a casino overnight, drinking alcohol and snorting cocaine as well as smoking cigarettes. As the night progressed, the patient became aware of chest discomfort that advanced to chest pain. He had had chest pain on previous occasions, but this time it lasted longer and was more severe. He became scared and came to the ER. The patient does not have a family physician but does see a psychiatrist intermittently for his bipolar I disorder and is taking Lamictal 100mg daily for this condition. The patient was admitted after the EKG was found to be abnormal and the patient's troponin lab values were elevated. The admitting diagnosis was rule out myocardial infarction. Cardiology consultation was obtained. During his hospital stay the patient was monitored on cardiac telemetry and the myocardial infarction was ruled out. A chest x-ray showed evidence of bilateral basilar pneumonia. He did have subsequent episodes of chest pain but refused further cardiac workup and insisted on being discharged on day 3. The family practice physician assigned to the patient provided the following final diagnoses: Angina; cocaine addiction; alcohol abuse; tobacco dependence; pneumonia; and bipolar I disorder. The patient was given instructions to call the physician's office for an appointment within 1 week.

Principal Diagnosis: _____

Secondary Diagnoses: _____

Principal Procedure: _____

Secondary Procedures: _____

13

The physician went to the nursing home to see his 83-year-old male patient who was complaining of difficulty breathing and fatigue. The patient was known to have congestive heart failure. The physician diagnosed the patient as having chronic diastolic heart failure in addition to the congestive heart failure and ordered new medications. He instructed the nurses at the nursing home to closely monitor the patient and notify him if the patient's symptoms worsened, as the patient may have to be admitted to the hospital for treatment if that occurred.

First-Listed Diagnosis: _____

Secondary Diagnoses: _____

First-Listed Procedure: _____

Secondary Procedures: _____

14

The same patient described in question 13, an 83-year-old male resident of a nursing home, developed more significant shortness of breath, increased edema in his legs, and chest pain during the next two days after the physician had evaluated the patient in the nursing home. The patient was admitted to the hospital and treated for congestive heart failure with acute exacerbation of his chronic diastolic heart failure. In addition, the patient continues to receive treatment for his hypertension and Type II diabetes with peripheral neuropathy. The patient improved with treatments and was transferred to a skilled nursing facility for further recovery.

Principal Diagnosis: _____

Secondary Diagnoses: _____

Principal Procedure: _____

Secondary Procedures: _____

15

The patient is a 62-year-old man who was initially admitted to Hospital A and diagnosed with an acute ST elevation anterolateral wall myocardial infarction (STEMI). He had a cardiac catheterization done at Hospital A with the findings of native vessel coronary artery disease in four vessels. The patient's condition was stabilized, and the patient elected to be transferred to a larger hospital for recommended angioplasty and coronary artery stenting. Records and films were transferred with the patient directly to Hospital B. At Hospital B, the patient had percutaneous transluminal angioplasty of three vessels with coronary artery disease. In addition, two non-drug-eluting stents were inserted into two coronary arteries. The patient had an uncomplicated recovery and was scheduled to begin the cardiac rehabilitation program in four weeks. Code for Hospital B.

Principal Diagnosis: _____

Secondary Diagnoses: _____

Principal Procedure: _____

Secondary Procedures: _____

Chapter 11

Diseases of the Respiratory System

Coding Scenarios for *Basic ICD-9-CM Coding*

The following case studies are organized by chapter following the sequence of the *Basic ICD-9-CM Coding* textbook. The objective of the case studies is to provide the student with more detailed clinical information to code, rather than one- or two-line diagnostic and procedure statements. Depending on whether the case study describes an inpatient hospital admission or an outpatient visit, the student is asked to provide the necessary diagnosis and procedure codes in the appropriate sequence—with principal diagnosis code listed first for inpatient admissions and main reason for visit code listed first for outpatient visits.

1

A 70-year-old male patient with longstanding chronic obstructive pulmonary disease (COPD) was admitted through the emergency department with increasing shortness of breath, weakness, and fatigue. His admitting diagnosis was acute respiratory insufficiency. Treatment included respiratory therapy and medications. It was confirmed with the patient that he has not resumed his 50-year history of smoking, and he was encouraged to remain smoke-free. The final diagnoses written by the physician was acute respiratory insufficiency due to acute exacerbation of COPD. History of smoking.

Principal Diagnosis: _____

Secondary Diagnoses: _____

Principal Procedure: _____

Secondary Procedures: _____

2

An 80-year-old female patient from a nursing home was admitted to the hospital with symptoms of weakness, coughing, shortness of breath, and mental status changes. Swallowing studies revealed she had difficulty swallowing and easily aspirated particles into her respiratory tract. It was determined that she suffered from aspiration pneumonia. She also was found to have a superimposed bacterial pneumonia. Both conditions were treated with intravenous antibiotics, and the patient's condition improved. She was transferred back to the long-term care facility for care.

Principal Diagnosis: _____

Secondary Diagnoses: _____

Principal Procedure: _____

Secondary Procedures: _____

3

A 10-year-old boy was treated in the allergist's office for childhood asthma. He was treated for his allergic rhinitis due to pollen and animal dander with his asthma. The patient's conditions were well controlled with his current medications.

First-Listed Diagnosis: _____

Secondary Diagnoses: _____

First-Listed Procedure: _____

Secondary Procedures: _____

4

A bilateral tonsillectomy and adenoidectomy was performed on a 9-year-old patient to resolve his recurring infections due to adenotonsillar hyperplasia. No infection was present at the time of the surgery. The patient was admitted as an inpatient for an overnight stay.

Principal Diagnosis: _____

Secondary Diagnoses: _____

Principal Procedure: _____

Secondary Procedures: _____

5

The patient is a 65-year-old man who is receiving chemotherapy for multiple myeloma from an oncologist on staff at this hospital. The patient came to the emergency department stating he had a cough, fever, chills, and felt extremely weak. The patient was admitted. The chest x-ray at the time of admission showed evidence of a left lower lobe pneumonia. During the hospitalization, the patient received respiratory therapy treatments, intravenous antibiotics, and supportive care. His chemistry profiles showed an abnormal BUN and glucose. Cultures of the sputum showed no pathologic organism. Blood cultures were negative. The patient's hemogram was abnormal with a hemoglobin of 9.3, hematocrit of 27, white blood cell count of 3,200 and platelets 126,000. A repeat CBC showed the hemogram had dropped to 7.5 with the hematocrit at 22. There was no evidence of GI or other source of bleeding. His oncologist also followed his care during the hospital stay and determined the pancytopenia shown on the CBC was a result of the chemotherapy the patient was receiving. For this reason, the patient was given two units of leukocyte-poor packed red blood cells. Follow-up CBC test showed hemoglobin at 9.6 and hematocrit at 28.

Follow-up chest x-ray showed significant clearing of the pneumonic process. The patient was switched to oral antibiotics at the time of discharge and given a prescription to continue taking both antibiotics for another week. The patient appeared significantly depressed, and this was discussed with him. A psychiatric consultation and possible medications were recommended, which the patient refused. The patient has a follow-up appointment with his oncologist and with the private physician within the next 10 days.

Principal Diagnosis: _____

Secondary Diagnoses: _____

Principal Procedure: _____

Secondary Procedures: _____

6

The patient is a 45-year-old man who comes to the physician's office for his 3-month follow-up visit for asthma. He is using a bronchodilator and steroid for control of his asthma. He is having no problems with the asthma at this time. He denies a change in cough and reports no increase in shortness of breath, no fluid retention, no increase in wheezing. He is taking his medication regularly and not missing any doses. Upon physical examination, the lungs are clear with decreased breath sounds in both lung fields, heart is regular rhythm with no murmurs, and extremities are free of edema. Oximetry and pulmonary function tests have not changed since the last visit. The patient's diagnosis is stable asthma, on long-term steroid therapy. The patient was advised to continue his present medications and return for a follow-up visit in 3 months.

First-Listed Diagnosis: _____

Secondary Diagnoses: _____

First-Listed Procedure: _____

Secondary Procedures: _____

7

The patient is a 19-year-old man who comes to the physician's office complaining of sore throat with fever for the past 4 days with pain in his right ear. He has difficulty swallowing and has been taking Tylenol for fever and throat lozenges for the sore throat. He feels weaker today. He has no known allergies. Physical examination showed the tonsillar arch reddened with tonsillar exudates. There are enlarged anterior cervical lymph nodes. The examination of the ears showed acute suppurative otitis media in both ears, but worse in the right ear.

A rapid strep screening test was positive. The diagnosis given was "Possible early tonsillar abscess, strep pharyngitis with acute suppurative otitis media." The patient was given an injection of antibiotics and a prescription.

First-Listed Diagnosis: _____

Secondary Diagnoses: _____

First-Listed Procedure: _____

Secondary Procedures: _____

8

A physician in private practice admitted this patient to the hospital. The patient is a 78-year-old woman who has coronary artery disease and is status post coronary artery bypass graft 8 years ago. She is also under treatment for hypertension and mild congestive heart failure. The patient was admitted at this time for shortness of breath starting 2 days prior to admission and worse on the day of admission. She complained of wheezing and cough productive of white sputum. She thought she had a mild fever this morning but was afebrile on admission. She had no chills, nausea, or vomiting. Her paroxysmal nocturnal dyspnea and orthopnea remain unchanged. Physical examination showed the patient to be in mild distress but alert and oriented. Her blood pressure was 150/70 mmHg, heart rate 70, and respiratory rate 16. Cardiovascular system examination revealed regular rate and rhythm. Lungs had poor air entry and patient was wheezing. Abdomen was soft, nontender. The extremities were 2+ edema bilaterally. Neurologically her left upper extremity and left lower extremity have weakness as the result of a CVA 2 years ago. The patient was admitted with COPD acute exacerbation. She responded well to respiratory therapy treatments and intravenous medications. She was discharged home on the following prescriptions: Prednisone, aspirin enteric-coated tablet, Albuterol inhaler, Persantine, Captopril, Theophylline, Diltiazem, Nitro paste, Lasix, and Digoxin. She will be seen in the office in 5 days. Discharge diagnoses are acute and chronic bronchitis/COPD, hypertension, CAD, status post CABG, CHF, old CVA with weakness/hemiparesis, left side in a right-handed woman.

Principal Diagnosis: _____

Secondary Diagnoses: _____

Principal Procedure: _____

Secondary Procedures: _____

9

The patient is a 9-year-old boy who is brought to the pediatrician's office by his mother because of the following: runny nose, fever, yellow discharge from the nose, swelling around the eyes, and tenderness in the cheeks. The child is snoring during sleep. The mother had given the child Children's Tylenol. Physical examination confirmed most of the subjective complaints and detected fluid in the sinuses. A prescription was given for 14-day oral antibiotic treatment and the doctor recommended to continue Children's Tylenol for fever. The doctor concluded the child had acute sinusitis in the frontal and maxillary sinuses.

First-Listed Diagnosis: _____

Secondary Diagnoses: _____

First-Listed Procedure: _____

Secondary Procedures: _____

10

A 62-year-old woman, on disability because of emphysema, is brought to the emergency department from home by fire department ambulance. The patient complained of sudden sharp chest pain, shortness of breath, and a nonproductive hacking cough. The patient has been under treatment for COPD and emphysema for more than 5 years and is dependent on oxygen. The patient described the pain as being on the left side with referred pain up to the shoulder. The patient was cautious when moving to protect her chest and shoulder. In the emergency department, a chest x-ray and continuous pulse oximetry was ordered. Pulse oximetry showed low oxygen saturation. Physical examination revealed diminished breath sounds bilaterally, but significantly worse on the left side. The chest x-ray revealed a collapsed lung on the left side and fluid in the pleural space. The patient was admitted. A chest tube was inserted to aspirate air and re-expand the lung. Follow-up chest x-ray showed the lung had re-expanded to its normal size, and the pleural effusion's fluid appeared to be reabsorbed and resolved. The physician's discharge diagnoses were COPD and emphysema with left side spontaneous pneumothorax and pleural effusion.

Principal Diagnosis: _____

Secondary Diagnoses: _____

Principal Procedure: _____

Secondary Procedures: _____

11

The patient is a 50-year-old female with known systemic lupus erythematosus with nephritis. Her renal function has been worsening over the past several months. Today the patient came to the emergency room complaining of pain in her chest that was worse when she coughed or took a deep breath. The ER physician heard a "friction rub," but a chest x-ray did not show any pleural effusion. The patient was admitted to the hospital. It was determined that the patient had pleurisy, but it was uncertain if it was related to her lupus. The patient also had diarrhea, dehydration with hyponatremia, hypokalemia, and azotemia. Intravenous fluids and medications were administered to correct her metabolic disorders, diarrhea, relieve the pain of the pleurisy, and treat her worsening renal function.

Principal Diagnosis: _____

Secondary Diagnoses: _____

Principal Procedure: _____

Secondary Procedures: _____

12

The patient is an 89-year-old man with advanced COPD who was admitted to the hospital complaining of cough, shortness of breath, and fever. It was determined that he was suffering from COPD with acute bronchitis. He is supplemental oxygen dependent and also has cor pulmonale. He was treated with bronchodilators, antibiotics, and a tapering dose of steroids. The patient was on "do not resuscitate" (DNR) status. The patient was becoming progressively weaker with more respiratory distress. During this hospital stay, the family members decided to initiate comfort care measures after speaking with the physician about the patient's prognosis. The family elected to receive hospice care and took the patient home to receive home end-of-life and comfort care.

Principal Diagnosis: _____

Secondary Diagnoses: _____

Principal Procedure: _____

Secondary Procedures: _____

13

A 5-year-old male was brought to the emergency room by his mother who gave the patient's history of having a 2-day history of increasing lethargy, decreased appetite, and vomiting. The mother stated the child's sister had similar symptoms and was seen in the doctor's office and diagnosed with viral syndrome during the past week. A physical examination and laboratory tests were performed on the 5-year-old male that showed evidence of dehydration and decreased breath sounds. A chest x-ray showed some diffuse areas in the right lower lobe possibly involving pneumonia. The admitting diagnosis was possible pneumonia of a viral or bacterial type with dehydration. During the hospital stay the child received IV antibiotics and fluids to treat the infection and dehydration. Within 12 hours the child became alert, active, and back to normal per his mother. He was given a clear liquid diet and later wanted more to eat, with no vomiting reported. Repeat chemistry, hematology, and urinalysis lab tests were repeated the following morning and showed results back to normal. The child was discharged to his mother's care on day 2 with a follow-up appointment made in the primary care physician's office for day 5. The physician's conclusion on the discharge summary written the day of discharge was "pneumonia, possibly viral origin, complicated by dehydration."

Principal Diagnosis: _____

Secondary Diagnoses: _____

Principal Procedure: _____

Secondary Procedures: _____

14

The patient was a 59-year-old man brought to the emergency room by ambulance with increasing shortness of breath and worsening color. The patient was mottled below the knees. Due to shortness of breath, the patient was not able to give any history in the emergency room before his family arrived. When they arrived, his family reported that he had become more lethargic at home over the past 24 hours. The patient had been a smoker for 45 years and had continued to smoke until one week ago. He had chronic obstructive asthma that was steroid dependent for many years and developed steroid-induced diabetes in the past 5 years. He was diagnosed with status asthmaticus upon admission. He was able to work up until the age of 55, when he received disability retirement benefits from his company and Social Security because of his poor health. Since his retirement he was also diagnosed with congestive heart failure. Recently he was found to have a large left chest mass when a chest CT exam was performed because of an increasing cough. After this finding was described to him, he refused any further workup and signed an advance directive that specified no heroic efforts in his final days. After admission, an order was written for "no code" per his advance directive, but the patient did allow respiratory therapy and intravenous medications for his heart and lung disease. Over the next 24 hours he seemed to improve with the breathing treatments of Solu-Medrol and Lasix, but his pulse oximetry was rarely above 80% without an oxygen mask. A portable chest x-ray showed his left lower lobe obstructing mass, larger than imaged one month ago, and pneumonia. Testing proved it to be pneumonia due to pseudomonas aeruginosa. His blood sugars improved, and he appeared to be stabilizing much to the surprise of his family and physicians. He had brief periods of alertness and was able to converse with his family and eat small meals. However, the evening before his passing, palliative care orders were written to make him as comfortable as possible, as his lung function was worsening again. Early in the morning of the third day he became unresponsive and then was noted to be without respirations or pulse at 0130. His wife and son were at his bedside when he was pronounced dead by the hospitalist on duty. His final diagnoses included pneumonia due to pseudomonas, steroid-dependent asthma in status asthmaticus, steroid-induced diabetes, large left lung mass, congestive heart failure, and respiratory failure—all probably related to his tobacco dependence. No autopsy was performed.

Principal Diagnosis: _____

Secondary Diagnoses: _____

Principal Procedure: _____

Secondary Procedures: _____

15

The patient, a 60-year-old man, was taken to the emergency room of a local hospital from a wedding reception after he developed symptoms of shortness of breath and chest pain. He also reported that he felt very tired after traveling to this city for the wedding and has learned he cannot tolerate as much walking as he had even one month ago. The patient knew he had lung cancer. The ER physician contacted his family physician, who told him the patient had small cell carcinoma of the left upper lobe of the lung, diagnosed 14 months ago, and he had been followed for possible malignant pleural effusion that resolved without treatment 3 months ago. The patient was placed in observation status and examined by an oncologist and cardiologist. After several tests were performed, it was determined the patient had exudative pleural effusion, which the oncologist referred to as "malignant pleural effusion." The cardiologist performed a therapeutic thoracentesis that provided immediate relief. The patient rested in the observation unit for 12 more hours and was discharged to the care of his family. The physicians advised the patient to rest at least 2 more days in this city before driving 250 miles with his family back to his hometown. Records were given to the patient to take to his oncologist at home.

First-Listed Diagnosis: _____

Secondary Diagnoses: _____

First-Listed Procedure: _____

Secondary Procedures: _____

Chapter 12

Diseases of the Digestive System

Coding Scenarios for *Basic ICD-9-CM Coding*

The following case studies are organized by chapter following the sequence of the *Basic ICD-9-CM Coding* textbook. The objective of the case studies is to provide the student with more detailed clinical information to code, rather than one- or two-line diagnostic and procedure statements. Depending on whether the case study describes an inpatient hospital admission or an outpatient visit, the student is asked to provide the necessary diagnosis and procedure codes in the appropriate sequence—with principal diagnosis code listed first for inpatient admissions and main reason for visit code listed first for outpatient visits.

1

A 40-year-old woman has been treated for symptoms of gallstones without improvement. The patient also was known to have chronic cholecystitis. She was admitted for a laparoscopic cholecystectomy. After the procedure was started, it was determined that the procedure could not be completed laparoscopically, and it was converted to an open procedure. The pathology report confirmed the preoperative diagnosis of chronic cholecystitis with cholelithiasis.

Principal Diagnosis: _____

Secondary Diagnoses: _____

Principal Procedure: _____

Secondary Procedures: _____

2

A 30-year-old woman has been treated for Crohn's disease of the small intestine since 18 years of age. She has had several exacerbations of the disease over the past years. At this time, the patient comes to the emergency department in extreme pain. A small bowel x-ray shows a small bowel obstruction. The patient was admitted to the hospital. Later the obstruction was found to be a result of mural thickening. The patient is taken to surgery and a partial resection of the terminal ileum is performed to release the obstruction. An end-to-end anastomosis is performed to close the small intestine. The patient was also noted to have flat, firm, hot, and red painful small lumps on the shins of both legs. Consultation with the wound-care physician determined the ulcers to be erythema nodosum, a known complication of Crohn's disease. The wound care physician prescribed oral and topical medications.

Principal Diagnosis: _____

Secondary Diagnoses: _____

Principal Procedure: _____

Secondary Procedures: _____

3

A 68-year-old man was admitted to the hospital for an inguinal hernia repair that could not be done on an outpatient basis because of anticipated extended recovery time required due to his other medical conditions. After being prepared for surgery and taken to the operating room, the patient complained of precordial chest pain. The surgery was cancelled, and the patient was returned to his room. Cardiac studies failed to find a reason for the chest pain, which resolved the same day. The patient's medications for his hypertension and COPD were also given.

Principal Diagnosis: _____

Secondary Diagnoses: _____

Principal Procedure: _____

Secondary Procedures: _____

4

A 70-year-old man who lives in another city and was visiting relatives in the area was brought to the emergency department by family members. The patient complained of vomiting blood and having very dark stools that appeared to have blood in them as well. The patient had gone out to dinner with relatives for a prime rib dinner. After he came home, he started vomiting and having diarrhea and blamed it on the large meal. He continued to have these symptoms overnight, and his family members insisted he come to the emergency department. The patient was admitted. The patient is taking Prinivil, Lanoxin, and Lasix for congestive heart failure and atrial fibrillation, and these medications were continued during the hospital stay. The gastroenterologist was called for a consultation and saw the patient. The patient agreed to an upper and lower GI endoscopic examination. The esophagogastroduodenoscopy (EGD) examination included a biopsy and cauterization of a gastric polyp and a biopsy of a pyloric ulcer. The findings of the EGD, confirmed by pathologic studies, were hiatal hernia, acute gastritis with bacteria determined to be helicobacter, gastric polyp, and a chronic deep pyloric ulceration. Hemorrhage was noted in the stomach, possibly from the ulcer as well as the polyp. The colonoscopy included a polyp at 80 cm that was removed with a hot biopsy forceps. Extensive diverticulosis was present but no areas of bleeding were seen. The attending physician agreed with the findings of the endoscopic examination as reasonable explanations for the patient's symptoms. The serial blood counts did not find any significant anemia. The patient was discharged, given prescriptions and copies of his medical records to take home for his private physician to review.

Principal Diagnosis: _____

Secondary Diagnoses: _____

Principal Procedure: _____

Secondary Procedures: _____

5

The patient is an 81-year-old woman who was admitted to the hospital for intractable emesis, near syncope, and extreme weakness and fatigue. The patient had been in the hospital 2 weeks previously for pneumonia, which was treated at that time. A visit in the physician's office 5 days ago revealed the pneumonia to be resolving. During this hospital stay it was determined the patient had a nonspecific form of gastroenteritis with resulting dehydration. Both conditions were treated. The patient is also known to have a hiatal hernia and reflux esophagitis, which were treated with her usual medications. A chest x-ray still showed the pneumonia to be present, and she was continued on oral antibiotics. The patient was discharged home to continue taking oral antibiotics and usual other medications.

Principal Diagnosis: _____

Secondary Diagnoses: _____

Principal Procedure: _____

Secondary Procedures: _____

6

A 75-year-old man was admitted to the hospital after coming to the emergency department after having a black melanotic stool the day before and on the day of admission. He had no pain, nausea, or vomiting but felt a little "light-headed." Testing in the emergency department found grossly guaiac positive stools. His admitting diagnosis was gastrointestinal bleeding. The patient has an extensive past medical and surgical history including:

1. Coronary artery bypass graft 7 years ago after a myocardial infarction with no symptoms today, but takes one baby aspirin a day

2. Recurrent deep vein thrombosis of lower extremity and recurrent pulmonary emboli, currently taking Coumadin to prevent recurrence

3. History of congestive heart failure currently taking Lanoxin and Dyazide

4. History of arthritis currently taking Tolectin

5. History of hyperlipidemia currently taking Lescol

6. Suspected carcinoma of the pancreas with an exploratory laparotomy 5 years ago that only proved pancreatitis to be present, no malignancy

7. Appendectomy, colon resection done years before for what sounds like a bowel obstruction and stomach surgery for what the patient calls a "blockage"

8. Large ventral hernia related to his left upper quadrant abdominal incision from past surgery, which is of no consequence at this time

During this hospital stay, he was given intravenous medications, vitamin K injection, and two units of fresh frozen plasma to reverse the effects of the Coumadin. Serial CBCs were done, which showed marginally low hemoglobin and hematocrit but nothing requiring treatment for anemia. An EGD was performed by the gastroenterologist, who documented a hiatal hernia with reflux esophagitis, a bleeding proximal jejunal ulcer, and evidence of a past gastrojejunostomy. The EGD was simply diagnostic, no biopsies were taken. The private physician used the diagnoses from the EGD and from the past medical and surgical history as the final diagnoses for the case. The patient continued to receive all of his medications in the hospital and was discharged home for follow-up in the physician's office in 1 week.

Principal Diagnosis: _____

Secondary Diagnoses: _____

Principal Procedure: _____

Secondary Procedures: _____

7

A 60-year-old man was acutely ill when admitted to the hospital for hematemesis. After study, the upper gastrointestinal (GI) bleeding was found to be due to a gastric varix that was caused by alcoholic cirrhosis of the liver and acute alcoholic hepatitis. The patient was known to have long-term chronic alcoholism with which he continues to struggle. The patient was also found to have esophageal varices, but these were not bleeding at this time. The surgery performed was the creation of a transjugular intrahepatic portosystemic (venous) shunt (TIPS). The patient was discharged to a skilled nursing facility for surgical recovery and ongoing management of his serious GI diseases.

Principal Diagnosis: _____

Secondary Diagnoses: _____

Principal Procedure: _____

Secondary Procedures: _____

8

A 55-year-old man was admitted to the hospital through the emergency department for suspected gallstone pancreatitis. After study it was found the patient had acute pancreatitis, radiologic evidence of gallstones, and possibly stones in the common bile duct. The patient was taken to surgery for an open cholecystectomy and common duct exploration. It was confirmed the patient had chronic cholecystitis with cholelithiasis and choledocholithiasis with obstruction of the biliary system. The physician stated the acute pancreatitis was a consequence of the bile duct stones, but the main reason for the patient's admission to the hospital and the need for surgery was the gallstones and the bile duct stones. The patient had a slow but steady recovery from surgery and was able to return home for further convalescence.

Principal Diagnosis: _____

Secondary Diagnoses: _____

Principal Procedure: _____

Secondary Procedures: _____

9

A 40-year-old man was admitted to the hospital through the emergency department for acute abdominal pain. The patient appeared to have alcoholic intoxication. He was treated with nasogastric suction, IV fluids, pain medications, and given multiple vitamins and mild tranquilizers as treatment for his alcohol withdrawal symptoms. The patient stated he was told by another physician at another hospital that he had chronic pancreatitis. The diagnosis of acute and chronic pancreatitis was made based on physical findings and laboratory and radiology test results. The patient stated he was supposed to take Dilantin for a "seizure disorder," but stopped taking them because his prescription ran out. He said he had not had a seizure in more than 1 year. A neurologist was consulted but declined to prescribe the Dilantin again, as the patient had no evidence of seizures while in the hospital. The patient was discharged and requested to come to the physician's office for follow-up in 5 days. The patient was advised to stop drinking and was referred to the outpatient substance abuse treatment center run by the hospital for counseling after discharge, which he agreed to do.

Principal Diagnosis: _____

Secondary Diagnoses: _____

Principal Procedure: _____

Secondary Procedures: _____

10

The patient is a 25-year-old woman with moderate mental retardation who needs dental extractions for dental caries in the pulp and chronic apical periodontitis. Prior to surgery, the patient was instructed to stop the anticoagulant drug, Coumadin, she is taking and begin taking Lovenox instead. The patient has a history of mitral valve and aortic valve replacements and needs subacute bacterial endocarditis prophylaxis before the surgery. She is taking the anticoagulation therapy because of her past heart surgery. She also needed to be monitored for therapeutic anticoagulant drug levels prior to surgery. Management of the anticoagulation was completed in 2 days, and the patient had the surgical dental extractions on day 3. The patient was allowed to return home on day 5 after the Coumadin was restarted on day 4 with no ill effects. The patient has follow-up appointments with the oral surgeon and the family physician in the next week.

Principal Diagnosis: _____

Secondary Diagnoses: _____

Principal Procedure: _____

Secondary Procedures: _____

11

The patient is an 84-year-old woman who was brought to the emergency department by her family upon the advice of the family physician. The patient said she had increasing abdominal pain, nausea, and some vomiting. This condition started 2–3 days ago, and the patient could not eat due to the nausea. Prior to this episode of illness, the patient had been reasonably well, receiving medications for hypertension and hypothyroidism. The patient was admitted. Overnight the patient appeared to become more acutely ill, developed respiratory distress, and the rapid response team evaluated her and obtained her physician's order to transfer her to the ICU. Soon after, the patient required intubation and mechanical ventilation for acute respiratory failure. The patient had signs and symptoms of septicemia and sepsis, possibly with an intra-abdominal source. Blood cultures grew E. coli. She was taken to the operating room, where she underwent an exploratory laparotomy. The surgeons found acute bowel ischemia and gangrene involving 100% of the small bowel and the right colon. This was an inoperable condition, and the laparotomy site was closed. The family was advised of the patient's very poor prognosis and offered hospice care, which they accepted. The mechanical ventilation was discontinued, and the patient was extubated. She was kept as comfortable as possible overnight and expired in the early morning hours of hospital day 4. The physician's final diagnoses were acute ischemic and gangrenous intestine, acute respiratory failure, E. coli septicemia, hypertension, and hypothyroidism.

Principal Diagnosis: _____

Secondary Diagnoses: _____

Principal Procedure: _____

Secondary Procedures: _____

12

A 39–year-old patient was transferred from the long-term acute care hospital to the hospital with a four-day history of diffuse and worsening abdominal pain. The patient is ventilator dependent, with a tracheostomy in place for chronic respiratory failure, and has severe polymyositis and dermatomyositis. She had evidence of sepsis and was later found to have E. coli septicemia with sepsis. She was taken to surgery with the preoperative diagnosis of acute abdomen with free intraperitoneal air. She was found to have a perforated transverse colon with intra-abdominal abscess. The tracheostomy was malfunctioning, too. The surgery performed was an exploratory laparotomy, transverse colectomy with primary end to end anastomosis, loop ileostomy, drainage of the intra-abdominal abscess, and revision of the tracheostomy. After a long stay in the intensive care unit and on the medical-surgical floor, the patient slowly recovered from this major illness. She was transferred back to the long-term acute care hospital for extended recovery time.

Principal Diagnosis: _____

Secondary Diagnoses: _____

Principal Procedure: _____

Secondary Procedures: _____

13

The patient is a 59-year-old male who was referred to the gastroenterologist by his primary care physician for evaluation of abdominal pain and black stools. The patient said he had acid indigestion and heartburn for many years and took Tums and Pepto-Bismol on a daily basis. Over the past several days, he had been experiencing burning and cramping epigastric pain that was not relieved by the usual medications. He also had noted black tarry stools, which was a new problem for him. His primary care physician had placed the patient on Pepcid. The patient's mother had a history of peptic ulcer disease, but there were no other major illnesses in the family. The gastroenterologist recommended the patient have an upper GI endoscopy to further evaluate the source of the problem and the patient consented. On an outpatient basis, the physician performed an esophagogastroduodenoscopy at the hospital. The findings included a normal appearing esophagus. There was a large hiatal hernia pouch extending about 4 cm below the junction to the diaphragmatic closure. The stomach body, angulus, and antrum were normal. The pyloric channel was normal. There was one solitary erosion measuring 3–4 mm in the duodenal bulb, but there was no evidence of recent bleeding. The descending duodenum was normal. No biopsies were taken. The physician's conclusion at the end of the examination was (1) gastroesophageal reflux, (2) hiatal hernia, and (3) small chronic duodenal ulcer. The physician recommended to the patient that he continue to take the Pepcid but discontinue the use of Pepto-Bismol because it possibly could cause the black tarry stools. The patient was to return to the gastroenterologist's office in one month and if symptoms continue, consider an abdominal ultrasound and work-up of the large bowel.

First-Listed Diagnosis: _____

Secondary Diagnoses: _____

First-Listed Procedure: _____

Secondary Procedures: _____

14

The patient is a 74 year old male who recently was in the hospital for a chronic bleeding duodenal ulcer. Because of significantly abnormal laboratory results, additional studies determined he had obstructive jaundice due to a suspected common bile duct stone. After discharge, the patient was seen again by the gastroenterologist who consulted on the patient in the hospital, and the patient was scheduled for an endoscopic retrograde cholangiopancreatography (ERCP) as an outpatient. The patient came to the hospital ambulatory surgery center on the morning the procedure was scheduled with continuing evidence of obstructive jaundice. An ERCP was performed with an Olympus video gastroduodenoscope. The duodenum was easily accessed. The ampulla was erythematous and widely patent. The catheter was placed into the pancreatic duct, and a pancreatogram was obtained. The catheter was repositioned into the common bile duct, and a guide wire was passed into the liver. The cholangiogram showed a filling defect within the common bile duct. A double channel papillotome was placed in the common bile duct and a 1 cm sphincterotomy was performed. The common bile duct was dilated and with an 11-mm balloon, the physician removed a large hard yellow stone without difficulty. Using contrast dye injected into the edges of the cut wound, hemostasis was achieved, and the scope was removed. The postoperative diagnoses for the procedure titled ERCP with sphincterotomy and stone extraction were (1) common duct stone and (2) chronic duodenal ulcer under treatment.

First-Listed Diagnosis: _____

Secondary Diagnoses: _____

First-Listed Procedure: _____

Secondary Procedures: _____

15

The patient is a 55-year-old man with a 35-year history of alcohol abuse. He came to the hospital emergency room after having one melenic stool at home. While in the ER he had another melenic stool. He is known to have esophageal varices secondary to alcoholic liver cirrhosis. He has had sclerotherapy for the varices in the past, but it was noted to be a failure. Patient had attempted to complete alcoholic rehabilitation on three occasions but has been unsuccessful and continues to drink—according to the patient, "only a couple of beers everyday." The patient is also known to have thrombocytopenia that may be the result of bone marrow suppressive affect of alcohol but not proven, and serial blood counts were performed during this admission. He has had gastrointestinal bleeding investigated during two previous admissions. The patient was seen in consultation by a gastroenterologist and a psychiatrist. The day after admission, the patient became increasingly tremulous and anxious, with anticipated alcohol withdrawal occurring. The withdrawal was successfully managed with medications, and the patient stayed in the hospital after threatening to leave against medical advice the evening of day 2. An upper GI endoscopy (EGD) was performed three days after admission. The findings of the exam were two small grade 1 distal esophageal varices 1 cm in length without stigmata. There were no gastric varices. The fundus and body of the stomach were within normal limits. There was mild peripyloric edema but no ulcers in the pylorus or duodenum. No sclerotherapy of the esophageal varices was necessary. It was suspected the GI bleeding had come from the esophageal varices, as there was no other source of bleeding found. The patient was given strong encouragement to continue work toward his sobriety, especially given the fact he had detoxification therapy while in the hospital to manage his withdrawal. He acknowledged it was a good time to return to Alcoholics Anonymous, which he acknowledged was a good program for him in the past, and take advantage of other community support systems for recovering alcoholics that the psychiatrist informed him about during this hospital stay, including two visits from gentlemen from the community program. The discharge summary prepared by his attending physician included the final diagnoses and procedures of bleeding esophageal varices in alcoholic liver disease, continuous alcoholism, alcoholic withdrawal, thrombocytopenia, EGD, and alcohol withdrawal treatment.

Principal Diagnosis: _____

Secondary Diagnoses: _____

Principal Procedure: _____

Secondary Procedures: _____

Chapter 13

Diseases of the Genitourinary System

Coding Scenarios for *Basic ICD-9-CM Coding*

The following case studies are organized by chapter following the sequence of the *Basic ICD-9-CM Coding* textbook. The objective of the case studies is to provide the student with more detailed clinical information to code, rather than one- or two-line diagnostic and procedure statements. Depending on whether the case study describes an inpatient hospital admission or an outpatient visit, the student is asked to provide the necessary diagnosis and procedure codes in the appropriate sequence—with principal diagnosis code listed first for inpatient admissions and main reason for visit code listed first for outpatient visits.

1

An 80-year-old female is admitted to the hospital with fever, malaise, and left flank pain. A urinalysis shows bacteria of more than 100,000/ml present in the urine and a subsequent urine culture shows Proteus growth as the cause of the infection. The patient was treated with intravenous antibiotics. Other preexisting conditions of hypertension, arteriosclerotic heart disease (ASHD), previous percutaneous transluminal coronary angioplasty (PTCA) but no history of coronary artery bypass graft (CABG), and long-term chronic obstructive pulmonary disease (COPD) were treated during the hospital stay. The patient also has a history of repeated urinary tract infections (UTI) over the past several years.

Principal Diagnosis: _____

Secondary Diagnoses: _____

Principal Procedure: _____

Secondary Procedures: _____

2

A 75-year-old man was admitted to the hospital in acute urinary retention. A transurethral resection of the prostate was performed, and the diagnosis of benign nodular hyperplasia of the prostate was made. The pathologist confirmed the hyperplasia diagnosis and also found microscopic foci of adenocarcinoma of the prostate. The attending physician listed both conditions as discharge diagnoses.

Principal Diagnosis: _____

Secondary Diagnoses: _____

Principal Procedure: _____

Secondary Procedures: _____

3

A 52-year-old woman was admitted to the hospital with urinary stress incontinence and is scheduled for surgical repair of a paravaginal cystocele. An anterior colporrhaphy is performed to repair the cystocele that was causing the incontinence. The patient has mild type II diabetes that is also treated during the hospital stay.

Principal Diagnosis: _____

Secondary Diagnoses: _____

Principal Procedure: _____

Secondary Procedures: _____

4

An 80-year-old man was brought to the emergency department with complaints of lower abdominal pain and the inability to urinate over the past 24 hours. An indwelling urinary catheter was placed in the patient and he was admitted. After study it was determined that the patient was in subacute to acute renal failure. The acute renal failure was caused by a urinary obstruction. The urologist concluded the urinary obstruction was a result of the patient's benign prostatic hypertrophy. An intravenous pyelogram was performed and confirmed the physician's diagnoses. The patient was treated with medications and the acute renal failure was resolved. The catheter remained in place for drainage. The patient would require a resection of the prostate but would return for prostate surgery the following week. The patient was discharged home.

Principal Diagnosis: _____

Secondary Diagnoses: _____

Principal Procedure: _____

Secondary Procedures: _____

5

A 60-year-old female patient is brought to a small community hospital complaining of flank and back pain, fever with chills, fatigue, and a general ill feeling. The patient was known to have essential hypertension and had a history of renal calculi treated six months ago. The patient was admitted with the diagnosis of possible urinary tract infection. Workup in the hospital showed evidence of acute pyelonephritis. She was treated with intravenous antibiotics, but while in the hospital the patient had a sudden loss of kidney function. A diagnosis was made of acute renal failure complicating the acute pyelonephritis. The physicians were concerned that the patient may need kidney dialysis, but this small community hospital did not have the equipment for dialysis. A urinary catheter was placed in the bladder, and a transfer of the patient to a larger hospital in the same city was quickly accomplished.

Principal Diagnosis: _____

Secondary Diagnoses: _____

Principal Procedure: _____

Secondary Procedures: _____

6

The patient is a 21-year-old man who is known to have polycystic kidney disease, which was diagnosed in the past year after he was found to have hypertension. Upon investigating the cause of hypertension in such a young individual, it was discovered he had polycystic kidney disease, an inherited condition. The hypertension was considered secondary to the kidney disease. On this occasion, the patient was admitted to the hospital because of worsening kidney function. After study, it was determined the patient had chronic kidney disease, stage III, as a result of the hypertension and polycystic kidney disease. This patient was referred to the university medical center for further management with hopes for better control of kidney function and avoidance of the need for kidney transplant.

Principal Diagnosis: _____

Secondary Diagnoses: _____

Principal Procedure: _____

Secondary Procedures: _____

7

The patient is a 46-year-old woman, gravida 3, para 3, admitted to the hospital for a scheduled vaginal hysterectomy and salpingo-oophorectomy. The patient has an extensive gynecological history and was most recently seen for dysmenorrhea and dyspareunia. She stated she was having prolonged, heavy menses with disturbing premenstrual syndrome that was lasting 3–4 days before the onset of the menses. Six months ago, an outpatient laparoscopy was performed and extensive endometriosis of the uterus, ovaries, tubes, and pelvic perito-neum was found. Lysis of adhesions and ablation of the endometriosis was attempted but due to the extensive nature of the disease, it was known the procedure would not be entirely suc-cessful. In addition, the patient has been diagnosed and treated for genital herpes on one occa-sion, molluscum contagiosum, diagnosed by vulvar biopsy, and cervical dysplasia described as mild to moderate that was investigated with 11 different biopsies. All subsequent pap smears have been normal. Despite continued treatment, the patient still suffers from chronic pelvic pain, dysmenorrhea, and dyspareunia. After discussing her treatment options, the patient con-sented to a vaginal hysterectomy and bilateral salpingo-oophorectomy to treat the extensive endometriosis of the various sites previously described. The surgery was accomplished without difficulty, and the patient was able to go home on day 3. An additional diagnosis was added to the record when the pathology report was reviewed by the surgeon. The pathologist's report confirmed the endometriosis as well as a small lesion of the cervix that was found to be car-cinoma in situ of the cervix.

Principal Diagnosis: _____

Secondary Diagnoses: _____

Principal Procedure: _____

Secondary Procedures: _____

8

The patient is a 25-year-old woman who is seen in the office today for a follow-up visit for a possible urinary tract infection. Last week the patient was in the office and had complained of pain and burning on urination, frequent urges to urinate, pressure in the lower abdomen, and foul-smelling urine. A urinalysis done last week showed a large number of white blood cells, and a urine culture was collected and sent to the laboratory. The culture confirmed the growth of more than 100,000 E. coli organisms. The diagnosis for this visit is more specifically acute cystitis due to E. coli organism. The patient has had frequent urinary tract infections in the past, and she is being referred to a urologist for further investigation and possible cystoscopy.

First-Listed Diagnosis: _____

Secondary Diagnoses: _____

First-Listed Procedure: _____

Secondary Procedures: _____

9

A patient is sent to the hospital outpatient radiology department with a physician's order for an intravenous pyelogram. Documented on the physician's order is the reason for the x-ray as "renal colic, possible kidney stone." The test is performed, and the diagnosis dictated by the physician on the IVP report is "renal colic due to bilateral nephrolithiasis with staghorn calculi." Following hospital and official coding guidelines, the hospital coder is able to use the radiologist's diagnosis as the reason for the outpatient test.

First-Listed Diagnosis: _____

Secondary Diagnoses: _____

First-Listed Procedure: _____

Secondary Procedures: _____

10

The patient is being admitted for the following procedure: transurethral ureteroscopic lithotripsy using high-energy shock waves. The patient is known to have several large ureteral stones, and other attempts to remove them have been unsuccessful. The lithotripsy procedure is performed without complications and the surgeon is satisfied that the ureteral stones were removed.

Principal Diagnosis: _____

Secondary Diagnoses: _____

Principal Procedure: _____

Secondary Procedures: _____

11

The patient is a 75-year-old man who was admitted to the hospital for severe weakness and falling multiple times at home over the past several days. The urinalysis performed in the Emergency Department showed evidence of a urinary tract infection, and for this reason he was admitted. The patient was also dehydrated. The patient also has bladder carcinoma, which has been an aggressive type treated by chemotherapy. He has bilateral nephrostomy tubes in place. There was some suspicion that there might be an obstruction in one of the nephrostomy tubes, but that was not found to be true. The patient also has coronary artery disease and is status post CABG with venous grafts. He has type II diabetes and hypercholesterolemia. The patient was seen in consultation by urology, oncology, and cardiology with his current and chronic conditions evaluated and treated with numerous medications, both intravenous and orally. The patient regained considerable strength and was able to return home with follow-up appointments made with 4 physicians.

Principal Diagnosis: _____

Secondary Diagnoses: _____

Principal Procedure: _____

Secondary Procedures: _____

12

The patient is a 45-year-old woman, gravida 2, para 2, who was electively admitted for a total abdominal hysterectomy and bilateral salpingo-oophorectomy primarily for her menometrorrhagia and severe dysmenorrhea with heavy flow and cramping. She also has uterine fibroids with the uterus being 15–16 weeks of gestation size. On the day of admission, a total abdominal hysterectomy and bilateral salpingo-oophorectomy was performed. She was found to have massive intraperitoneal adhesions that took an extended period of time to lyse. In the process of removing the adhesions, a small laceration was made in the small bowel. It was quickly repaired. During surgery she had profuse bleeding tendencies, apparently because of the continuous ingestion of ibuprofen she was taking for the pelvic pain she experienced. Bleeding tendencies are known to be an adverse effect of ibuprofen; the physician was not aware of the amount she was taking. After surgery, the patient experienced several complications. First, she was diagnosed with acute blood-loss anemia. She lost about 1500 ml of blood during surgery, according to the anesthesiologist. She had hypoxemia, which might be attributed to her current smoking, even though she tried to quit prior to surgery but was unsuccessful. She developed atelectasis and fever, both postoperative complications. Finally, during the postoperative management of her conditions, she complained of back pain and was found to have hydronephrosis, which may have been caused by the surgery, as so much packing was placed around the ureters to try to protect them. The urologist performed a cystoscopy, retrograde pyelogram, and inserted a stent into her right ureter. Within hours, the patient's problems immediately reverted. She became afebrile, the back pain and atelectasis disappeared. She was able to be discharged home on day 4 postop and has an appointment to see the surgeon in her office in two weeks.

Principal Diagnosis: _____

Secondary Diagnoses: _____

Principal Procedure: _____

Secondary Procedures: _____

13

A 46-year-old female was admitted to the hospital through the emergency room feeling tired, weak, and stating that she had not been feeling well for the past 3 days. She also stated she had diarrhea alternating with vomiting off and on for the past week. Laboratory tests were performed including an electrolyte panel, BUN, and creatinine all of which were abnormal. The impression written by the doctor on the history and physical examination report was "dehydration with suspected acute renal failure," and intravenous hydration was started. The patient was monitored closely by the nursing staff, including the documentation of fluid intake and output. The patient did not have diarrhea or vomiting. Laboratory tests including the BUN and creatinine were repeated over the next 48 hours. Given the patient's general healthy history and the other tests performed, there was no underlying chronic kidney condition. No reason for the patient's diarrhea and vomiting that occurred prior to admission was found. No dialysis was required, as the patient's normal kidney function returned as the patient was rehydrated. The physician concluded the patient's condition was acute renal failure due to dehydration.

Principal Diagnosis: _____

Secondary Diagnoses: _____

Principal Procedure: _____

Secondary Procedures: _____

14

The patient is a 68-year-old female who had a hysterectomy 22 years ago and had a cystocele repair 8 years ago. Now the patient has very significant urinary stress incontinence for the past 2 years and is admitted at this time for surgical treatment. She had failed conservative management with medications that had provided no improvement of her stress incontinence. The patient required inpatient recovery and monitoring because of her oxygen dependence due to severe COPD. The day of admission the patient was taken to surgery for a suprapubic sling operation. The procedure is a suspension of urethra from the suprapubic periosteum to restore support to the bladder and urethra. The patient was able to be released from the hospital late in the afternoon of the day after surgery, with no complications from the anesthesia and her lung function returned to her baseline status. Home health care services were ordered for the patient, and a follow-up appointment in the urologist office was scheduled for 7 days after surgery.

Principal Diagnosis: _____

Secondary Diagnoses: _____

Principal Procedure: _____

Secondary Procedures: _____

15

The patient is a 26-year-old female who is gravida 4, para 3, AB 1 with two past cesarean deliveries and one normal spontaneous vaginal delivery. She had one voluntary interruption of pregnancy at 10 weeks prior to the birth of her children. The patient states she does not want any more children and cannot tolerate oral contraceptives because of the side effects of nausea and vomiting. She also complains of irregular menstrual and intermenstrual uterine bleeding with 2 periods a month that last between 5 and 7 days. The patient is given the facts about the proposed procedures, the alternatives, risks, complications, and possible failure rate. Nevertheless the patient consents to the surgery to be performed on an outpatient basis at the hospital. The procedures performed are a dilatation and curettage with a diagnostic laparoscopy with bilateral tubal Falope ring application. The pre- and post-operative diagnoses are the same: dysfunctional uterine bleeding and desire for elective sterilization.

First-Listed Diagnosis: _____

Secondary Diagnoses: _____

First-Listed Procedure: _____

Secondary Procedures: _____

Chapter 14

Complications of Pregnancy, Childbirth, and the Puerperium

Coding Scenarios for *Basic ICD-9-CM Coding*

The following case studies are organized by chapter following the sequence of the *Basic ICD-9-CM Coding* textbook. The objective of the case studies is to provide the student with more detailed clinical information to code, rather than one- or two-line diagnostic and procedure statements. Depending on whether the case study describes an inpatient hospital admission or an outpatient visit, the student is asked to provide the necessary diagnosis and procedure codes in the appropriate sequence—with principal diagnosis code listed first for inpatient admissions and main reason for visit code listed first for outpatient visits.

1

A 35-year-old woman at 22-weeks of pregnancy underwent a 1-hour glucose screening test that was found to be abnormal, with a blood sugar level reported to be over 200 mg/dL. The patient was sent to the outpatient laboratory for a 3-hour glucose tolerance test. The reason for the laboratory test was documented on the order as "rule out gestational diabetes; abnormal glucose tolerance on screening during pregnancy."

First-Listed Diagnosis: _____

Secondary Diagnoses: _____

First-Listed Procedure: _____

Secondary Procedures: _____

2

The patient is a 26-year-old female, gravida 2, para 1, in her 10th week of pregnancy. While at work, she developed severe cramping and vaginal bleeding. Co-workers brought her to the hospital emergency department, and she was admitted to the hospital. After examination, the physician described her condition as an "inevitable abortion." When the physician was asked to further define her condition, she stated that an inevitable abortion meant the cervix was dilated and fetal and placental material probably had already passed from the patient's body. According to the physician, another description of this condition was an incomplete early spontaneous abortion. During this pregnancy the patient had been treated for transient hypertension of pregnancy, for which she was monitored during this hospital stay. She was taken to the operating room where a dilation and curettage was performed to treat the abortion. There were no complications from the procedure.

Principal Diagnosis: _____

Secondary Diagnoses: _____

Principal Procedure: _____

Secondary Procedures: _____

3

A 34-year-old female is admitted in active labor during week 39 of pregnancy. She had a previous cesarean section 2 years ago as a result of fetal distress and cephalopelvic disproportion (CPD). No fetal distress was found during this admission, but it was determined that the patient still had CPD; therefore, a repeat low cervical cesarean section had to be performed. A healthy 8 lb, 10 oz female was safely delivered.

Principal Diagnosis: _____

Secondary Diagnoses: _____

Principal Procedure: _____

Secondary Procedures: _____

4

A 45-year-old woman, gravida 1, para 0, was admitted in labor to the hospital obstetrical department. Unexpectedly but happily, this woman found herself pregnant after 15 years of marriage. She had been under the care of a physician who specialized in high-risk pregnancies. Because of her age, the woman was thought to be at higher risk for complications, but her pregnancy was uneventful. The physician described her as an "elderly primigravida, full term pregnancy." She had a manually assisted vaginal delivery of a healthy 7 lb, 5 oz girl. Mother and baby were able to leave the hospital on day 2 after delivery.

Principal Diagnosis: _____

Secondary Diagnoses: _____

Principal Procedure: _____

Secondary Procedures: _____

5

The patient is a 30-year-old woman, gravida 3, para 2, in week 40 of pregnancy. The patient is admitted for "induction of labor at term." There is no other reason documented by the physician as the reason for labor induction. The patient was not in labor at the time of admission. The induction is performed by artificial rupture of membranes. Labor proceeds normally, and the woman delivers a healthy male infant vaginally without complications. The mother and baby were able to be discharged on the hospital day 2.

Principal Diagnosis: _____

Secondary Diagnoses: _____

Principal Procedure: _____

Secondary Procedures: _____

6

The patient is seen for her third antepartum visit in the high-risk OB clinic. The woman has admitted to using cocaine both prior to and during her current pregnancy. A drug screen performed during this visit is positive for cocaine. She feels she is unable to quit using the drug on her own, but wishes to become drug-free for the safety of her baby and herself. The patient has consented to admission to a specialized antepartum unit at a nearby hospital for drug detoxification. The patient will be seen again in the OB clinic in 1 month for continued antepartum care. The patient is also being treated for a urinary tract infection during the pregnancy.

First-Listed Diagnosis: _____

Secondary Diagnoses: _____

Principal Procedure: _____

Secondary Procedures: _____

7

The patient is seen in her OB physician's office 2 weeks after a normal vaginal delivery that produced a healthy full-term female infant. The patient has been breast-feeding the infant, but over the past 2 days has developed redness, pain, and swelling of her right breast. Upon examination there appears to be a hard lump in the right breast, and the diagnosis of a postpartum breast abscess is made. The patient is given a prescription for an antibiotic and advised she may take an anti-inflammatory drug to reduce the pain and inflammation. She is also advised to discontinue breast feeding until the infection resolves. The patient will return to the office within 7 days for a re-evaluation.

First-Listed Diagnosis: _____

Secondary Diagnoses: _____

Principal Procedure: _____

Secondary Procedures: _____

8

The patient is admitted to the hospital 6 weeks after delivering a healthy female infant following a full-term pregnancy with the admitting diagnosis of acute cholecystitis with cholelithiasis. The patient was known to have gallstones prior to her pregnancy and had symptoms of the disease recur during the pregnancy and become more serious during the immediate postpartum period. A laparoscopic cholecystectomy is performed without complications. Pathologic examination confirmed the admitting diagnosis. The patient is able to go home 1 day after the surgery.

Principal Diagnosis: _____

Secondary Diagnoses: _____

Principal Procedure: _____

Secondary Procedures: _____

9

The patient is admitted to the hospital with excessive vaginal bleeding 2 days following an elective abortion at an outpatient surgical facility. The patient is immediately taken to surgery for a dilatation and curettage. The pathology report describes the tissue removed as "retained products of conception." The previous elective abortion was not completed as expected. At the time of the procedure it was determined the patient had anemia due to the blood loss and it was treated. The physician's final diagnosis is "delayed hemorrhage following elective abortion, now completed, anemia of pregnancy due to blood loss." The patient is able to be discharged the next day.

Principal Diagnosis: _____

Secondary Diagnoses: _____

Principal Procedure: _____

Secondary Procedures: _____

10

A pregnant woman is admitted to the hospital during week 12 of her pregnancy. The patient had called her physician describing vague symptoms, and the physician ordered a complete obstetrical ultrasound. The fetus is seen in utero, but no fetal heart tones are detected and further examination confirms the fetus is dead. The physician describes the condition in one progress note as an inevitable abortion and in another progress note as a missed abortion. No medical or obstetrical complication can be found to explain the loss of the pregnancy. A D&C is performed to complete the missed abortion. The mother receives grief counseling and is able to be discharged 1 day after the procedure.

Principal Diagnosis: _____

Secondary Diagnoses: _____

Principal Procedure: _____

Secondary Procedures: _____

11

The patient was admitted from home on May 31 with vaginal bleeding. This is the patient's third admission to labor and delivery during this pregnancy. The patient is 33 years old, gravida 1, para 0, with an estimated date of confinement of July 9. She has twin gestation and complete placenta previa. Because of this last episode of bleeding, it was decided to keep her at bedrest in labor and delivery at the hospital so that, should any further excessive bleeding occur, she would be available for emergency cesarean delivery if necessary. The intent was to keep her until she reached 36 weeks gestation as recommended by the perinatologist in consultation. On June 10 she had bright red bleeding from the vagina. There were contractions noted. Because she was one day short of 36 weeks gestation, it was decided to go forward with a primary low cervical cesarean delivery for the complete placenta previa with hemorrhage. She delivered a 4 pound, 9 ounce viable female with Apgars of 8 and 9 at 16:01 p.m. She delivered a 4 pound, 15 ounce viable male with Apgars of 7 and 9 at 16:02 p.m. Intraoperative blood loss was approximately 1 liter. She was anemic due to blood loss prior to surgery. She had a good recovery from the surgery and her hemoglobin stabilized at 8.2 gm. She was discharged home to follow up in the office in 2 weeks for an incision check. Her twin infants remained in the premature nursery for further treatment.

Principal Diagnosis: _____

Secondary Diagnoses: _____

Principal Procedure: _____

Secondary Procedures: _____

12

The patient was admitted to the hospital from the obstetrician's office at 38 and 3/7 weeks gestation. She came to the office today complaining of not feeling well and noticing a lack of fetal movement over the past day or two. She had been in the office 3 days ago and the baby was reactive. The biophysical profile in the office today was 6/8 with no breathing movement. The nonstress test was reactive. The patient also has severe iron deficiency anemia of pregnancy and hypertension complicating her pregnancy. She desires a tubal ligation during this delivery for her grand multiparity. She is 38 years old and gravida 6, para 3, AB 2 with an estimated date of delivery of June 30. She has had two previous cesarean deliveries, one in 1995 and one in 2005. Her oldest child was delivered vaginally in 1993. Because of the decreased fetal movement, a repeat low cesarean delivery was performed on June 19, 2008. A bilateral tubal ligation was also performed by ligation and crushing. Delivered at 4:55 p.m. was a 6 pound, 2 ounce live female infant with Apgar scores of 7 and 8. The patient had an uneventful recovery from the delivery, was continued on her medications for anemia and gestational hypertension, and asked to return to the office in 2 weeks. Mother and daughter were discharged home together on post-op day 3.

Principal Diagnosis: _____

Secondary Diagnoses: _____

Principal Procedure: _____

Secondary Procedures: _____

13

The patient is a 23-year-old female , gravida 2, para 1, AB 0, who was admitted to the hospital in the early morning hours reporting she had sporadic contractions for the past 24 hours. She is 38 and 1/7 weeks gestation. At 2:45 a.m. she had an artificial rupture of membrane, her cervix was 4-5 cm dilated and 90% effaced. She had some variable fetal heart rate decelerations on the external fetal monitor. She was pushing with some of her contractions, and the fetal distress appeared to worsen. Presentation was vertex, and station was minus 1 for most of the morning. The fetal head came down to about zero station. However, since the fetal distress did not abate, a long discussion was held with the patient and her mother about a change in the management of her anticipated delivery. The doctor recommended a cesarean delivery for the intrauterine pregnancy be performed because of the fetal distress caused by fetal heart rate decelerations, and the patient consented to it. A low transverse primary cervical cesarean section was performed at 10 a.m. under spinal anesthesia. A viable male infant with spontaneous respiration and cry was delivered. The cord was doubly clamped and cut, and the infant was placed in the warmer and examined by the pediatrician. The mother's placenta was removed, uterine cavity cleaned, and the uterine incision closed in two layers. Careful inspection of the uterus, fallopian tubes, and ovaries did not reveal any unusual findings or bleeding. The peritoneum was closed vertically, and the fascia was closed. Subcutaneous tissue was closed with plain silk, and the skin was closed with subcuticular sutures followed by staples. The patient received Pitocin and a gram of Ancef, per protocol. The patient's estimated blood loss was about 500 cc with no surgical complications. Postoperatively the patient complained of the typical abdominal discomfort from the incision. The patient was known to have microcytic anemia during her pregnancy, and the anemia was present at the time of delivery and at discharge as well. The anemia continued to be treated. The patient was discharged with her newborn son on day 3 with a follow-up appointment in the obstetrician's office in 10 days.

Principal Diagnosis: _____

Secondary Diagnoses: _____

Principal Procedure: _____

Secondary Procedures: _____

14

The 45-year-old female was admitted to the hospital in premature labor at 36 and 4/7th weeks gestation with 5 cm dilation. The patient is gravida 6, para 5 with five daughters at home ranging in age from 8 to 18 years. This was a "surprise" pregnancy to this elderly multigravida patient and her husband. Two antepartum ultrasounds predicted the birth of a male infant, which has brought considerable excitement to the family. The patient's labor was augmented with Pitocin drip, and she was placed on an external fetal monitor. The patient has a known cystocele that was monitored during the pregnancy and will probably require surgical treatment in the near future. After a short period of labor, the patient had a manually assisted delivery of a healthy male infant at 4 lb 2 oz with Apgar scores of 8 and 9 at one and five minutes. When the patient was visited by the delivering physician in her room later the same day, the patient asked if it was "too late" for tubal ligation, as she and her husband concluded their family was complete and she desired permanent sterilization. The next day the patient was taken to the operating room for a postpartum endoscopic tubal ligation by division and ligation, which was completed uneventfully. The patient was discharged home on day 3, but the male infant remained in the nursery for observation and weight gain. Discharge instructions and a follow-up appointment with her obstetrician were given to the patient.

Principal Diagnosis: _____

Secondary Diagnoses: _____

Principal Procedure: _____

Secondary Procedures: _____

15

HISTORY: The patient is a 28-year-old, gravida 2, para 1, with complete/total placenta previa with four bleeding episodes. She has a previous cesarean section for her first child. The patient has received steroids and has consented for a repeat preterm cesarean delivery because of the placenta previa and the threat-to-life hemorrhage that could occur again as the pregnancy continued or during a vaginal delivery. The patient is aware that a hysterectomy may need to be performed if the placenta cannot be removed but will be avoided if at all possible. The patient also is known to have the baby in a double footling breech presentation and had gestational hypertension during this pregnancy. Labor was not allowed to occur in this patient. The patient is a 32 5/7 week gestation.

FINDINGS:

1. Complete placenta previa

2. Viable male infant in double footling breech presentation. Weight 5 pounds even. Apgar scores were 6 at one minute, 8 at five minutes, and 9 at ten minutes. The uterus did not have to be removed. There were normal-appearing tubes and ovaries. Of note: the pathologist reported on examination of the placenta that mild-to-moderate amnionitis was present in this mid third-trimester placenta.

DESCRIPTION OF PROCEDURE: The patient was taken to the operating room, where a spinal anesthesia was found to be adequate. She was then prepped and draped in the normal, sterile fashion in the dorsal supine position with a left-ward tilt. A Pfannenstiel skin incision was made with the scalpel and carried through to the underlying layer of the fascia. The fascia was incised in the midline, and the incision extended laterally with the use of Mayo scissors. The superior aspect of the fascial incision was then grasped with the Kocher clamps, and the underlying rectus muscles were dissected with the Mayo scissors. Attention was then turned to the inferior aspect of this incision, which in a similar fashion was grasped with the pickups and entered, and the underlying rectus muscles were dissected with the Mayo scissors. The rectus muscle was spread in the midline, and the peritoneum was entered bluntly. The peritoneum was extended superiorly and inferiorly, with good visualization of the bladder, using the Metzenbaum scissors. The bladder blade was placed and the vesico-uterine peritoneum was identified, tented up, and entered sharply with the Metzenbaum scissors. A bladder flap was then created digitally, and the bladder blade was replaced. The uterine incision was made about a centimeter and a half higher than usual due to the placenta previa, and the incision was widened with blunt force. At this time we were able to reach past the placenta previa and were able to grab both feet. At this point, the bag seemed to rupture. The infant was delivered in double footling breech with the typical breech maneuvers. The head delivered atraumatically. The nose and mouth were bulb suctioned. The cord was doubly clamped and cut. The infant was handed off to the waiting pediatrician. Cord gases and blood were obtained. The placenta was removed. The uterus was exteriorized and cleared of all clots and debris. The uterine incision was then repaired with a 0 Vicryl in a running, locked fashion, and a second layer of the same was used to ensure excellent hemostasis. The uterus was then replaced into the abdomen and the gutters were irrigated and cleared of all clots and debris. The peritoneum was repaired with a 2-0 Vicryl. The 0 Vicryl was then used to reapproximate the rectus muscle in the midline. The fascia was repaired with a 0 Vicryl in a running fashion. The subcutaneous layer was then closed with plain 2-0 silk on a GI needle. The skin was closed with staples. The sponge, lap, and needle counts were correct times two. The patient had been given a gram of Ancef at cord clamp. The patient was taken to the recovery room in stable condition.

Principal Diagnosis: _____

Secondary Diagnoses: _____

Principal Procedure: _____

Secondary Procedures: _____

Chapter 15

Diseases of the Skin and Subcutaneous Tissue

Coding Scenarios for *Basic ICD-9-CM Coding*

The following case studies are organized by chapter following the sequence of the *Basic ICD-9-CM Coding* textbook. The objective of the case studies is to provide the student with more detailed clinical information to code, rather than one- or two-line diagnostic and procedure statements. Depending on whether the case study describes an inpatient hospital admission or an outpatient visit, the student is asked to provide the necessary diagnosis and procedure codes in the appropriate sequence—with principal diagnosis code listed first for inpatient admissions and main reason for visit code listed first for outpatient visits.

1

A 90-year-old woman, a resident of a long-term care facility, was admitted to the hospital with a severe decubitus ulcer on the right buttock described as a stage III pressure ulcer. The patient also had a small chronic ulcer on the right heel. The patient also has generalized atherosclerosis. Treatments of the skin conditions were an excisional debridement of the skin of the heel and an excisional debridement into the muscle of the buttock. The wound care nurse closely monitored the patient after surgery and gave detailed instructions to the nurses at the long-term care facility who would be taking care of the patient after discharge. The patient was transferred back to the long-term care facility. The wound care physician and nurse would visit the patient in the long-term care facility within 1 week to monitor the healing of the pressure and chronic ulcers.

Principal Diagnosis: _____

Secondary Diagnoses: _____

Principal Procedure: _____

Secondary Procedures: _____

2

A 20-year-old woman was scheduled for an outpatient procedure to treat a pilonidal cyst that had become abscessed. The procedure performed was an incision and drainage of the pilonidal sinus. The patient will continue to take oral antibiotics to resolve the infection. The patient was discharged home with a follow-up appointment in 7 days with the surgeon who performed the procedure.

First-Listed Diagnosis: _____

Secondary Diagnoses: _____

Principal Procedure: _____

Secondary Procedures: _____

3

A 19-year-old woman was seen in the dermatologist's office with extensive inflammation and irritation of the skin on her eyelids and under her eyebrows that was spreading to her temples and forehead. Upon questioning the patient, the physician learned that she had recently used new eye cosmetics. The physician had examined the patient during a prior visit for cystic acne. During this visit, the physician also examined the patient's cystic acne on her forehead and jawline. He advised her to continue to use the medication he had prescribed previously. The physician's diagnosis was contact dermatitis due to cosmetics and cystic acne. He advised the patient to immediately discontinue use of any make-up on the face until the next follow-up visit. The patient was given a topical medication to resolve the inflammation.

First-Listed Diagnosis: _____

Secondary Diagnoses: _____

Principal Procedure: _____

Secondary Procedures: _____

4

A 50-year-old woman was seen in her primary care physician's office complaining of warmth and redness of her left anterior lower leg. Last weekend she was doing yard work and received a small puncture wound on the same area of her leg. She did not think she had a foreign body in the wound. Over the next couple of days the area became red and began to show slight swelling. Upon physical examination, the physician found a tiny puncture point with obvious cellulitis tracking down her leg from below the knee almost to the ankle. The wound itself required no treatment. The physician recommended the patient take a short-term course of antibiotics and return for a follow-up visit in 5 days. The diagnosis written on the encounter form was puncture wound resulting in cellulitis of the lower leg.

First-Listed Diagnosis: _____

Secondary Diagnoses: _____

First-Listed Procedure: _____

Secondary Procedures: _____

5

A 60-year-old man was sent to the dermatologist's office by his primary care physician for evaluation of several lesions on his arms and legs. The patient states he spends a lot of time out of doors as a mailman and golfing every weekend. The patient expresses the concern that he may have skin cancer. He remembers that his father, a farmer, had many of these same type of lesions on his arms and neck through the years. After performing a thorough skin examination, the physician finds multiple brown annular keratotic lesions on the patient's arms and lower legs with patchy dry areas around them. The physician performs a skin biopsy and examines the lesion microscopically. No cancer type cells are seen. Given the patient's history of the same lesions in the family and his frequent exposure to ultraviolet sunlight, the physician explains to the patient that he has what is referred to as DSAP or disseminated superficial actinic porokeratosis. Further he explains there is no treatment to prevent these lesions from returning once removed. The patient elects not to have any lesions removed at this time but will consider it and make an appointment in the future if he decides to have them removed.

First-Listed Diagnosis: _____

Secondary Diagnoses: _____

First-Listed Procedure: _____

Secondary Procedures: _____

6

The 25-year-old patient is seen in the dermatologist's office upon the advice of the family practice physician with the complaint of excessive sweating in particular areas of her body, such as her underarms, soles of her feet, and the palms of her hands. The patient notes that the excessive sweating started when she was a young teenager. She describes this condition as very embarrassing and difficult to manage, as, nearly every day, she has to take extra clothing with her in order to change her blouse at work. The physician takes a complete history and cannot find any medical condition that might be causing this problem. The physical examination confirms, however, excessive moisture under the arms and on her hands and feet. The physician is certain the patient suffers from primary hyperhidrosis. Her primary care physician had given her a prescription for a certain antiperspirant designed for this condition. The patient had tried the antiperspirant but found it to be ineffective as well as irritating to her underarm skin. The dermatologist recommends injections of botulinum toxin at the sites where excessive sweating is occurring. The drug promptly freezes the nerve that would normally stimulate the sweat gland. He had used this therapy for other patients who were pleased with the results. The patient immediately wants the procedure. The physician injects both axillae with the "botox" under sterile technique. The patient is to return in 4 weeks to report on the results or sooner if problems are detected. The physician states that if the patient has a positive response, the injections will need to be repeated every 6 to 9 months.

First-Listed Diagnosis: _____

Secondary Diagnoses: _____

Principal Procedure: _____

Secondary Procedures: _____

7

Upon the advice of his family physician, the patient made an appointment with a dermatologist to evaluate an itching, red, blistering condition that recently appeared on his lower arms and lower legs. The patient is a 26-year-old man who works as a salesman in a computer store. The dermatologist asks the patient questions about his recent contact with new soaps, detergents, chemicals, fabrics, fragrances, and outdoor or indoor plants, but the patient reports he has had no new experiences with these items. Upon further questioning, the doctor learns the patient had a new roommate move in 1 month ago with a dog that had taken a strong liking to the patient and followed him everywhere. The physician is then certain the patient's condition is a contact dermatitis resulting from exposure to animal dander. The physician gives the patient samples of a topical ointment and a prescription for a topical corticosteroid medication to reduce the inflammation and relieve the itching. The patient is told this condition is likely to continue as long as the animal resides with him. The patient is advised to return in 2 weeks for a follow-up visit.

First-Listed Diagnosis: _____

Secondary Diagnoses: _____

First-Listed Procedure: _____

Secondary Procedures: _____

8

The patient is a 54-year-old woman who has suffered from left-side chronic ulcerative colitis for many years. Today she is seen in her physician's office for a follow-up visit. Of most concern to the patient today are the "red bumps" that are present on her right lower leg. The patient has had similar lesions before now, but the lesions have recently returned and are larger in size than previously. The physician recognizes the lesions as a recurrence of erythema nodosum, which is a complication of her underlying systemic condition. The tender red nodules appear to be coinciding with the worsening of her colitis. The patient thinks she might have bumped her leg against a grocery cart the previous week and blamed that for the tender nodules that appeared first. A topical ointment is prescribed, and the physician advises the patient that the nodules will probably heal as her colitis becomes more controlled with the medication she is currently receiving. The physician treats both the colitis and the erythema nodosum during the visit today.

First-Listed Diagnosis: _____

Secondary Diagnoses: _____

First-Listed Procedure: _____

Secondary Procedures: _____

9

A 60-year-old man returns to the Wound Care Clinic today for a follow-up visit for treatment of his diabetic foot ulcer. The patient is a type I diabetic with an ulcer on the heel of his foot that is attributed to his diabetes. The wound was infected when the patient was first seen in the Wound Care Clinic, but today the ulcer is much smaller in size and is no longer infected. Close surveillance, wound dressings, and the appropriate use of antibiotics were successful in treating this man's foot ulcer and prevented it from becoming gangrenous. The patient receives ongoing education about proper skin and foot care as his diabetic condition makes him at risk for more ulcers. The patient will return in 2 weeks for a follow-up visit.

First-Listed Diagnosis: _____

Secondary Diagnoses: _____

First-Listed Procedure: _____

Secondary Procedures: _____

10

The patient is a 47-year-old woman who returns to her dermatologist's office after a 1-year absence with pityriasis rosea, a condition she has had several times before. Usually in the spring of the year, the patient suffers from this skin condition. She explains to the physician that she first noticed a 3–4 cm annular or ring-shaped lesion on her trunk that was followed a few days later with many smaller ring-shaped and pustular lesions parallel to the skin folds on her chest and abdomen. The physician notes the red and brown lesions with a trailing scale. Once again, the patient describes the condition as extremely itchy and is seeking another prescription for the topical glucocorticoid cream the physician prescribed in the past. The physician is agreeable to renewing the prescription and offers the patient the option of UV-B (ultraviolet light) phototherapy, as the outbreak seems to be more severe this year. The patient states she will try the cream first and make another appointment for the phototherapy if there is no improvement.

First-Listed Diagnosis: _____

Secondary Diagnoses: _____

First-Listed Procedure: _____

Secondary Procedures: _____

11

The patient was registered as an outpatient for same-day surgery. The 53-year-old man had two lesions on his scalp. One lesion was 1.2 cm × 1.3 cm × 1.0 cm on the posterior scalp and was slightly raised and slightly erythematous. After injection of local anesthesia in the center of the lesion, a 3-mm punch biopsy was performed. The biopsied tissue was then removed and sent for frozen section to pathology. The frozen section was positive for basal cell carcinoma. A 5-0 Prolene stitch was used to close the defect. The patient had a second lesion about 2 cm away from the first lesion and measuring 0.5 cm × 0.2 cm. The lesion was excised by using sharpened scalpel to penetrate the skin and dermis on both sides. This lesion was then removed and sent to pathology. The second lesion was reported to be an actinic keratosis and removed in its entirety. It was closed with a 5-0 Prolene stitch times 2. Steri-strips were applied. We informed the patient that we will refer him to a plastic surgeon for removal of the basal cell carcinoma, as this may require significant undermining and wound closure may be problematic because of the size of the lesion. There is quite a bit of tension on the patient's scalp, and the excision of the basal cell carcinoma will require the skills of a plastic surgeon. The patient will be seen for follow up in this surgeon's office in 7 days and was given the name and phone number of the plastic surgeon to call for an appointment within the next 2 weeks.

First-Listed Diagnosis: _____

Secondary Diagnoses: _____

First-Listed Procedure: _____

Secondary Procedures: _____

12

The patient is a 56-year-old woman admitted to the hospital after being seen in the physician's office for two large draining abscesses on her back. One was on the upper-left back and the other on the right-lower back skin. Both lesions were large, actively draining, and showed some necrotic features to the surrounding tissue. These areas on the back were warm to the touch and tender. Because of the size of the lesions, the patient was admitted as an inpatient for surgery. The surgeon performed an incision and drainage on two areas of the back. The right-lower back actually had two areas of abscess with necrotic tissue present. These were widely opened with sharp debridement with a cavity that connected the two abscesses. A third incision was made in this area because the fluctuance had penetrated deeper down, and the entire area required debridement of necrotic tissue and copious irrigation. A Penrose drain was placed to keep the tracks open. The left-upper back had an area of fluctuance of 3 cm × 5 cm. A transverse incision was made deep into the subcutaneous cavity, and all the purulent material was removed from the widely opened area. It was copiously irrigated. Specimens were collected from all these areas for cultures. The fluid cultures grew Methicillin-resistant staphylococcus aureus susceptible to Clindamycin. While in the hospital, the patient received intravenous antibiotics. The patient was continued on this antibiotic orally for one more week. The drain was left in for the surgeon to remove about 3 days after discharge. The patient was known to have hypertension, and it was treated during the hospital stay. The patient had two fasting glucose tests performed in the hospital, and both were significantly elevated at 160 and 180. A hemoglobin A1c was performed with a finding of 9.5. The patient was informed that she had type II diabetes, poorly controlled. She had a dietary consultation in the hospital and will attend diabetic education classes after discharge. She was discharged with a glucose monitoring kit and a prescription for oral diabetic medication. She will be seen in the primary care physician's office in 1 week.

Principal Diagnosis: _____

Secondary Diagnoses: _____

Principal Procedure: _____

Secondary Procedures: _____

13

The patient was a 69-year-old man who had many previous admissions for cellulitis and alcoholic cirrhosis of the liver proven by biopsy. He had hepatic encephalopathy on several occasions and hepatorenal failure two times when he was previously hospitalized. He also has marked exogenous obesity. On this occasion he was admitted for an abrupt elevation of temperature with diaphoresis on the night of admission following a dinner party. His lower abdominal area was the site of marked reddening and induration at the fold of his paniculus adiposis. His admitting diagnosis was cellulitis of abdominal tissues, and he was started on intravenous antibiotics. He was seen in consultation by infectious disease physician and a nephrologist. It appeared his cellulitis this time was triggered by edema of the extremities. His abdominal cellulitis responded virtually overnight to the intravenous cephazolin. He also had stasis dermatitis and cellulitis of his legs, but the legs were less red and indurated than his lower abdomen. He was also proven to be hypoalbuminemic. Blood cultures were drawn and pseudomonas aeruginosa was found in his blood. This organism was not susceptible to the antibiotic he received for the first four days of his hospitalization. Because the antibiotics he was receiving would not have been expected to kill the pseudomonas, it was speculated that the process involving the lower abdominal wall was due to gram positive coccal organisms such as staphylococcus or streptococcus, which is why the abdominal cellulitis responded so quickly to the cephalosporin antibiotics. The organism causing the abdominal cellulitis was not proven. But it was not surprising to find the pseudomonas in his blood by virtue of his anatomic problems as well as his poor hepatic function, which leaves him prone to bacteremia. However, the bacteremia produced no symptoms in this patient with a well established history of cirrhosis. He was anicteric and did not have any evidence of encephalopathy. He was continued on treatment with the best antipseudomonal agent and continued with gentle diuresis to remove the edema fluid in both lower extremities that produce the leg cellulitis. His liver function studies were not any worse than previously noted, but the doctors again encouraged the patient to completely eliminate alcohol consumption. Because the patient travels extensively for business and pleasure, the doctors emphasized the need to take all of his medications faithfully in order to maintain his apparent resilience in the knowledge of his extensive liver disease and to carry antibiotics with him so that any early onset of cellulitis might be aborted by early treatment. The patient agreed and was discharged after an 11-day hospital stay. His discharge diagnoses were documented as cellulitis, anterior abdominal wall, gram-negative bacteremia (pseudomonas), stasis dermatitis and cellulitis bilateral lower extremities, advanced alcoholic liver cirrhosis with hypoalbuminemia, and morbid obesity.

Principal Diagnosis: _____

Secondary Diagnoses: _____

Principal Procedure: _____

Secondary Procedures: _____

14

The 4-year-old female was admitted to the hospital directly from her pediatrician's office because of symmetrical raised red skin lesions over 20% of her body. She also has edema of her eyelids. The child had been treated with a penicillin-type drug for an upper respiratory infection, and it was suspected the child was having a reaction to that drug. A pediatric infectious disease specialist examined the patient immediately. After reviewing laboratory results, the consultant concluded the patient had Stevens-Johnson Syndrome, which is a toxic epidermal necrolysis that produces the skin lesions seen on this child. The consultant attributed the edema of the eyelids to the same syndrome. The patient received a 4-day treatment of intravenous immunoglobulin drugs and made an excellent recovery. The consultant stated the 20–25% exfoliation of her skin surface caused by the Stevens-Johnson Syndrome was an adverse effect of the penicillin this child received for the respiratory infection. The child was discharged home to her parents' care with pediatric home health nursing follow-up.

Principal Diagnosis: _____

Secondary Diagnoses: _____

Principal Procedure: _____

Secondary Procedures: _____

15

The patient is an 89-year-old female admitted to the hospital from the nursing home for surgical treatment of her Stage IV pressure ulcer of the coccyx. The patient was taken to surgery, and the physician dictated an operative report that described a debridement of the coccyx wound with sharp excision down to the fascia and the bone. The patient was transferred back to the nursing home two days later to be visited by the surgeon and the wound care clinical nurse specialist in one week. While the patient was in the hospital she continued to receive treatment for her chronic diastolic heart failure, coronary artery (native vessel) disease with known total chronic occlusion in at least 2 coronary vessels.

Principal Diagnosis: _____

Secondary Diagnoses: _____

Principal Procedure: _____

Secondary Procedures: _____

Chapter 16

Diseases of the Musculoskeletal System and Connective Tissue

Coding Scenarios for *Basic ICD-9-CM Coding*

The following case studies are organized by chapter following the sequence of the *Basic ICD-9-CM Coding* textbook. The objective of the case studies is to provide the student with more detailed clinical information to code, rather than one- or two-line diagnostic and procedure statements. Depending on whether the case study describes an inpatient hospital admission or an outpatient visit, the student is asked to provide the necessary diagnosis and procedure codes in the appropriate sequence—with principal diagnosis code listed first for inpatient admissions and main reason for visit code listed first for outpatient visits.

1

A 50-year-old man is treated for severe low back pain and numbness on the left leg over several weeks. The patient thinks the pain is the result of lifting heavy boxes during a recent move to a new residence, but the physician cannot conclude that this was the cause. Diagnostic studies reveal that the patient has a herniated disc. The patient is also found to have osteoarthritis of the spine. The patient is admitted for a laminotomy and excision of the intervertebral disc at L4-L5 to treat the herniated disc. The patient has an uneventful postoperative recovery and is discharged home to begin rehabilitation therapy in the near future. How would the diagnosis and procedures be coded with ICD-9-CM?

Principal Diagnosis: _____

Secondary Diagnoses: _____

Principal Procedure: _____

Secondary Procedures: _____

2

An 82-year-old woman had been treated by her family physician for chronic low back pain. One morning upon awakening she could not get out of bed due to severe back pain. She was brought to the emergency department and admitted. X-rays show several severe compression fractures of the lumbar vertebrae as a result of senile osteoporosis. An injection of anesthetic agents is administered into the spinal canal to help alleviate her pain.

Principal Diagnosis: _____

Secondary Diagnoses: _____

Principal Procedure: _____

Secondary Procedures: _____

3

This 60-year-old patient is seen again in his primary care physician's office for care of his arthritis. He has generalized degenerative arthritis of the knees, hips, and of the lumbosacral spine. His condition is becoming progressively worse, and different medications have been tried to alleviate the pain and discomfort. Because of his long-standing hypertension, which has not been well-controlled, and angina due to coronary artery disease (with disease in the vein bypass grafts after previous CABG 10 years previously), the patient is not a good candidate for joint replacement surgery. A new arthritis medication is prescribed, and his antihypertensive and cardiac medication prescriptions are renewed.

First-Listed Diagnosis: _____

Secondary Diagnoses: _____

Principal Procedure: _____

Secondary Procedures: _____

4

A 40-year-old woman is admitted to the hospital for chemotherapy for systemic lupus erythematosus (SLE). She is going to receive the next course of intravenous infusion of glucocorticoids and cyclophosphamide, an effective but highly toxic chemotherapy drug, to treat the SLE. The patient has several complications as a result of SLE, including nephritic syndrome, inflammatory myopathy, anemia of chronic disease, and swan-neck deformities of her fingers. During the hospital stay, the patient receives other medications to manage the complications. Intravenous infusion is started on day 1. She is monitored for toxicity, but none is detected and she is able to go home on day 3.

Principal Diagnosis: _____

Secondary Diagnoses: _____

Principal Procedure: _____

Secondary Procedures: _____

5

The patient is a 25-year-old woman who returns to the orthopedic clinic to see her sports medicine physician complaining of gradually increasing pain in her shinbones that used to abate when she resorted to walking instead of running but now is not relieved by such a walking rest. The woman runs several miles 4 days a week. Two weeks ago the physician had ordered x-rays of both lower legs. The results were negative for fractures. Because the patient now complained of pain in her right foot, today the physician ordered the x-rays of the legs to be repeated and an x-ray of the right foot to be performed. The radiologist concluded there was a stress reaction in the right and left lower distal tibias and a stress fracture of the second metatarsal of the right foot. Given the patient's history, physical findings, and radiological evidence, the physician makes the diagnosis of bilateral stress fractures of the tibias and stress fracture of the right second metatarsal. The patient is instructed to rest and keep off her feet as much as possible for the next 8 weeks, specifically with no running or other exercising. Based on her complaints of back pain, the physician also describes the patient as having an acute lumbosacral strain. The patient is to return in 4 weeks for repeat x-rays. The physician concluded that her injuries were the result of cumulative trauma from the repetitive impact of running on hard surfaces.

First-Listed Diagnosis: _____

Secondary Diagnoses: _____

First-Listed Procedure: _____

Secondary Procedures: _____

6

The patient is admitted to the hospital for an incision and drainage of the right fibula with debridement of the bone. After multiple outpatient diagnostic tests are performed, the diagnosis of subperiosteal abscess of the right fibula as a result of acute osteomyelitis localized in the right fibula due to a staphylococcal infection is made in this 9-year-old boy. The child began complaining of pain below the right knee and difficulty walking over the past 2 weeks. The patient denied any trauma to the leg but, as an active boy who plays soccer and softball, trauma could not be ruled out, although no evidence of an injury was found on the leg. To prevent bone destruction as well as the possibility of the infection spreading to other bones and joints in the lower leg, the child is admitted for surgery. The procedure is an incision-drainage of the subperiosteal abscess of the bone and debridement of the proximal fibula. The child withstands the procedure well and is discharged to his parents for at-home recovery 1 day after surgery.

Principal Diagnosis: _____

Secondary Diagnoses: _____

Principal Procedure: _____

Secondary Procedures: _____

7

The patient is a 65-year-old man who had a total knee replacement on the right side 9 years previously. Up until 6 months ago, the patient enjoyed an active retirement, golfing on a daily basis and enjoying walks with his wife around a nearby nature reserve. The patient began to experience pain in the thigh near the knee and in the lower leg on the same side where the joint replacement had occurred. The patient returns to his orthopedic physician with these complaints and x-rays are taken. It appears the prosthetic joint is not in good position. The doctor makes the diagnosis of "aseptic loosening" of the prosthetic joint and recommends total knee revision arthroplasty. The patient consents to surgery and is admitted for the procedure. The physician finds he has to replace the femoral, tibial, and patellar components in order to take advantage of the new more durable prosthetic components that were not available when the patient originally had his knee replaced. The patient also was found to have mild gouty arthritis, which was treated with medications during the hospital stay. The patient is discharged day 5 after surgery to receive physical therapy at home.

Principal Diagnosis: _____

Secondary Diagnoses: _____

Principal Procedure: _____

Secondary Procedures: _____

8

The patient is a 70-year-old woman who is diagnosed with prosthetic articular-bearing surface wear of a hip joint that was replaced 15 years previously as a result of osteoarthritis, localized to the hip. The patient had been having pain in the hip for nearly 1 year before she visited a new orthopedic surgeon for treatment. The surgeon who performed her original surgery had retired. Based on her physical findings and radiological studies, the new physician strongly suspects that the surface of the artificial joint is worn down due to everyday use over the past 15 years. The surgeon recommends a revision hip arthroplasty. The patient consents to surgery and is admitted for the procedure. During the hospital stay, the patient is also treated for hypertension and GERD. The physician performs an isolated modular femoral head and acetabular liner exchange to treat the surface wear, which was found to be extensive. This included revision of the femoral head and acetabular liner by removing and exchanging the modular femoral head and acetabular liner with new implants made with a ceramic surface. The doctor describes the new implants as "ceramic-on-ceramic" devices. The patient is discharged to receive physical therapy at home.

Principal Diagnosis: _____

Secondary Diagnoses: _____

Principal Procedure: _____

Secondary Procedures: _____

9

The patient comes to the orthopedic surgeon's office complaining of pain, swelling and tenderness, as well as extreme morning stiffness, in the fingers, hands, wrists, knees, and especially the feet. She also complains of fatigue, anorexia, and unintended weight loss. The patient is a 40-year-old woman who is a partner in a large corporate law firm. Upon physical examination, the physician notes warmth in the joints, especially the knees. The doctor also notes that the patient has simultaneous involvement of the same joints bilaterally. The patient reports that another orthopedic surgeon had told her this condition was simply osteoarthritis, but the patient remains concerned about the other symptoms she has been experiencing. Her grandmother had rheumatoid arthritis, and the patient suspects she has the same disease. The orthopedic surgeon agrees this is a possibility and recommends the patient see a rheumatologist for further investigation. The physician wrote "rule out rheumatoid arthritis" on the progress note he completed for this office visit.

First-Listed Diagnosis: _____

Secondary Diagnoses: _____

Principal Procedure: _____

Secondary Procedures: _____

10

The patient is a 30-year-old man who comes to the emergency department complaining of joint pain in his shoulder. The patient, who was a state champion wrestler during his college years, reports that his shoulder has dislocated on several occasions since college when he had several traumatic dislocations of the same shoulder. On this occasion, the patient was lifting a box overhead to place on a shelf in his garage. X-rays were taken to examine the shoulder. The ED physician is unable to reduce the dislocation on the initial attempt. With light intravenous sedation, the physician completes a closed reduction of shoulder dislocation. The physician wrote "chronic recurrent dislocation of right shoulder and traumatic arthritis of the right shoulder" as the final diagnosis on the ED record.

First-Listed Diagnosis: _____

Secondary Diagnoses: _____

Principal Procedure: _____

Secondary Procedures: _____

11

The patient, a 48-year-old female, was admitted to the hospital for surgical repair of a massive rotator cuff tear of her right shoulder. The patient was known to have hypertension, but it was well controlled and she received medical clearance for surgery. The patient has had pain, weakness, and limited range of motion in her right shoulder, which has been present for several years and has been getting progressively worse. Several years ago she had a fall and injured her right hip but doesn't remember her shoulder being injured at that time. The patient was taken to surgery and placed under general anesthesia. The surgeon found a complete tear of the rotator cuff that appeared nontraumatic, and significant tenosynovitis of the shoulder. The surgeon performed a rotator cuff repair, first attempting through an arthroscope, and finishing with a mini-open approach because of the size of the rotator cuff tear. A synovectomy of the shoulder was also performed through the arthroscope. The patient was kept overnight in the hospital, received her antihypertensive medication, and was discharged to home on day 2 with a follow-up appointment with the surgeon in 10 days.

Principal Diagnosis: _____

Secondary Diagnoses: _____

Principal Procedure: _____

Secondary Procedures: _____

12

The patient is a 56-year-old man with significant hypertensive heart disease who was admitted to the hospital for an arthroscopic partial medial meniscectomy on his right knee. Given his hypertension and heart disease, the cardiologist advised the orthopedic surgeon to admit the patient to the hospital for at least overnight monitoring after the procedure. During a previous orthopedic surgery, this patient had a hypertensive crisis and was placed in the intensive care unit for monitoring. This surgery was performed uneventfully. The patient had an arthroscopic partial medial meniscectomy of the posterior horn of the medial meniscus. This was determined to be an old tear, likely from a football playing injury. There were no loose bodies in the medial and lateral gutters. The articular cartilage surfaces were in reasonably good condition. The notches of the anterior cruciate and posterior cruciate ligaments were intact. Within the lateral compartment, the meniscus was intact and the articular cartilage surfaces in good condition. At the conclusion of the procedure, all excess fluid was drained, the portal incisions closed with nylon sutures, an injection of Marcaine was administered for pain control, and sterile dressings were applied. The patient was taken to the recovery room and then transferred to a regular bed. He was discharged the following morning with a follow up-appointment with the surgeon in 10 days.

Principal Diagnosis: _____

Secondary Diagnoses: _____

Principal Procedure: _____

Secondary Procedures: _____

13

Normally a patient with this type of foot condition would be treated as an outpatient for surgery. However this patient is a 28-year-old female with severe chronic asthmatic bronchitis and a congenital heart condition—ventricular septal defect—that has been treated and monitored for several years. At this time the patient has very painful bunions on both feet that makes walking increasingly difficult with the fact she is unable to wear a shoe on her left foot. She has acquired this condition rather quickly over the past couple of years. The patient was admitted as an inpatient for the podiatrist to perform the surgery and to allow her cardiologist to continue to monitor her condition for possible postoperative complications. The patient is taken to surgery on the day of admission with the pre-operative diagnosis of hallux abductovalgus, both feet, worse on the left. The procedure was performed on the left foot with intravenous antibiotic administered for prophylaxis. The patient consented to a McBride bunionectomy with soft tissue correction. The procedure includes a distal soft tissue release and correction of the soft tissue deformity at the MTP joint by releasing the tight lateral capsule, ligament complex, and adductor tendon. There is reefing of the loose medial capsule with resection of the medial eminence to correct the bunion protrusion. Pre-, intra- and postoperatively her respiratory and cardiac functions were monitored. No complications occurred. Respiratory therapy treatments were given postoperatively to prevent a worsening of her asthmatic bronchitis. An echocardiogram was performed postoperatively to compare to a recent echo performed during her surgical clearance for this procedure, and no appreciable changes were noted in her heart function. The patient complained of typical postoperative pain in her foot, but the pain was well managed with appropriate analgesic medications. The patient was discharged with follow-up appointments in her podiatrist's office in one week and her cardiologist's office in one month. A decision will be made during her recovery period when to perform similar surgery on her other foot.

Principal Diagnosis: _____

Secondary Diagnoses: _____

Principal Procedure: _____

Secondary Procedures: _____

14

The patient is a 48-year-old woman who was diagnosed with an aggressive form of breast carcinoma in the past year and had a radical mastectomy followed by chemotherapy. She has also developed secondary myelofibrosis with therapy-related low grade myelodysplastic syndrome, presumably due to the antineoplastic chemotherapy she has received. On this occasion, the patient called her physician reporting excruciating low back pain that had developed rapidly over the past two days and was told to go to the emergency room. It was feared the patient had a compression fracture or similar condition due to metastatic bone cancer. The patient was admitted and examined by her attending physician, oncologist, and consulting orthopedic surgeon. X-rays of the spine, bone scan, and CT scans of her lumbar spine failed to find any pathology, including no metastatic disease, much to the relief of the patient, family, and physicians. The physicians could not explain the rapid onset of low back pain, which was treated with pain medications. On day 3, the patient reported less back pain and better ambulation and was allowed to go home with her family. Chemotherapy will be performed on schedule in the next two weeks, and the patient continued to receive treatment for her myelofibrosis and myelodysplastic syndrome.

Principal Diagnosis: _____

Secondary Diagnoses: _____

Principal Procedure: _____

Secondary Procedures: _____

15

The patient is a 19-year-old female college scholar-athlete who is a scholarship basketball player at the state university. She has had repeated injuries to her knees over the past 7 years while she has played in competitive sports, including basketball, softball, and soccer. Over the past 3 months she had noted a feeling of instability in the right knee, more than usual and with increasing pain over the medial compartment, as a result of these old injuries. The physicians who had treated her over the past year were fairly confident that she had a torn anterior cruciate ligament and possible tears to the medial meniscus and medial collateral ligament. She was admitted to the hospital for reconstructive surgery, with a planned transfer to a sports rehabilitation unit at the university hospital. At surgery, the orthopedic surgeon found a grossly positive Lachman's sign and anterior drawer in neutral, internal, and external rotation. The medial meniscus was torn at the posterior horn in a complex fashion posteriorly. There was no repairable tissue. The medial collateral ligament was torn. The good news was the surfaces of the patellofemoral joint, medial compartment, and lateral compartments were in good condition. The anterior cruciate ligament was completely torn. The posterior cruciate ligament was intact, and the patellar tendons rode laterally in the notch. At the conclusion of the procedure, the knee was stable to Lachman and drawer testing. The procedures performed were an arthroscopic reconstruction or repair of the anterior cruciate ligament using patellar tendon graft and repair of the medial meniscus and medial collateral ligament, also known as the triad knee repair or O'Donoghue procedure. After 3 days of post operative recovery, the patient was transferred to the sports rehabilitation unit for a complex rehabilitation program.

Principal Diagnosis: _____

Secondary Diagnoses: _____

Principal Procedure: _____

Secondary Procedures: _____

Chapter 17

Congenital Anomalies and Certain Conditions Originating in the Perinatal Period

Coding Scenarios for *Basic ICD-9-CM Coding*

The following case studies are organized by chapter following the sequence of the *Basic ICD-9-CM Coding* textbook. The objective of the case studies is to provide the student with more detailed clinical information to code, rather than one- or two-line diagnostic and procedure statements. Depending on whether the case study describes an inpatient hospital admission or an outpatient visit, the student is asked to provide the necessary diagnosis and procedure codes in the appropriate sequence—with principal diagnosis code listed first for inpatient admissions and main reason for visit code listed first for outpatient visits.

1

A 6-month-old infant, born with a congenital anomaly of the ear with impairment of hearing, is admitted for surgery to treat his mixed hearing loss. The patient is taken to surgery to place bilateral cochlear hearing implants. He quickly recovers from the procedure and anesthesia and is discharged home.

Principal Diagnosis: _____

Secondary Diagnoses: _____

Principal Procedure: _____

Secondary Procedures: _____

2

A 3-month-old infant is born with a biliary atresia. The patient has severe obstructive jaundice due to the congenital condition. The patient was admitted and the diagnosis is confirmed by surgical exploration with operative cholangiography. The biliary atresia is treated with roux-en-Y cholecystojejunostomy of the gallbladder.

Principal Diagnosis: _____

Secondary Diagnoses: _____

Principal Procedure: _____

Secondary Procedures: _____

3

A 2-month-old female infant, who has been in critical condition and in the NICU since being transferred to this hospital one day after her birth, is brought to the operating room for excisional repair of the coarctation of the aorta with end-to-end anastomosis done with the pump oxygenator.

Principal Diagnosis: _____

Secondary Diagnoses: _____

Principal Procedure: _____

Secondary Procedures: _____

4

A 2-day-old infant is transferred to the larger community hospital for evaluation and treatment from a small rural hospital where he was born. The baby's mother has type I diabetes mellitus. The infant was large at birth (more than 10 pounds) and exhibited hypoglycemia, transient tachypnea, and possibly other endocrine disorders that are characteristic of a syndrome of infants born to diabetic mothers. The baby required special surveillance because, as an "infant of a diabetic mother," he was at increased risk for a variety of complications and congenital defects. The baby was also observed for suspected sepsis or other infectious process. Fortunately, no major problems are found. The infant was discharged to his parents 3 days after admission to be followed closely by a pediatric specialist.

Principal Diagnosis: _____

Secondary Diagnoses: _____

Principal Procedure: _____

Secondary Procedures: _____

5

The patient is admitted to the children's hospital for open heart surgery to repair her congenital heart defects. The patient is a 7-year-old girl who was born with Tetralogy of Fallot that was corrected by surgical repair at age 2 years. She has been seen by the pediatric cardiologist every 6 months since that surgery, with a known fact that further surgery would be necessary later in childhood. Since birth, it has also been known that she suffers from the following diagnoses as listed on her discharge summary: "Stenosis of the pulmonary valve with right ventricular outflow obstruction causing pulmonary insufficiency and stenosis of the left pulmonary artery; status post previous cardiac surgery; surgically repaired congenital heart defects 5 years ago." The corrective surgery for these conditions is "right ventricular outflow reconstruction with replacement of pulmonary valve with homograft; left pulmonary artery reconstruction to hilum with patch arterioplasty; right pulmonary artery stenosis arterioplasty." The surgery is performed under cardiopulmonary bypass and an intraoperative transesophageal echocardiogram is performed.

Principal Diagnosis: _____

Secondary Diagnoses: _____

Principal Procedure: _____

Secondary Procedures: _____

6

A 12-hour-old infant was transferred to the university hospital neonatal intensive care unit for respiratory problems after being born at a community hospital by vaginal delivery to a woman who had just completed her 39th week of pregnancy. The infant was exhibiting respiratory symptoms consistent with aspiration of meconium at the time of the delivery. The infant had low Apgar scores of 5 and 6 with tachypnea and cyanosis. Within 1 day, the infant's chest x-ray demonstrated patchy infiltrates. The neonatologist diagnosed the infant as having meconium aspiration pneumonia with no signs of pulmonary hypertension as a consequence of the pneumonia. The physician also described the infant as "small for dates," weighing 2200 grams.

Principal Diagnosis: _____

Secondary Diagnoses: _____

Principal Procedure: _____

Secondary Procedures: _____

7

The patient is an 18-month-old boy who was born with a complete bilateral cleft lip and palate deformity. He is seen in the University Hospital's outpatient pediatric clinic. The child has had reconstruction surgery to correct the congenital defect. The child continues to have feeding difficulties. While he is free of infection now, he has had a couple of ear infections. Both the feeding and ear problems are attributed to the cleft lip and palate that appears to be incompletely repaired. The physician recommended to the parents that one more surgery should be performed to improve the symmetry of the palate and lip and alleviate the feeding problems and ear infections. However, it is possible that the child well need ear tubes placed in the future because of the chronic ear infections. A revision of the cleft palate and advancement flap graft is scheduled for the next month.

First-Listed Diagnosis: _____

Secondary Diagnoses: _____

First-Listed Procedure: _____

Secondary Procedures: _____

8

A three-week-old infant was brought by her parents to the University Hospital's outpatient high-risk pediatric clinic for her first post-hospital discharge examination. The physician examined the patient and was most concerned about the child's fetal growth retardation. The physician was pleased to see the child had gained weight since leaving the hospital. The physician described the child's condition as premature infant with fetal growth retardation, 36 week gestation, with a birth weight of 1600 grams. The parents will bring the child back to the clinic in three weeks.

First-Listed Diagnosis: _____

Secondary Diagnoses: _____

First-Listed Procedure: _____

Secondary Procedures: _____

9

A 25-day-old infant is brought to the university hospital's high-risk pediatric clinic by her foster mother for evaluation of her status as a "crack baby." The child's mother was dependent on cocaine, and the baby had a positive drug screen for cocaine at birth and exhibited several symptoms. The baby continues to exhibit transitory tachypnea of newborn. The physician orders a continuation of pediatric home health services to monitor the child's respiratory status and the effect of the noxious substance (cocaine) on the baby. The reason for the clinic visit documented by the physician is crack baby with continued transitory tachypnea. The baby will be brought back to the clinic in 2 weeks.

First-Listed Diagnosis: _____

Secondary Diagnoses: _____

First-Listed Procedure: _____

Secondary Procedures: _____

10

The parents of a 10-day-old baby bring the newborn to the pediatrician's office to evaluate her feeding problems. The child vomits after bottle feedings. When the baby was born, the umbilical cord was found loosely wrapped around the newborn's neck. It was quickly removed by the obstetrician, and the baby was observed for respiratory and other difficulties. Feeding problems were evident while the baby was in the hospital, and the pediatricians considered the nuchal cord problem as the cause. The physician recommends a change in baby formula and different feeding bottles. The physician also orders pediatric home health services to assist the parents in the child's care at home. A follow-up appointment is scheduled to return to the office in 2 weeks. The physician's diagnosis is feeding problems in an infant born with nuchal cord around his neck.

First-Listed Diagnosis: _____

Secondary Diagnoses: _____

First-Listed Procedure: _____

Secondary Procedures: _____

11

This male infant was born today at 32-3/7th weeks premature weighing 1920 grams by a repeat cesarean delivery. The baby had Apgar scores of 8 and 9. He had bag-mask inhalation for 30 seconds. His oxygen saturation was then 99 on room air. The baby was brought to the premature nursery and placed on monitors. He was observed for a suspected infection but found to have none. Otherwise his physical exam showed no abnormalities, and he remained in the nursery after his mother's discharge for additional monitoring and weight gain. He was discharged at day 10 to be followed by pediatric home care nurses. No circumcision was performed.

Principal Diagnosis: _____

Secondary Diagnoses: _____

Principal Procedure: _____

Secondary Procedures: _____

12

This female infant was born to a 17-year-old mother, gravida 1, para 0, by spontaneous vaginal delivery with vertex presentation. She was born at 34 4/7 weeks gestation, weighing 2035 grams (4 pounds, 4 ounces). Her Apgar scores were 4 and 9. The baby required bag-mask inhalation for 2 minutes and 30 seconds and was transferred to the neonatal intensive care nursery for continuing monitoring and treatment. Initially the baby had transient tachypnea, respiratory distress, and metabolic acidosis. She had hypermagnesemia, as her mother received magnesium therapy. She also had neonatal hyperbilirubinemia of prematurity. She was observed for possible sepsis, but none was found. The intravenous antibiotics were discontinued after 2 days. The baby's physical examination on discharge was within normal limits for a premature infant as her condition improved with laboratory data showing more normal findings. She was discharged at age 5 days to be followed by pediatric home care nurses with an appointment in the physician's office 2 days after discharge.

Principal Diagnosis: _____

Secondary Diagnoses: _____

Principal Procedure: _____

Secondary Procedures: _____

13

A 32-year-old female patient returns to her obstetrician-gynecologist's office to review the findings of her recent transvaginal uterine ultrasound. The patient has been married for 3 years and has not become pregnant as desired. The doctor informs the patient that the ultrasound examination showed that she had a bicornuate uterus, which is sometimes described as a heart-shaped uterus because of the distinct shape of the uterus when viewed externally, for example, on an ultrasound. The doctor also explained this is a congenital condition that occurs when the uterine fundus fails to fuse. The patient's condition is a partial bicornuate uterus with an evidenced cleft in the uterine dome. Given the fact that patients with this type of Mullerian abnormality often have a kidney abnormality as well, the patient was given an order to return to the radiology department for a renal ultrasound. The physician's review of the literature about this condition found that reproductive function is generally good in patients with partial bicornuate uteri, but the patient will be referred to a reproductive endocrinologist if the patient does not become pregnant within the next 6 months. The patient will return to this physician's office in 2 weeks to discuss the results of the renal ultrasound if an abnormality is found.

First-Listed Diagnosis: _____

Secondary Diagnoses: _____

First-Listed Procedure: _____

Secondary Procedures: _____

14

A full-term male infant was born at Community Hospital to a mother who acquired a severe case of herpes simplex virus (HSV) during her pregnancy. At the age of one day old, the infant was transferred to University Hospital's special care unit to "rule out HSV visceral and/ or central nervous system (CNS) infection." The infant was diagnosed with congenital HSV but did not develop a visceral or CNS specific infection. The infant was treated with intravenous acyclovir for 10 days. An additional diagnosis of small-for-dates was made for the infant, who weighed 2,040 grams with a gestational age of 38 1/7th weeks. The infant was discharged to his mother's care with neonatal home nursing services to follow the infant's care at home. Code for the infant at University Hospital only.

Principal Diagnosis: _____

Secondary Diagnoses: _____

Principal Procedure: _____

Secondary Procedures: _____

15

A pre-term male infant was born at Community Hospital at 33 and 5/7th weeks to a primigravida 30-year-old female. The infant was having respiratory difficulties and was transferred within hours to University Hospital to care for his prematurity and to rule out respiratory distress syndrome. While in the neonatal intensive care unit, the infant's respiratory symptoms abated. A thorough evaluation of the infant included laboratory and imaging studies. One unexpected diagnosis established through the imaging studies was the diagnosis of spina bifida occulta, the mildest form of spina bifida. Only through imaging examinations could the physician see an opening in the vertebrae of the spinal column, with no apparent damage to the spinal cord, which is the definition of spina bifida occulta. The infant remained in the hospital for 4 weeks gaining weight and maturing. The infant was discharged with the final diagnoses of preterm infant, 33 5/7th weeks gestation, birthweight of 1,600 grams with spina bifida occulta. The infant was discharged to the care of his parents with neonatal home nursing services to follow the infant's care at home. An appointment was made for the parents to return with the infant to see a pediatric neurologist in 4 weeks. Code for the infant at University Hospital only.

Principal Diagnosis: _____

Secondary Diagnoses: _____

Principal Procedure: _____

Secondary Procedures: _____

Chapter 18

Symptoms, Signs, and Ill-Defined Conditions

Coding Scenarios for *Basic ICD-9-CM Coding*

The following case studies are organized by chapter following the sequence of the *Basic ICD-9-CM Coding* textbook. The objective of the case studies is to provide the student with more detailed clinical information to code, rather than one- or two-line diagnostic and procedure statements. Depending on whether the case study describes an inpatient hospital admission or an outpatient visit, the student is asked to provide the necessary diagnosis and procedure codes in the appropriate sequence—with principal diagnosis code listed first for inpatient admissions and main reason for visit code listed first for outpatient visits.

1

A 50-year-old man is scheduled for an outpatient colonoscopy. The reason for the colonoscopy is stated as "change in bowel habits, family history of colon cancer, and possible colonic polyp." A colonoscopy is performed. At the conclusion of the colonoscopy, the physician documents the final diagnosis as (1) change in bowel habits, unexplained, (2) normal colon examination.

First-Listed Diagnosis: _____

Secondary Diagnoses: _____

First-Listed Procedure: _____

Secondary Procedures: _____

2

A 59-year-old woman is referred by her primary care physician to the hospital outpatient radiology department with an order for a CT scan of the abdomen. The patient has been complaining of generalized abdominal pain, fatigue, and nausea but no vomiting over the past several weeks. Previous x-rays taken were abnormal. The doctor's diagnosis on the order is "abnormal radiology findings of GI tract, require further definition by CT exam, generalized abdominal pain, fatigue, nausea, rule out abdominal malignancy."

First-Listed Diagnosis: _____

Secondary Diagnoses: _____

First-Listed Procedure: _____

Secondary Procedures: _____

3

A patient is admitted for a bronchoscopy with a transbronchial lung biopsy to determine the etiology of a lung mass found on recent x-ray and CT studies. The patient had been complaining of a cough and chest pressure over the past several weeks. The patient is taken to the outpatient endoscopy suite. Following administration of conscious sedation, the fiberoptic bronchoscopy is performed. During the process to obtain the transbronchial biopsy, the patient experiences a prolonged episode of bradycardia, and the physician terminates the procedure before the biopsy is obtained. The procedure will be rescheduled after the cardiologist evaluates the patient.

Principal Diagnosis: _____

Secondary Diagnoses: _____

Principal Procedure: _____

Secondary Procedures: _____

4

A 50-year-old man is admitted through the emergency department (ED) with a complaint of chest pain. The EKG and laboratory tests done in the ED are inconclusive, but an acute myocardial infarction is ruled out. During the hospital stay, the cardiovascular workup could not disprove the existence of coronary artery disease. Results of a thallium cardiac stress test were mildly abnormal. The patient did not want to have a cardiac catheterization study performed. Gastrointestinal studies, including an EGD, found some abnormalities including evidence of gastroesophageal reflux disease. Given the conflicting information, the physician concludes the patient had "atypical chest pain due to either angina or GERD." The patient is requested to visit both a cardiologist and gastroenterologist for additional testing.

Principal Diagnosis: _____

Secondary Diagnoses: _____

Principal Procedure: _____

Secondary Procedures: _____

5

A 38-year-old woman comes to her physician's office for the results of recent diagnostic studies. The woman had several complaints including numbness of her legs, difficulty in walking, and lack of coordination and trembling in her hands. The symptoms are not present all the time but have occurred more frequently over the past couple of weeks. The patient had also been examined by a neurologist. The patient was told the MRI and neurological tests, as well as the conclusion of the neurologist, consider her condition to be consistent with multiple sclerosis (MS.) When the patient asked whether the doctor was certain that she had MS, he said he was not 100% certain and made arrangements for her to be examined by physicians in a neurology group that specializes in treating patient with MS.

First-Listed Diagnosis: _____

Secondary Diagnoses: _____

First-Listed Procedure: _____

Secondary Procedures: _____

6

A 52-year-old woman with known fibrocystic disease of the right breast has an appointment for a diagnostic mammogram at the hospital outpatient department. A screening mammogram done 3 days previously was abnormal with a suspicious lesion noted in the upper quadrant of the left breast. Findings of fibrocystic disease of the right breast were noted again. The diagnostic mammogram is performed and interpreted by the radiologist. The patient's physician meets with the radiologist to review the findings. The patient's physician agrees with the radiologist's findings of "microcalcifications of breast tissue, left breast" and advises the patient of the benign findings. The status of the fibrocystic disease of the right breast had not changed since last year's mammogram. The patient will have a follow-up diagnostic mammogram in 6 months.

First-Listed Diagnosis: _____

Secondary Diagnoses: _____

First-Listed Procedure: _____

Secondary Procedures: _____

7

A 30-year-old woman has a repeat visit in her gynecologist's office to review the results of a recent abnormal Pap smear. Over the past year, the woman had experienced genital warts that appear and disappear on the external areas of her genitals. During the last visit, the gynecologist had performed a colposcopy and a Pap smear. Cells were scraped from the cervix and sent for cytological and DNA testing. The patient is advised today that the conclusion of the test is "DNA positive for cervical high-risk human papillomavirus (HPV)." The patient consents to a cervical biopsy which is scheduled for the following week. The patient's genital warts on her external genitalia today were examined and appear to be decreasing.

First-Listed Diagnosis: _____

Secondary Diagnoses: _____

First-Listed Procedure: _____

Secondary Procedures: _____

8

A mother brought her 7-week-old infant to the pediatrician's office for intermittent diarrhea. The physician examines the infant and takes a comprehensive history, including the baby's food history and eating pattern. The physician considers the possibility that the baby is allergic to the infant formula being fed to the patient, which includes milk products. The physician recommends certain laboratory tests be performed and includes the following diagnosis on the order for the tests "Failure to thrive, possible milk allergy, diarrhea."

First-Listed Diagnosis: _____

Secondary Diagnoses: _____

First-Listed Procedure: _____

Secondary Procedures: _____

9

Family members bring a 19-year-old man to the hospital emergency department. The patient had stated he had a severe headache, fever, and nausea and vomiting. A thorough physical examination is performed including a spinal tap. The physician arranges for the transfer of the patient to a larger hospital with the diagnosis of "Rule out meningitis." All records and test results are transferred with the patient. In addition to the physical complaints stated by the patient, the physician adds the diagnosis of meningismus.

First-Listed Diagnosis: _____

Secondary Diagnoses: _____

First-Listed Procedure: _____

Secondary Procedures: _____

10

A 56-year-old woman is admitted through the emergency department complaining of right upper quadrant abdominal pain. In addition, the patient says she is having nausea and had vomited several times at home. The patient is admitted with the diagnosis of possible cholecystitis. Several tests are performed, and all results are normal, except those of an ultrasound of the abdomen. It is also discovered that the patient has elevated blood pressure readings, but a diagnosis of hypertension is not made. The physician stated "no conclusive diagnosis found." When asked for more documentation concerning the patient diagnosis, the physician stated that the only conclusive findings were the patient's initial complaints, her elevated blood pressure readings, and the abnormal ultrasound of the GI abdominal area. The patient is discharged for outpatient management.

Principal Diagnosis: _____

Secondary Diagnoses: _____

Principal Procedure: _____

Secondary Procedures: _____

11

The patient is a 66-year-old woman who was admitted to the hospital after being seen in her physician's office with the complaint of difficulty in swallowing, first solid food and now difficulty with swallowing liquids. She was found to be dehydrated and was admitted. A gastroenterology consult was obtained, and the physician recommended an esophagogastro-duodenoscopy to rule out esophageal stricture or obstruction. The patient became very anxious during the start of the EGD, and it was postponed. After discussion with the patient and the primary care physician, the gastroenterologist recommended the procedure be performed under general anesthesia, which was accomplished. The EGD was performed, and no obstruction, stricture, or other disease was found in the esophagus, in the stomach, or small bowel, which was also examined. After being reassured that there was no disease or cancer present in her upper GI tract, the patient appeared very relieved. That evening she was able to eat a soft diet meal and drink liquids. The primary care physician listed the final diagnoses as dysphagia, cause unknown; anxiety disorder; and dehydration.

Principal Diagnosis: _____

Secondary Diagnoses: _____

Principal Procedure: _____

Secondary Procedures: _____

12

The patient is a 15-year-old female who has experienced a fever of 102 with chills overnight and was brought to the Emergency Department by her mother at 5 a.m.. Laboratory tests, including a complete blood count and urinalysis, were performed with normal results produced. The patient also complained of body aches, weakness, and fatigue. The patient's family physician was contacted and advised the patient be discharged home and come to his office the same afternoon if she did not feel better. The Emergency Department physician wrote the final diagnosis as "fever with chills, possible viral syndrome."

First-Listed Diagnosis: _____

Secondary Diagnoses: _____

First-Listed Procedure: _____

Secondary Procedures: _____

13

The patient is a 45-year-old man who was referred by his primary care physician to the cardiologist in his office "to diagnosis and treat for possible cardiac disease." Three days earlier the patient had an abnormal test stress study that was done for preventive health purposes. The patient did not have any complaints typical of cardiac disease. When the nurse in the cardiologist's office was taking the patient's history and recording the vital signs, she noted the patient's blood pressure to be 138/88. The patient admitted to being somewhat "stressed-out" by being there, so the nurse waited 10 minutes and took the blood pressure again. This time the blood pressure values were 138/84. After the cardiologist reviewed the patient's history with him and completed the physical examination, the physician personally took the patient's blood pressure and found it to be 136/86. The physician explained to the patient that it was possible that he had hypertension, but he would not make the diagnosis during the first patient visit. The patient was prescribed a mild diuretic and given a follow-up appointment to return in 2 weeks. The doctor completed his progress note about the visit with the impressions of (1) Abnormal cardiovascular stress test, (2) Elevated blood pressure readings, rule out hypertension.

First-Listed Diagnosis: _____

Secondary Diagnoses: _____

First-Listed Procedure: _____

Secondary Procedures: _____

14

A 58-year-old woman requested a same-day appointment with her primary care physician because of recurrent jaw and shoulder pain that had occurred over the past 2 days and was increasing in intensity. The physician examined the patient and had the nurse perform an immediate electrocardiogram (EKG) on the patient. The physician recognized these symptoms as a possible acute myocardial infarction (AMI). When the physician noted the EKG was markedly abnormal, he had the staff call for an ambulance immediately and transferred the patient to the nearest hospital's emergency room. The diagnoses recorded by the physician on the progress note for the visit was jaw and shoulder pain, rule out AMI.

First-Listed Diagnosis: _____

Secondary Diagnoses: _____

First-Listed Procedure: _____

Secondary Procedures: _____

15

The parents of a seven-week-old female infant returned to the pediatrician's office for a follow-up visit to examine the baby, who had been previously diagnosed with "colic." Laboratory work performed during the last visit was reported with normal values. The parents stated there had not been much change in the baby since their last appointment, 2 weeks ago. The infant was inconsolable 3 or 4 times a week with symptoms that lasted 4–5 hours, from the late afternoon through the evening hours. Some of the physician's recommended calming techniques worked, such as the "football hold," placing the baby face down along the length of the father's arm, as well as putting the baby in the car seat and driving around for several hours, but other efforts failed. The breast-feeding mother had eliminated recommended items from her diet, including caffeine, chocolate, and gas-producing foods. The pediatrician encouraged the parents that he had seen many babies like their baby and fortunately most of the babies did not experience as much colic after the age of 12–14 weeks. The parents' made note of additional calming techniques recommended by the physician and his nurse. The physician's examination of the infant during this visit found an otherwise healthy infant. A follow-up appointment was made for 3 weeks later. The final diagnosis recorded for the visit was full-term female infant with colic.

First-Listed Diagnosis: _____

Secondary Diagnoses: _____

First-Listed Procedure: _____

Secondary Procedures: _____

Chapter 19

Injuries

Coding Scenarios for *Basic ICD-9-CM Coding*

The following case studies are organized by chapter following the sequence of the *Basic ICD-9-CM Coding* textbook. The objective of the case studies is to provide the student with more detailed clinical information to code, rather than one- or two-line diagnostic and procedure statements. Depending on whether the case study describes an inpatient hospital admission or an outpatient visit, the student is asked to provide the necessary diagnosis and procedure codes in the appropriate sequence—with principal diagnosis code listed first for inpatient admissions and main reason for visit code listed first for outpatient visits.

1

A 16-year-old boy is brought to the emergency department with second- and third-degree burns of the chest and first- and second-degree burns of the upper arms. The total body surface burn is 25 percent with 9 percent being third-degree. The patient is transferred to the burn unit at the city's university hospital.

Note: List all applicable codes *excluding* the E code.

First-Listed Diagnosis: _____

Secondary Diagnoses: _____

First-Listed Procedure: _____

Secondary Procedures: _____

2

The patient, a 22-year-old man, was brought to the emergency department by friends after being involved in a fight. The patient complains of severe jaw pain, and his face appears asymmetrical with the left side of his face appearing out of alignment. The physician obtains x-rays of the man's facial bones and jaw and is advised by the radiologist that a dislocation of the mandible exists. Multiple lacerations were noted on both hands. One laceration in particular across the metacarpal area of the right hand required suturing, which was done in the emergency department. The patient is admitted to the hospital. The next morning the patient is taken to surgery for a closed reduction of the fracture of the mandible. The patient is discharged the next day with a follow-up appointment scheduled with the surgeon in 10 days.

Note: List all applicable codes *excluding* the E code.

Principal Diagnosis: _____

Secondary Diagnoses: _____

Principal Procedure: _____

Secondary Procedures: _____

3

A 42-year-old man was in an auto accident that involved the collision of his vehicle into the expressway median divider. He was brought to emergency department complaining of leg and foot pain. X-rays showed a left supracondylar femur fracture and a fracture of the talus (tarsal) bone of the left foot. He was admitted to the hospital and taken to the operating room for an immediate open reduction with internal fixation for both fractures.

Note: List all applicable codes *excluding* the E code.

Principal Diagnosis: _____

Secondary Diagnoses: _____

Principal Procedure: _____

Secondary Procedures: _____

4

The patient is a semiprofessional baseball player who is a pitcher. He is seen in the orthopedic sports medicine physician's office because of a painful right shoulder. The patient felt a pain in his right shoulder while pitching during a game within the past three days. After the game, he felt more severe muscular pain in the shoulder and was unable to use his arm. The physician suspects a severe injury to the biceps tendon and muscles of the shoulder. The patient consents to exploratory surgery and shoulder repair if indicated. The patient is admitted to the hospital for the surgery. During the open procedure, the physician examines the superior labrum that attaches the biceps tendon to the bones of the shoulder. The physician finds the superior labrum is torn from front to back. An immediate repair or arthroplasty of the shoulder is done to repair the labrum and reattach it to the bones of the shoulder joint. The physician describes the injury as a SLAP, or superior glenoid labrum lesion. The physician advises the patient-athlete that the injury is fairly common among athletes who use their upper extremities in strenuous activities. Physical therapy and athletic training will be the next plan of care for the patient so that he may return to playing baseball.

Note: List all applicable codes *excluding* the E code.

Principal Diagnosis: _____

Secondary Diagnoses: _____

Principal Procedure: _____

Secondary Procedures: _____

5

The patient is a 19-year-old man who is brought to the emergency department (ED) by fire department ambulance after being called to the scene of a street fight by neighbors. Apparently the patient was beaten by rival gang members. The patient was unconscious when found by the paramedics. The ED physician performs a comprehensive physical examination, and the patient is taken for an MRI of the brain. The patient regains consciousness within 40 minutes of arriving in the ED, less than an hour after being found by the paramedics. The MRI is negative for fractures or internal bleeding. The patient is admitted to the ICU for monitoring. The physician describes the injury as a closed head injury with loss of consciousness of less than 1 hour. The patient also has multiple lacerations on the face, including his cheek, forehead, lip, and jaw. There are abrasions on his hands as well as multiple contusions on the abdominal wall and the knees and lower legs. The lacerations are suture repaired in the ICU after the patient is stabilized. The patient is transferred out of the ICU within 48 hours with no signs of permanent neurological injury. He is discharged home 7 days after his injury occurred.

Note: List all applicable codes *excluding* the E code.

Principal Diagnosis: _____

Secondary Diagnoses: _____

Principal Procedure: _____

Secondary Procedures: _____

6

The patient is a 25-year-old man brought to the emergency department (ED) after being shot in the abdomen during a drive-by shooting. The trauma team assembled in the ED, and it was quickly determined that the gunshot wound of the abdomen was complicated by injury to the abdominal aorta, with the retained bullets remaining in the abdominal fascia. The trauma surgeons attempt to control the bleeding and prepare the patient for surgery to repair the aorta, but the damage to the vascular system is too great, and the patient expires prior to being admitted and taken to surgery.

Note: List all applicable codes *excluding* the E code.

First-Listed Diagnosis: _____

Secondary Diagnoses: _____

First-Listed Procedure: _____

Secondary Procedures: _____

7

The patient is a 44-year-old woman who works as a road construction flag holder. The patient was directing traffic on an expressway where road resurfacing was being performed. A truck came too close to the worker and its tires rolled over her left foot. The patient is brought to the nearest hospital's emergency department where the physician on duty immediately examines the patient and x-rays are performed. The physician describes the patient's trauma as a crush injury of the foot with open fractures. The radiologist's impression documented on the radiology report describes the injury as open fractures of all five metatarsals of the foot. The orthopedic surgeon on call came to the hospital, and the patient is taken to surgery for an open reduction and internal fixation of the metatarsal bones with a fasciotomy. The patient remains in the hospital 3 days before being discharged to home health services follow-up care, with an appointment to see the orthopedic surgeon in 7 days.

Note: List all applicable codes *excluding* the E code.

Principal Diagnosis: _____

Secondary Diagnoses: _____

Principal Procedure: _____

Secondary Procedures: _____

8

The patient is a 50-year-old man brought to the emergency department (ED) by fire department ambulance that was called to a restaurant in which the patient was eating dinner with friends. The patient was eating steak when he felt something stick in his chest. He could not dislodge it, and was becoming rather panicky because of the intense epigastric pain. He was still able to breathe unassisted and able to speak. The emergency department physician examines the patient and immediately calls the gastroenterologist for what the ED physician describes as "Steakhouse Syndrome." The patient is examined by the gastroenterologist who suspects that food is lodged in the patient's esophagus. The patient is taken immediately to the gastroenterology procedure suite, and an upper GI endoscopy is performed. The physician finds several large pieces of poorly chewed meat at the level of the lower esophagogastric sphincter. The physician is able to remove some of the obstruction, but smaller pieces of meat had already passed into the stomach. The physician also documents that reflux esophagitis is present. The physician is able to examine the upper GI tract, including the stomach, and no injury to the mucosa is found. The patient is admitted to the hospital overnight and discharged the next morning.

Note: List all applicable codes *excluding* the E code.

Principal Diagnosis: _____

Secondary Diagnoses: _____

Principal Procedure: _____

Secondary Procedures: _____

9

The patient is a 15-year-old girl who is brought to the emergency department by ambulance from a motor vehicle accident where she was thrown from the car. After a complete history and physical examination, multiple radiological studies are obtained. The trauma physician determines the patient has an unstable fracture of the L2-L3 vertebrae, but there is no evidence of spinal cord injury. With the parents' consent, the patient is admitted and taken to surgery for repair of her injury. The physician performs an open reduction of the L2-L3 fracture. He also performs a posterior spinal fusion of L2-L3 with posterior segmental fixation with instrumentation. The procedure also includes L2-L3 interspinous process wiring. Bone is harvested from the right posterior iliac crest for bone grafting. The primary closure includes a L1-L2 laminotomy. The patient tolerates the surgical procedure and is taken to the surgical ICU. Fifteen days later the patient is transferred to an acute rehabilitation facility for ongoing therapy and recovery.

Note: List all applicable codes *excluding* the E code.

Principal Diagnosis: _____

Secondary Diagnoses: _____

Principal Procedure: _____

Secondary Procedures: _____

10

The patient is a 40-year-old man brought to the emergency department by fire department ambulance after falling off a ladder at home while doing home repairs. Apparently, in an attempt to catch himself, his left hand and wrist broke a window, and he was cut severely by the broken glass. The ED physician examines the patient and orders x-rays of the fingers, hand, and wrist. No fractures are seen. Based on the physical examination, the physician concludes there is a minor injury to the ulnar nerve and the tendon in addition to the laceration of the wrist. The physician repairs the laceration loosely and makes arrangements for the patient to be transferred to another hospital in the city where a hand surgeon waits to examine him and possibly take him to surgery for definitive repair. The patient is transferred by private ambulance to the nearby hospital.

Note: List all applicable codes *excluding* the E code.

First-Listed Diagnosis: _____

Secondary Diagnoses: _____

First-Listed Procedure: _____

Secondary Procedures: _____

11

The patient is a 20-year-old man who sustained a drunken fall through a plate-glass window and was cut by the broken glass. He was brought to the Level I trauma emergency department at a local hospital. On examination the patient had a large penetrating wound to the right thoracoabdominal region. The patient had no memory of the event and could not describe how it happened. According to friends, he had been told to leave the nightclub/bar. They saw him leave alone and agreed he was "drunk." The fall through the glass of a store occurred about a half a block down on the same street. The patient was hemodynamically stable in the ER but the CT scan revealed several retained objects in the right upper quadrant that had violated the liver, as well as possible violation of the right kidney. The patient was taken by the trauma surgeons to the operating room for an exploratory laparotomy. The injuries found during the procedure were a major laceration through and through of the liver, a laceration of the jejunum, and a hematoma of the right kidney. Exploratory laparotomy was performed with repair of the liver laceration, repair of the jejunum laceration, examination of the right kidney, and removal of 3 fragments of leaded glass from the abdominal cavity. Examination of the colon revealed no injuries. A #10 JP drain was placed into the right upper quadrant for postoperative drainage. The fascia, subcutaneous tissue, and skin edges were closed with sutures and staples. The patient was taken to the recovery area in stable condition. In addition to the injuries described with the operative findings, the patient was treated for acute alcoholic poisoning and multiple small skin lacerations (that did not need repair) of the right upper and lower extremity. After an extended hospital stay that included physical therapy, antibiotic and postoperative treatment, wound care management, and substance abuse preventative counseling, the patient was discharged home.

Note: List all applicable codes *excluding* the E code.

First-Listed Diagnosis: _____

Secondary Diagnoses: _____

First-Listed Procedure: _____

Secondary Procedures: _____

12

Fire department ambulance and paramedics brought a 14-year-old boy to the Level I trauma emergency room after he was shot in the head by a drive-by shooter while standing with some friends on a neighbor's porch. The entrance was into the right posterior parietal area of the skull, and the bullet was lodged in the occipital area. The inlet gunshot wound was hemorrhaging. The injury traumatized a major portion of the brain. When the patient arrived at the hospital, he was deeply comatose with cerebrate rigidity. His pupils were fixed and dilated with severe respiratory compromise. He was intubated and placed on a ventilator and taken to the pediatric ICU. After discussing his condition with his parents, consent was obtained and the patient was taken to surgery, even though everyone understood the patient was in extremely critical condition. The following procedures were performed: decompressive craniotomy, duraplasty, and insertion of an intracranial pressure (ICP) monitor. Massive injuries to the brain were found as a result of the gunshot wound: comminuted skull fractures of the parietal bone, cerebral contusion, subdural hemorrhaging, diffuse cerebral edema, and herniation of the brain stem. The patient never regained consciousness. It became evident that the patient could not recover from these injuries, and the family consented to organ donation of his lungs, liver, kidneys, skin, and other tissue. The family did not consent to donating his heart. A flexible fiberoptic bronchoscopy was performed to examine the lung to determine the suitability for donation, and no injuries or inflammation was found. The patient was pronounced dead approximately 50 hours after the original injury.

Note: List all applicable codes *excluding* the E code.

First-Listed Diagnosis: _____

Secondary Diagnoses: _____

First-Listed Procedure: _____

Secondary Procedures: _____

13

The patient is a 21-year-old male who was found by a passing police car sitting on the side of a city street with a bleeding face and dazed appearance. A fire ambulance brought the patient to the emergency room. The patient claimed to have no memory of what happened or chose not to tell the healthcare providers the circumstances that caused his injury. He did remember being on the street, walking home from a friend's house. Alcohol and drug screens were negative, but the patient was extremely quiet and sleepy. He did not complain of the amount of pain the physicians would have expected in a patient with the injuries found, which were bilateral mandibular angle fractures, laceration of the jaw, and fractured teeth. The patient was admitted and taken to surgery the following morning and given IV antibiotics to prevent infection. The procedures performed were an open reduction and internal fixation of the mandibular fracture, a repair of the jaw laceration, and forceps extraction of one fractured tooth. The patient had no complications during or after the procedure. The preoperative urinalysis and subsequent urine culture showed a urinary tract infection, which was treated. X-rays of his skull and neck showed no fractures or injuries. The patient also had abrasions on both hands that were cleaned and bandaged. At the time of discharge, the patient still claimed to have no memory of what happened to him but otherwise appeared to be alert, cooperative, and thinking clearly. City police interviewed the patient during the hospital stay to investigate a possible crime but were unable to gain any information and found no witnesses to the event. He was discharged to the care of his older sister, whom he lives with, and follow-up appointments were given, primarily for care of his fractured mandible.

Note: List all applicable codes *excluding* the E code.

Principal Diagnosis: _____

Secondary Diagnoses: _____

Principal Procedure: _____

Secondary Procedures: _____

14

The patient is a 30-year-old man brought to the emergency department by his mother after being injured in an argument with a male neighbor two days ago. The patient fell down his front steps at this home trying to grab the neighbor, who had come to the patient's home complaining of loud music. The patient complained of pain and significant swelling of his right leg, near his knee, which had been replaced 2 years ago. Neither the patient nor the mother could tell the doctor the reason for the knee replacement other than it "collapsed" and had to be replaced. The patient also has had hemophilia A disease since birth and was diagnosed as HIV positive ten years ago. He is asymptomatic related to his HIV status and has had no infections or consequences of it. X-ray of the leg showed a right tibia fracture at the upper or proximal end. Because of his hemophilia, the fact the patient had a replaced joint near the site of the fracture, and the potential complications of an open reduction type treatment, the patient was admitted to the hospital. The leg was splinted and elevated for 48 hours until the swelling was under control. He was taken to the operating room on day 3, and a closed reduction, closely monitored under imaging, was performed, and an excellent reduction was achieved.

A cast was applied. He complained of severe pain from the time of admission, and this was managed fairly well with injectable and oral analgesic medications. He was also given 3,000 units of Factor VIII on a daily basis for the hemophilia status. The patient and his mother were instructed that the patient was to use the wheelchair they had at home to get around and not to put any weight on the right leg. Home healthcare services were ordered, and a medical car was arranged to take the patient home and get him into the house. A follow-up appointment with his orthopedic surgeon for fracture care was given to the patient, and he was encouraged to contact his hematologist at University Hospital as soon as possible. Copies of his record were given to the patient.

Note: List all applicable codes *excluding* the E code.

Principal Diagnosis: _____

Secondary Diagnoses: _____

Principal Procedure: _____

Secondary Procedures: _____

15

The patient is an 80-year-old female who fell out of bed and injured her left ankle. Examination in the emergency room revealed pain, swelling, and deformity around the left ankle. The patient denied any other pain or injury. She was admitted to the orthopedic floor and seen promptly by an orthopedic surgeon and her attending physician. X-rays were taken that showed a trimalleolar fracture of the left ankle with displacement. The patient had a significant past medical history with a previous cerebrovascular accident (CVA) last year in this right-handed lady. The left hemiplegia was due to an old cerebral infarction of the distribution of the right middle cerebral artery. She had vigorous physical therapy following this and had been doing well with ambulation and self care since that time. She is also has type II diabetes of long standing and ischemic heart disease that continues under treatment. While she was in the hospital she continued to receive her oral diabetic medication. An EKG show inferior lateral ischemia that was not a new finding. The day after admission, the orthopedic surgeon performed a closed reduction and casting of the left ankle. X-rays taken following the reduction revealed alignment to be in good position. The patient tolerated the procedure well and had no intra- or postoperative complications. A slight urinary tract infection was noted, and an antibiotic was prescribed. The patient was discharged home with home health services ordered.

Note: List all applicable codes *excluding* the E code.

Principal Diagnosis: _____

Secondary Diagnoses: _____

Principal Procedure: _____

Secondary Procedures: _____

Chapter 20

Poisoning, Adverse Effects, and Complications

Coding Scenarios for *Basic ICD-9-CM Coding*

The following case studies are organized by chapter following the sequence of the *Basic ICD-9-CM Coding* textbook. The objective of the case studies is to provide the student with more detailed clinical information to code, rather than one- or two-line diagnostic and procedure statements. Depending on whether the case study describes an inpatient hospital admission or an outpatient visit, the student is asked to provide the necessary diagnosis and procedure codes in the appropriate sequence—with principal diagnosis code listed first for inpatient admissions and main reason for visit code listed first for outpatient visits.

1

A 25-year-old woman was found unresponsive in her apartment by her roommate and brought to the hospital by fire ambulance paramedics. She had recently been treated for depression, and her roommate found the patient's prescription bottle of antidepressant medication empty. The patient's other prescription bottle of lorazepam was also empty. The emergency department (ED) staff talked to the patient's psychiatrist and confirmed these medications had been prescribed for depression. An empty bottle of vodka was found in the bedroom near the patient's body. The ED examination and toxicology studies confirm a drug overdose of these two medications and alcohol. Another friend received a suicide e-mail note from the patient the same afternoon. While the patient was receiving treatment in the ED, she suffered a cardio-pulmonary arrest and died.

Note: List all applicable codes *including* the E code.

First-Listed Diagnosis: _____

Secondary Diagnoses: _____

First-Listed Procedure: _____

Secondary Procedures: _____

2

A patient with congestive heart failure and 6 weeks status post acute MI had been prescribed and was correctly taking Lanoxin (digoxin). She began to experience nausea and vomiting with extreme fatigue. She was admitted to the hospital. Blood drug levels are taken and it is determined the patient is experiencing a side effect of the medication. A different medication is prescribed for her heart disease to avoid these symptoms. The patient's cardiac conditions are evaluated and found to be stable.

Note: List all applicable codes *including* the E code.

Principal Diagnosis: _____

Secondary Diagnoses: _____

Principal Procedure: _____

Secondary Procedures: _____

3

The patient had surgery 1 week previously for acute appendicitis with a peritoneal abscess. She is admitted now for fever, pain, and redness at the operative site. There is evidence of cellulitis of the operative wound, and cultures of the abdominal wall wound drainage confirm Staphylococcus aureus, methicillin resistant, as the cause. She receives intravenous (IV) antibiotics for the infection and also receives treatment for type II diabetes mellitus. The physician's diagnoses on discharge were: status postappendectomy with wound infection, MRSA (methicillin resistant staphylococcus aureus); diabetes type II.

Principal Diagnosis: _____

Secondary Diagnoses: _____

Principal Procedure: _____

Secondary Procedures: _____

4

An 80-year-old man was brought to the emergency department (ED) by his family with the chief complaint of "nose bleed." The patient is taking Coumadin under prescription by his internist for atrial fibrillation. The patient is also known to have congestive heart failure. The patient said his nose began bleeding about 2 hours ago and he was unable to stop the bleeding with other methods he had used in the past. He reported that he had these nose bleeds before today. However, today the bleeding is more pronounced and could not be stopped at home. In the ED, the physician is able to control the bleeding somewhat but recognized that an ENT physician should be called in for consultation. The patient's laboratory work revealed anemia and an EKG showed the existing atrial fibrillation. Because of his various conditions, his internist admits him to the hospital. He was seen by the ENT physician, who was able to stop the bleeding with an anterior and posterior packing. The packing was removed on day 2 and the epistaxis had stopped. Repeated laboratory work confirmed the doctor's diagnosis of "chronic blood loss anemia." The patient continues to receive medications for the atrial fibrillation and congestive heart failure, and new medications are started to treat the anemia. The patient's Coumadin was continued, but the dosage is lowered. In the physician's discharge progress note, he wrote "Epistaxis due to Coumadin therapy with resulting chronic blood loss anemia in a patient with atrial fibrillation and congestive heart failure.

Note: List all applicable codes *including* the E code.

Principal Diagnosis: _____

Secondary Diagnoses: _____

Principal Procedure: _____

Secondary Procedures: _____

5

A 12-year-old girl is brought to the primary care physician's office by her mother. The mother states that she had taken the child to the Urgent Care Center 5 days previously because the child had acute otitis media. The Urgent Care doctor had prescribed azithromycin. The child's condition did not improve, and, in fact, she developed red spots and itchiness on her arms and chest. The primary care physician examines the patient and concludes that the child has an allergy to the medication. The acute otitis media is still present as the medication seemed to have no effect on the infection. The physician tells the mother to discontinue the azithromycin medication and a new prescription is given. On the encounter form the physician writes "drug allergy and acute otitis media."

Note: List all applicable codes *including* the E code.

First-Listed Diagnosis: _____

Secondary Diagnoses: _____

First-Listed Procedure: _____

Secondary Procedures: _____

6

The patient, a 35-year-old man, is brought to the emergency department (ED) by friends who report that the patient has chest pain. Upon questioning, the patient admitted to being a cocaine addict and to having used cocaine several times over the past 24 hours. The patient stated "maybe I overdosed," as he experienced chest pain on a previous occasion when he used more cocaine than he normally used. The patient is placed on telemetry in the ED and is later admitted to a telemetry bed on a nursing unit. Further cardiovascular testing finds no evidence of an acute myocardial infarction or respiratory disease. However, it is determined that the patient has hypertension that had never been treated. The physician determines that this event is a cocaine overdose that occurred accidentally with the consequence of chest pain. The patient is also treated for hypertension and is strongly advised to continue the antihypertensive medications and to seek help to overcome the cocaine addiction, as the two conditions have serious consequences on his long-term health. A referral is given to the local community mental health center, which offers a drug counseling service. The patient agrees and is discharged accompanied by his brother who had surgery 1 week previously for acute appendicitis with a peritoneal abscess.

Note: List all applicable codes *including* the E code.

Principal Diagnosis: _____

Secondary Diagnoses: _____

Principal Procedure: _____

Secondary Procedures: _____

7

The patient is a 67-year-old man who comes to his cardiologist's office with complaints of pain and warmth around the pacemaker generator pocket in his left upper chest wall. The physician examines the patient and determines the patient has cellulitis of the chest wall due to an infected pacemaker pocket and needs to have the pacemaker generator moved to a different location of the chest wall to allow the infected pocket to heal. The patient has a history of a MRSA infection being treated in the past. The type of infection that appears present at this time will be investigated to check for a recurrence. The physician makes arrangements for the patient to have outpatient surgery the next day.

Note: List all applicable codes *including* the E code.

First-Listed Diagnosis: _____

Secondary Diagnoses: _____

First-Listed Procedure: _____

Secondary Procedures: _____

8

The family practice physician examines a 56-year-old male established patient who comes to the office with his wife. The patient states that he has felt dizzy and lightheaded over the past three days. The patient is on medications for hypertension and states he has been taking all as prescribed. The physician and the physician's nurse take the patient's blood pressure and find it to be 100/70 mm Hg, which is much lower than the patient's pressure as normally recorded. The patient had been taking antihypertensive medications of irbesartan (Avapro) and metoprolol (Toprol) with a low-dose diuretic. The physician is unable to determine which medication was the cause but is certain the patient's symptoms of vertigo and light-headedness are the side effects of the antihypertensive medications. New prescriptions are issued for adjusted dosages of the medications, and the patient is advised to go to the emergency department and call this physician if the symptoms get worse over the next 24 hours.

Note: List all applicable codes *including* the E code.

First-Listed Diagnosis: _____

Secondary Diagnoses: _____

First-Listed Procedure: _____

Secondary Procedures: _____

9

The patient is a 25-year-old woman who was prescribed Cipro by her family physician for an E. coli urinary tract infection and advised to take one 250-mg tablet every 12 hours for 10 days. Because she was leaving on a vacation cruise on Saturday, the patient doubled up the dosages and for the past 3 days had taken two 250-mg tablets every 12 hours. Over the past 24 hours, the patient had diarrhea severe enough for her to come to the emergency department (ED). A urinalysis shows bacteria still present to support the diagnosis of UTI. The physician recognizes these symptoms as not only side effects of the medication but, in this patient's situation, an accidental overdose of Cipro (antibiotic), as she had not followed the physician's directions in the amount of the medication she was to take. The ED physician advises her to continue taking the medication as prescribed without alterations.

Note: List all applicable codes *including* the E code.

First-Listed Diagnosis: _____

Secondary Diagnoses: _____

First-Listed Procedure: _____

Secondary Procedures: _____

10

The patient had surgery 2 weeks previously for insertion of a central venous vascular catheter for infusion to treat colon carcinoma. The patient is admitted to the hospital extremely ill with the admitting diagnosis of "sepsis." The patient's signs and symptoms include elevated temperature, rapid heart rate and respirations, and elevated white blood cell count. After study, the physician determines that the patient has sepsis due to the vascular catheter that apparently is the source of the infection. The physician and consultants further describe the patient's condition as systemic inflammatory response syndrome or sepsis in a patient with an infection. Blood cultures show evidence of methicillin susceptible staphylococcal aureus (MSSA) organisms as the cause of the septicemia or bloodstream infection. Intravenous antibiotic medications and other therapy are given for the infection and the carcinoma. The partially implantable venous access device is removed. The patient recovers and is discharged home in 10 days to be followed in the oncology clinic in 1 week.

Principal Diagnosis: _____

Secondary Diagnoses: _____

Principal Procedure: _____

Secondary Procedures: _____

11

The patient is an 80-year-old man with multiple medical problems: Parkinson's disease, glaucoma, near total blindness in both eyes, old MI 6 months ago, recent abnormal cardiac stress test, status post right total knee replacement, and osteoarthrosis, generalized. On this occasion he is admitted to the hospital for a planned revision of his right total knee arthroplasty. The patient has been evaluated by cardiology and cleared for surgery. He had been seen by the orthopedic surgeon several weeks ago and scheduled for this revision arthroplasty. About 10–12 years ago the patient had a total knee replacement on the right side for osteoarthritis. He developed increasing pain in his knee, and the orthopedic evaluation found aseptic loosening of the tibial component of his knee. The patient was taken to surgery on the day of admission and had a revision right knee arthroplasty of the tibial component. The surgeon found femoral and patellar components of the previous knee replacement to be stable and in good working order. The tibial component was found to be grossly loose and was able to be removed with little effort. The tibial tray had divided completely from the cement mantle. The orthopedic surgeon proceeded to replace the tibial component only. The patient recovered well from surgery without complications and was transferred to a skilled unit facility for rehabilitation and to increase his ability to perform activities of daily living independently. All of his medical conditions were monitored and treated while he was in the hospital for this surgery.

Principal Diagnosis: _____

Secondary Diagnoses: _____

Principal Procedure: _____

Secondary Procedures: _____

12

Four days ago this 33-year-old female delivered a premature infant, which expired within hours after birth at another hospital. She is admitted to this hospital today for wound dehiscence of her recent cesarean section postoperative wound. The patient is morbidly obese with a body mass index of 45.0 postpartum. During her pregnancy, she was told she had cardiomyopathy and received treatment. The wound dehiscence was treated medically by the obstetrician, and she received evaluation and management from a cardiologist for her cardiomyopathy and obesity. The patient was able to be discharged home on day 4 with home health nursing follow up care and appointments with her physicians within 2 weeks.

Principal Diagnosis: _____

Secondary Diagnoses: _____

Principal Procedure: _____

Secondary Procedures: _____

13

One year ago this 40-year-old female received a left kidney transplant from an unrelated donor to treat her end-stage renal disease. The doctors were notified by the transplant network that the donor was diagnosed with low grade lymphoma, and the transplant patient was tested for any evidence of the lymphoma in the donated kidney. Unfortunately the transplanted kidney was proven by biopsy to have non-Hodgkin's lymphoma. The patient was admitted to the hospital. A nephrectomy was performed to remove the transplanted kidney. The patient was put back on hemodialysis for the end-stage kidney disease still present. The patient had an uneventful recovery and was discharged home with home health services.

Principal Diagnosis: _____

Secondary Diagnoses: _____

Principal Procedure: _____

Secondary Procedures: _____

14

The patient is a 24-year-old male who received an orthotopic liver transplant 2 months ago to treat his primary biliary cirrhosis. The patient was admitted at this time after a transplant clinic visit on the same day because of a generalized macular rash on his chest. The patient also complained of diarrhea and an enlarging abdomen that the doctors identified as ascites. A skin biopsy was performed and revealed a significant number of donor lymphocytes due to acute graft-versus-host (GVH) disease. The doctors informed the patient that his acute GVH disease is a complication of his liver transplant but can be treated with medications such as corticosteroids, immunosuppressants, antibiotics, and immunoglobulins. The patient remained in the hospital for 5 days and started on a medication regimen with relief of his diarrhea and lessening of the symptoms of the ascites and the rash. The patient was discharged home with home health services and an appointment with the transplant clinic in 2 weeks.

Principal Diagnosis: _____

Secondary Diagnoses: _____

Principal Procedure: _____

Secondary Procedures: _____

15

The patient is a 7-year-old male who was brought to the emergency department by his mother because of a suspected allergic reaction. The patient was experiencing wheezing, urticaria, and itching and tingling on his lips and in his mouth. The patient was at a party at school and ate cookies that contained small bits of peanuts, unknown to him at the time. The mother states he has a known allergy to peanuts and has had reactions in the past when exposed to peanuts, even without eating them. The physician described the patient's condition as a relatively mild anaphylactic reaction to food (peanuts), and the patient received an injection of epinephrine. He was observed in the emergency room for another 3 hours and had a complete resolution of his symptoms.

First-Listed Diagnosis: _____

Secondary Diagnoses: _____

First-Listed Procedure: _____

Secondary Procedures: _____

Chapter 21

Supplementary Classifications—E-Codes

Coding Scenarios for *Basic ICD-9-CM Coding*

Note: Assign only E codes for the following scenarios.

An E code from the categories E800–E999 may be used with any code in the range of 001–V91 that indicates an injury, poisoning, or adverse effect due to an external cause.

An additional E code from category E849 can be used to indicate the place of occurrence to describe the place where the event occurred, but not the patient's activity at the time of the event.

An activity E code from categories E001–E030 may be used with any code in the range of 001–V89. The activity code indicates that an injury or other health condition resulting from an activity or the activity contributed to the condition. The activity codes are not applicable to poisonings, adverse effects, misadventures, or late effects.

An external cause status E code from category E000 should be assigned whenever any other E code is assigned, including an activity E code, except for the events noted next. Assign a code from category E000 to indicate the work status of the person at the time the event occurred. The external cause status E codes are not applicable to poisonings, adverse effects, misadventures, or late effects. Do not assign a code from category E000 if no other E codes (cause, activity) are applicable to the encounter. Do not assign code E000.9, unspecified external cause status, if the status is not stated.

1. Injury in a fight between spectators at a football game; location was a sports stadium. Patient is a student and was a spectator at the sports event.

   E code(s): _____

2. Self-inflicted gunshot wound using a handgun, stated to be intentional; location was his garage at home. Patient is an unemployed worker.

   E code(s): _____

3. Driver injured in a motor vehicle accident involving a collision with another motor vehicle on a highway. Patient is an employed driver for a delivery company.

   E code(s): _____

4. Patient is a construction worker who fell off scaffolding at a construction site. Patient is an employed construction worker.

    E code(s): _____

5. Homeowner fell off a ladder while washing windows at his home. Patient is an unemployed homeowner.

    E code(s): _____

6. Patient was the driver of a motor vehicle that struck a bridge abutment on a highway. Patient is a student driving his vehicle while talking on a handheld cellular phone.

    E code(s): _____

7. Patient was a passenger on a commercial airplane flight who was injured when the plane experienced a hard landing at the city public airport. Patient was flying to a vacation destination.

    E code(s): _____

8. Patient was a vacationer who stepped on broken glass in the sand on the beach at the oceanside resort. Patient was on vacation and walking on the beach.

    E code(s): _____

9. Child was injured when he dove into the swimming pool at the next-door neighbor's home and struck the side of the pool with his leg. Patient was a student and diving off a springboard platform.

    E code(s): _____

10. Patient was brought to the emergency department with wounds suffered in a drive-by gang shooting using a handgun, which appeared to be a homicide attempt. Shooting occurred on a public street. Patient was a student.

    E code(s): _____

11. A hospital patient fell out of bed and injured his hip while in the hospital. Patient was a retired individual in the hospital.

    E code(s): _____

12. A patient was assaulted by an acquaintance and was stabbed in the abdomen with a knife during the argument, which occurred in a parking lot. Patient was an unemployed worker.

    E code(s): _____

13. The patient has a closed head injury as result of a tree falling on him during a tornado. The accident occurred at his home. Patient was off work on vacation at home.

    E code(s): _____

14. The child was scalded with hot tap water while in the bath. This is judged as child abuse. The abuser was the boyfriend of the child's mother, and the incident occurred in the home. Patient was a student.

    E code(s): _____

15. The patient was overcome by heat exhaustion while working near a blast furnace in a steel mill. Patient was an employed steel worker in the mill.

    E code(s): _____

16. The patient was working as a paid landscaper and injured his back by lifting heavy stones being placed for a decorative border around the entrance to a city park.

    E code(s): _____

17. A teenager was brought to the emergency room with an injured right wrist that was the result of the patient running and falling while wearing "heelies" or athletic shoes with a single wheel housed in the heel of the shoes. The accident occurred in a parking lot of a grocery store. The patient was a student in high school.

    E code(s): _____

18. A 30-year-old man was brought to the emergency room complaining of back and neck pain from a fall that occurred after he collided with another player while playing basketball at the local outdoor basketball court. The patient was spending leisure time playing basketball.

    E code(s): _____

19. A 50-year-old man was brought to the emergency room and diagnosed with a right hip fracture that was a result of a fall off his skis while snow skiing at a local ski resort. Patient was on vacation at the ski resort.

    E code(s): _____

20. A child was struck by a car and dragged several feet when he ran across the street in front of his home. He sustained head injuries and multiple fractures and was admitted to the trauma intensive care unit at the hospital after being brought to the emergency department by fire ambulance. Patient was a student who was running and playing.

    E code(s): _____

Chapter 22

Late Effects

Coding Scenarios for *Basic ICD-9-CM Coding*

The following case studies are organized by chapter following the sequence of the *Basic ICD-9-CM Coding* textbook. The objective of the case studies is to provide the student with more detailed clinical information to code, rather than one- or two-line diagnostic and procedure statements. Depending on whether the case study describes an inpatient hospital admission or an outpatient visit, the student is asked to provide the necessary diagnosis and procedure codes in the appropriate sequence—with principal diagnosis code listed first for inpatient admissions and main reason for visit code listed first for outpatient visits.

1

Six months after a house fire in which the patient sustained burns of his right leg, he has developed severe scarring as a result of the third-degree burns. The patient is evaluated in the plastic surgeon's office and scheduled for reconstructive surgery in the near future.

Note: List all applicable codes *including* the E code.

First-Listed Diagnosis: _____

Secondary Diagnoses: _____

First-Listed Procedure: _____

Secondary Procedures: _____

2

A patient comes to the pain clinic for management of chronic neck and shoulder pain that she has suffered since an auto accident that occurred 10 months previously. The patient has difficulty sleeping due to the pain and has trouble lifting or moving anything with her left shoulder or arm. After taking a complete history and performing a thorough physical examination, the pain management physician diagnoses the condition as "cervicobrachial syndrome, due to auto accident 10 months ago and past injury to nerve roots, spinal area."

Note: List all applicable codes *including* the E code.

First-Listed Diagnosis: _____

Secondary Diagnoses: _____

First-Listed Procedure: _____

Secondary Procedures: _____

3

The patient is seen in the neurology clinic at the request of her family physician for assessment of her limb-kinetic apraxia due to her past cerebrovascular accident (CVA). The patient has expressive aphasia and facial weakness due to her past CVA, which is also evaluated during the visit.

Note: List all applicable codes *including* the E code.

First-Listed Diagnosis: _____

Secondary Diagnoses: _____

First-Listed Procedure: _____

Secondary Procedures: _____

4

The patient is seen in the orthopedic clinic for a complaint of muscle wasting of the lower legs. In conducting a thorough history and physical examination, the physician learns that the patient had poliomyelitis 50 years previously. The physician determines the muscle wasting is a result of her old polio and describes it as postpolio syndrome. The physician recommends a trial of physical therapy to prevent further muscular wasting.

First-Listed Diagnosis: _____

Secondary Diagnoses: _____

First-Listed Procedure: _____

Secondary Procedures: _____

5

The patient is admitted to the hospital with chronic weakness, fatigue, and other central nervous system symptoms. The patient is known to have had infectious mononucleosis several months previously and has never felt well since that time. Laboratory tests and neurological studies are used to evaluate the patient's condition and possible underlying cause. The physician concludes that the current condition is late effect or chronic Epstein-Barr infection.

Principal Diagnosis: _____

Secondary Diagnoses: _____

Principal Procedure: _____

Secondary Procedures: _____

6

The patient is seen in the offices of an infectious disease specialist who treated her 1 year previously when she had Lyme disease. She complains of generalized joint pain and stiffness. Based on laboratory test results and physical examination, the physician concludes that the patient no longer has active Lyme disease. However, he concludes that her arthropathy of multiple joints is the residual effect of the cured Lyme disease.

First-Listed Diagnosis: _____

Secondary Diagnoses: _____

First-Listed Procedure: _____

Secondary Procedures: _____

7

The 57-year-old male patient is a resident of a long-term care facility after suffering a stroke 2 months previously, with bilateral quadriplegia as a result. The patient is being discharged from this facility to be readmitted to another long-term care facility that specializes in the type of care the patient requires for his paralytic syndrome.

Principal Diagnosis: _____

Secondary Diagnoses: _____

Principal Procedure: _____

Secondary Procedures: _____

8

A 75-year-old patient is admitted to the hospital with the acute onset of neurological symptoms including double vision, speech difficulty, and loss of balance. Because the patient had a cerebrovascular accident (CVA) 5 years previously, with residual hemiparesis on her nondominant side, the physician is concerned the patient is having another stroke. Physical and neurological examination along with CT scanning and blood tests prove the patient has not had another stroke. The physician describes this episode of illness as a "TIA" or transient ischemic attack. The patient's symptoms completely resolve, but she is seen by a physical therapist for her old CVA hemiparesis. The patient's essential hypertension is also treated. The stage II chronic kidney disease due to her Type II diabetes mellitus was monitored and treated. The patient is discharged on the hospital day 3 for follow-up in her physician's office in 1 week.

Principal Diagnosis: _____

Secondary Diagnoses: _____

Principal Procedure: _____

Secondary Procedures: _____

9

The patient is a 50-year-old woman who was previously treated by closed reduction and external fixation of a fracture of her right tibia that she suffered as the result of a fall. During follow-up care, it becomes evident that the fracture is not healing. X-rays demonstrate a nonunion of the distal tibia. The patient is admitted for surgical repair of the nonunion. The surgery performed is an open reduction of the tibia with bone grafting. Bone for the grafting is harvested from the patient's iliac crest. The tibial bone, at the site of the nonunion, is osteotomized and repositioned. The harvested bone graft is packed into the fracture site, and three screws are inserted to secure the area. The patient is discharged the day after surgery for recovery at home.

Note: List all applicable codes *including* the E code.

Principal Diagnosis: _____

Secondary Diagnoses: _____

Principal Procedure: _____

Secondary Procedures: _____

10

The patient, an active 60-year-old man, who suffered a fracture of the neck of the left femur in an automobile accident 10 years previously, is admitted to the hospital for a left total hip replacement. The patient has suffered progressive disability of his hip joint with pain on standing, sitting, and lying down. He also has difficulty walking. Given the fact the patient has little to no arthritis in any other joint, it is determined that the arthritis in his left hip is a result of the old fracture or trauma. The patient consents to a total hip replacement with ceramic-on-ceramic bearing surface. The patient is discharged home to be followed up by home health nurses and physical therapists.

Note: List all applicable codes *including* the E code.

Principal Diagnosis: _____

Secondary Diagnoses: _____

Principal Procedure: _____

Secondary Procedures: _____

11

The patient is a 77-year-old female who is a resident of a nursing home. She had a cerebral vascular accident 10 months ago and since that time has had several seizures that have been determined to be a consequence of her stroke. None of the seizures has been very significant, but the patient has been placed on anticonvulsant medication. Her doctor wrote in the last progress note documenting his visit the diagnosis of "Patient stable, seizure disorder over the last 9 months, due to her previous stroke."

First-Listed Diagnosis: _____

Secondary Diagnoses: _____

First-Listed Procedure: _____

Secondary Procedures: _____

12

The patient is a 25-year-old male Army veteran of the Iraq war who was discharged one year ago. He was in a vehicle that was slightly damaged by an improvised explosive device that did not hit the vehicle directly. However, the vehicle crashed into a wall as a result, and the four soldiers inside the vehicle had minor injuries. This patient recalls hitting his head on the side door of the vehicle when it crashed but otherwise was uninjured. Since the soldier has been discharged, his family at home describe him as exhibiting irritability and impulsive behaviors that are uncharacteristic of him. Today's visit at the Veterans Administration Outpatient Center is to review test results to explain his behavior change, which the patient also notices but cannot explain. Given the circumstances, the physician concludes the patient has "Late effect symptoms (irritability, impulsiveness) of traumatic brain injury." The patient was referred to a specialized treatment center that focuses on patients with traumatic brain injury.

First-Listed Diagnosis: _____

Secondary Diagnoses: _____

First-Listed Procedure: _____

Secondary Procedures: _____

13

A patient who had a cerebral vascular accident 7 months ago was admitted to the hospital for a surgical tendon transfer on his left hand and wrist. The patient acquired a contracture of the left hand and wrist as a result of the CVA. Otherwise the patient had recovered well from the stroke. During the hospital stay, the orthopedic surgeon performed a hand tendon transfer with no complications, and the patient was discharged from the hospital on the day after surgery. The patient also had two chronic conditions managed while in the hospital: essential hypertension and simple chronic bronchitis. The patient was discharged with instructions for post-operative care including a follow-up appointment in the orthopedic surgeon's office in 5 days.

Principal Diagnosis: _____

Secondary Diagnoses: _____

Principal Procedure: _____

Secondary Procedures: _____

14

This was the first admission to a long term acute care hospital (LTACH) for the 45-year-old male patient, who was unconscious and respiratory dependent because of his chronic respiratory failure. He acquired the respiratory failure after suffering a multi-drug overdose 2 weeks ago. According to his family, it was believed the patient was addicted to multiple illegal drugs but exactly which drugs was unknown. The patient had a tracheostomy in place for connection to the mechanical ventilator. The patient is admitted to the LTACH for managing his respiratory failure and possibly weaning from mechanical ventilation. All attempts to wean the patient from the ventilator were unsuccessful. After 30 days in the LTACH, the patient was transferred to a long term care ventilator unit at a skilled nursing facility for further care. His final diagnoses were noted to be chronic respiratory failure from multiple drug overdose, polysubstance dependence, ventilator dependency, and tracheostomy status. He remained on the ventilator the entire time he was in the LTACH.

Principal Diagnosis: _____

Secondary Diagnoses: _____

Principal Procedure: _____

Secondary Procedures: _____

15

The patient was previously treated by closed reduction with external fixation for a fracture on the surgical neck of the right humerus. There was a malunion of the fracture in the 80-year-old female patient, and she was admitted for an open reduction of the humerus with bone grafting. During the surgical procedure, the orthopedic surgeon harvested bone from the patient's iliac crest. The humeral fracture site was opened and the area of malnunion was osteotomized, cleaned, and repositioned. Internal fixation with screws was accomplished and the harvested bone was packed into the fracture site. The patient recovered from the procedure uneventfully and was discharged on the second hospital day. Other chronic conditions treated in the hospital were arteriosclerotic heart disease, chronic renal insufficiency, and type II diabetes mellitus. The patient was given an appointment to see the orthopedic surgeon in his office in 5 days and was going to be followed by home health nurses for postoperative care.

Principal Diagnosis: _____

Secondary Diagnoses: _____

Principal Procedure: _____

Secondary Procedures: _____

Chapter 23

Supplementary Classifications—V Codes

Coding Scenarios for *Basic ICD-9-CM Coding*

The following case studies are organized by chapter following the sequence of the *Basic ICD-9-CM Coding* textbook. The objective of the case studies is to provide the student with more detailed clinical information to code, rather than one- or two-line diagnostic and procedure statements. Depending on whether the case study describes an inpatient hospital admission or an outpatient visit, the student is asked to provide the necessary diagnosis and procedure codes in the appropriate sequence—with principal diagnosis code listed first for inpatient admissions and main reason for visit code listed first for outpatient visits.

1

A 27-completed-week gestation infant is delivered by cesarean section. The baby weighs 945 grams. The baby's lungs are immature, and she subsequently develops respiratory distress syndrome, requiring a long stay in the neonatal intensive care unit. The baby eventually is able to go home with her family. The physician's diagnosis is "liveborn infant, delivered by cesarean section, extreme immaturity with a birthweight of 945 grams at 27 weeks of gestation, with resulting respiratory distress syndrome."

Principal Diagnosis: _____

Secondary Diagnoses: _____

Principal Procedure: _____

Secondary Procedures: _____

2

The 60-year-old male patient is scheduled for an outpatient cystoscopy. This is a follow-up visit because the patient has a history of bladder carcinoma that was resected 7 years previously. At that time, the patient received chemotherapy but has not been treated for the cancer for nearly 6 years. He has had yearly cystoscopic examinations, and no recurrence of the bladder cancer has been found. The cystoscopy is performed by the urologist, who documents as the post-operative diagnosis "history of transitional cell carcinoma of the bladder with no recurrence found, follow-up examination, mild benign prostatic hypertrophy evaluated."

First-Listed Diagnosis: _____

Secondary Diagnoses: _____

First-Listed Procedure: _____

Secondary Procedures: _____

3

A 35-year-old patient, gravida 6, para 6, requests a tubal ligation/sterilization to be performed by her OB-GYN physician as she does not want to have more children. An outpatient procedure is scheduled. The physician performs the following procedure with the following diagnosis: laparoscopic tubal ligation using Falope rings, admission for desired sterilization and multiparity.

First-Listed Diagnosis: _____

Secondary Diagnoses: _____

First-Listed Procedure: _____

Secondary Procedures: _____

4

A full-term, 38-week gestation infant is born by vaginal birth in the hospital to a 35-year-old woman who develops gestational diabetes during the pregnancy. The mother requires close monitoring during the pregnancy because of rather severe fluctuations in blood glucose level. The infant, weighing 8 lb, 5 oz, appears normal and healthy. However, because of the mother's gestational diabetes, the infant is kept in the hospital 2 days longer than usual to observe for possible metabolic disorders as a result of his mother's condition. No symptoms are exhibited by the infant, and the results of diagnostic studies performed are negative. The pediatrician writes the discharge diagnosis as normal, full-term infant, observed for possible effects of mother's gestational diabetes.

Principal Diagnosis: _____

Secondary Diagnoses: _____

Principal Procedure: _____

Secondary Procedures: _____

5

A 75-year-old retired nun has a total hip replacement for localized osteoarthritis of the hip. After surgery, she experiences significant difficulty in ambulating, along with gait abnormalities. Physical therapists treat the patient while she is in the hospital, but on day 6, she is discharged to home to be followed up by home health services.

Code for the home health services received: The patient is seen three times a week by a nurse and physical therapists. The patient receives an anticoagulant drug to prevent clots. This requires the nurse to draw blood for a PT/PTT laboratory test weekly. Physical therapists treat the patient for her gait abnormality as part of her aftercare following the hip joint replacement. Physical therapy performed includes gait training and strengthening exercises to increase the patient's mobility.

First-Listed Diagnosis: _____

Secondary Diagnoses: _____

First-Listed Procedure: _____

Secondary Procedures: _____

6

A premature twin infant with a liveborn mate is admitted to the special care nursery after the cesarean delivery during which he was delivered. The infant is treated for his prematurity and low birth weight as well as neonatal jaundice associated with the preterm delivery. The infant receives phototherapy for the jaundice and is discharged to his parents after 1 month in the hospital. The pediatrician's discharge diagnoses were "premature twin infant, result of a 34-week pregnancy, with a birthweight of 1800 grams."

Principal Diagnosis: _____

Secondary Diagnoses: _____

Principal Procedure: _____

Secondary Procedures: _____

7

The fire ambulance brings a family to the hospital emergency department (ED) after a serious car accident. The father and mother were seriously injured and are admitted to the hospital with multiple fractures and head trauma. During the accident, the 10-month-old baby was secured in a rear-facing child seat in the backseat. The ED physicians examine the baby carefully and request several x-rays to be performed. All x-rays are negative, but the physicians are still particularly concerned about the infant, given the serious nature of the accident. They decide to admit the baby to the hospital for monitoring and further testing for undetected injuries. After day 2, no injuries can be found in the infant, and he is discharged to the care of his maternal grandparents.

Principal Diagnosis: _____

Secondary Diagnoses: _____

Principal Procedure: _____

Secondary Procedures: _____

8

The patient is a 32-year-old woman who is 24 weeks pregnant. She is being followed up by her physician as a high-risk pregnancy because of her history of having a hydatidiform mole 10 years previously. The patient is considered to have a history of infertility as the patient has not been pregnant since she was treated for the hydatidiform mole with surgical evacuation. The physician orders ongoing laboratory testing for monitoring of the current pregnancy and no problems have been detected. The patient will return for her next prenatal visit at 27 weeks.

First-Listed Diagnosis: _____

Secondary Diagnoses: _____

First-Listed Procedure: _____

Secondary Procedures: _____

9

The first visit of the day for this pediatrician is a 2-week-old infant who was born by vaginal delivery to a woman during the 39th week of pregnancy. All laboratory tests done in the hospital were normal and the baby was discharged with her mother on day 2. The mother reports that the infant has been nursing well and has generally been a delight. The pediatrician examines the infant and does not find any problems or abnormalities at the age of 14 days. The mother is counseled regarding infant care, nursing, and the recommended infant vaccinations to be performed during the follow-up visits.

First-Listed Diagnosis: _____

Secondary Diagnoses: _____

First-Listed Procedure: _____

Secondary Procedures: _____

10

The patient is a 28-year-old woman who is a third-grade school teacher. She is donating one of her kidneys for a young boy in her class who has polycystic kidney disease and is in need of a kidney transplant. The donor has a history of an allergy to latex, so she was protected from any exposure to latex supplies during her hospital stay. This allergy did not prevent her from being a donor. The teacher's surgery is performed uneventfully, and she is discharged to her home to recover.

Principal Diagnosis: _____

Secondary Diagnoses: _____

Principal Procedure: _____

Secondary Procedures: _____

11

The patient was seen in the physician's office for change of the dressings on both hands. The patient is a construction worker who was injured on the job 7 days ago. He was handling a rope used to pull up a heavy metal structure when the rope began to run through his gloved hands. He tried to stop the rope and states that his gloves actually caught fire. He developed pain to both of his hands, especially to the third and fourth fingers of both hands. He was brought to the Emergency Department of the hospital near the construction site. The ER physician applied cool dressings to the hands and removed some avulsed skin from several fingers. During this office visit, the patient's dressings were changed with Silvadene applied to the fingers. The wounds did not appear infected. The reason for the visit documented by the physician was "Change of dressings to protect the healing deep abrasions on multiple fingers of both hands."

First-Listed Diagnosis: _____

Secondary Diagnoses: _____

First-Listed Procedure: _____

Secondary Procedures: _____

12

The patient was seen in his primary care physician's office for fracture aftercare concerning the traumatic fractures of his pelvis that occurred 4 weeks ago. The patient was hit by a car, knocked down, and the car ran over his pelvis. The fractures did not require surgical treatment. During his hospital stay, he was diagnosed with diabetes mellitus, type II, and hypertriglyceridemia. He knew he had hypertension but was not taking any medication as he was uninsured. New antihypertensive medications were started. After the hospital stay, the patient was transferred to an acute rehabilitation facility, and he improved dramatically over the past 4 weeks. He was discharged from the rehabilitation facility 2 days ago and will begin outpatient physical therapy tomorrow. During this office visit, his medical conditions were monitored. The office staff was able to provide him with his oral medications through a program for the uninsured sponsored by the pharmaceutical company. The physician also reviewed and signed the physical therapy plan of treatment and orders for the patient to continue to receive fracture aftercare.

First-Listed Diagnosis: _____

Secondary Diagnoses: _____

First-Listed Procedure: _____

Secondary Procedures: _____

13

The patient, a 70-year-old man, was seen in his cardiologist's office for a report of the echocardiogram that was performed on the patient within the past week. The man had the mitral valve in his heart replaced about 20 years ago and has had some vague symptoms that led the doctor to order the echocardiogram. Based on the physical examination and the report of the echocardiogram, the cardiologist concluded the heart valve was near the end of its life and needed to be replaced. The doctor informed the patient that this was an expected event, that valves do not last forever, and that the need to replace it did not mean the valve was defective or causing a complication. To prevent the patient from experiencing serious problems by delaying the inevitable replacement, the doctor arranged for the patient to be admitted to the hospital the same evening, with consultation with the cardiothoracic surgeon immediately. Two days later the patient had the mitral valve replaced with a new prosthetic valve and had an uneventful recovery. (Diagnosis hint: Fitting, device)

Principal Diagnosis: _____

Secondary Diagnoses: _____

Principal Procedure: _____

Secondary Procedures: _____

14

The patient is a 17-year-old high school senior who was in his chemistry laboratory when another student spilled a chemical during a lab assignment. Other students in the classroom complained of nausea and shortness of breath. This patient had no symptoms or complaints. The student was examined by the Emergency Department physician and found to be well. The diagnosis written by the doctor on the record was "Well adolescent, exposed to hazardous chemical, no injury or disease found."

First-Listed Diagnosis: _____

Secondary Diagnoses: _____

First-Listed Procedure: _____

Secondary Procedures: _____

15

A five-month-old female was brought by her mother to the pediatrician's office for her scheduled "Synagis" shot. Synagis is a medication given prophylactically to high-risk infants to protect them from acquiring the respiratory syncytial virus (RSV) and avoid an acute respiratory illness. The doctor's progress note for the visit concludes with his impression of "Ex-30 week premature infant here for Synagis injection, completed."

First-Listed Diagnosis: _____

Secondary Diagnoses: _____

First-Listed Procedure: _____

Secondary Procedures: _____

Answer Key for Coding Scenarios

Chapter 2

Procedures

1. **Principal Diagnosis:** Acute duodenal ulcer with hemorrhage, 532.00
    Secondary Diagnoses: Diverticulosis of colon, 562.10
    Principal Procedure: EGD with biopsy, 45.16
    Secondary Procedures: Colonoscopy, 45.23

2. **Principal Diagnosis:** Adenocarcinoma of endometrium, 182.0
    Secondary Diagnoses: Cyst of ovary, 620.1; Type II diabetes, 250.00
    Principal Procedure: Total abdominal hysterectomy, 68.4
    Secondary Procedures: Bilateral salpingo-oophorectomy, 65.61

3. **Principal Diagnosis:** Coronary atherosclerosis, native arteries, 414.01
    Secondary Diagnoses: Angina, pectoris 413.9; hypertension, 401.9
    Principal Procedure: Left heart catheterization, 37.22
    Secondary Procedures: Left ventriculogram, 88.53; Coronary arteriography using two catheters, 88.56

4. **Principal Diagnosis:** Calculus of ureter, 592.1
    Secondary Diagnoses: Hydronephrosis, 591; Urinary tract infection, unspecified, 599.0
    Principal Procedure: Ureteral catheterization (for stent insertion), 59.8
    Secondary Procedures: Cystoscopy, 57.32 (this code is optional as it is understood the procedure was done endoscopically); retrograde pyelogram, 87.74

5. **Principal Diagnosis:** Malignant neoplasm, female breast, upper inner quadrant, 174.2

    Secondary Diagnoses: History, family, malignant neoplasm, breast, V16.3

    Principal Procedure: Local excision of lesion of breast, 85.21

    Secondary Procedures: None indicated by the documentation provided

6. **Principal Diagnosis:** Inguinal hernia, without mention of obstruction or gangrene, unilateral, recurrent, 550.91

    Secondary Diagnoses: None indicated by the documentation provided

    Principal Procedure: Unilateral repair of inguinal hernia, indirect with direct, 53.01

    Secondary Procedures: None indicated by the documentation provided

7. **Principal Diagnosis:** Chondromalacia of patella, 717.7

    Secondary Diagnoses: Bursitis, prepatellar, 726.65

    NOTE: The instruction for coding case 7 is to focus on coding the surgical procedure and not the entire record. It is difficult to determine the principal diagnosis without the complete record. It appears that one of the following conditions woulds be coded with the principal diagnosis based on the circumstances of the admission, with other diagnoses listed as secondary diagnoses: Duodenal ulcer, 532.90; GERD, 530.81, BPH, 600.01; Retention, urinary, 788.20.

    Principal Procedure: Local excision or destruction of lesion of joint (debridement), 80.86

    Secondary Procedures: (Arthroscopy of the knee [80.26] is not a required secondary code as it is the surgical approach. Some hospitals, however, may require the code to be used for internal data reporting purposes.)

8. **Principal Diagnosis:** Displacement of lumbar vertebral disc without myelopathy, 722.10

    Secondary Diagnoses: Carpal tunnel syndrome or syndrome, carpal tunnel, 354.0

    Principal Procedure: Excision of intervertebral disc, 80.51

    Secondary Procedures: None indicated by the documentation provided

9. **Principal Diagnosis:** Fracture distal end radius with ulna, closed, 813.44

    Secondary Diagnoses: Pedal cycle accident injuring pedal cyclist, E826.1; Injury occurring at the home, E849.0; Activities including bike riding, E006.4

    Principal Procedure: Closed reduction of fracture with internal fixation of radius/ulna, 79.12

    Secondary Procedures: None indicated by the documentation provided

10. **Principal Diagnosis:** Calculus of the gallbladder with cholecystitis, without mention of obstruction, 574.10
    Secondary Diagnoses: Benign neoplasm of liver/biliary passages, 211.5
    Principal Procedure: Laparoscopic cholecystectomy, 51.23
    Secondary Procedures: Diagnostic procedure (biopsy) on liver, 50.19

11. **Principal Diagnosis:** Small bowel obstruction due to adhesions, 560.81
    Secondary Diagnoses: Hypothyroidism, 244.9; Hypertension, 401.9; Dyslipidemia, 272.4; Anxiety, 300.00; Elevated blood pressure, 796.2
    Principal Procedure: Lysis of adhesions, intestine, 54.59
    Secondary Procedures: Application, adhesion barrier substance, 99.77

12. **Principal Diagnosis:** Effusion, pleural, 511.9
    Secondary Diagnoses: Failure, respiratory, acute, 518.81; Neoplasm, malignant, esophagogastric junction; 151.0
    Principal Procedure: Insertion, chest tube, 34.04
    Secondary Procedures: Intubation, endotracheal, 96.04; Ventilation, mechanical, (24 hours) 96.71

13. **Principal Diagnosis:** Neoplasm, malignant, primary, rectum with colon (rectosigmoid), 154.0
    Secondary Diagnoses: Disease, artery, coronary, 414.01, Status, angioplasty, coronary V45.82; Angina, pectoris, 413.9: Hypercholesterolemia, 272.0
    Principal Procedure: Resection, rectum, anterior, 48.63
    Secondary Procedures: None indicated by documentation provided

14. **Principal Diagnosis:** Fracture, femur, subcapital, 820.09
    Secondary Diagnoses: Hypertension, 401.9; Fall (external cause) E888.9; Accident, occurring at parking lot, E849.8; Activity, walking, E001.0; Activity status, (retired) recreation, E001.8
    Principal Procedure: Fixation, bone, internal, femur, 78.55
    Secondary Procedures: None indicated by documentation provided

15. **Principal Diagnosis:** Stenosis, Aortic valve, with mitral insufficiency, 396.2
    Secondary Diagnoses: Failure, heart, diastolic, chronic, 428.32; Failure, heart, congestive, 428.0; Hypertension with renal involvement, with failure, 403.91; Disease, renal, end stage, 585.6; Anemia, of chronic disease, 285.29; Dyslipidemia, 272.4; History, hepatitis C, V12.09
    Principal Procedure: Replacement, heart valve, aortic with tissue graft, 35.21
    Secondary Procedures: Annuloplasty, 35.33; Bypass, cardiopulmonary, 39.61; Insertion, Swan-Ganz catheter, 89.64

Chapter 3

Coding for Prospective Payment: Principal Diagnosis, Additional Diagnoses and Procedures

1. **Principal Diagnosis:** Systolic heart failure, acute on chronic, 428.23
   Secondary Diagnoses: Type II diabetes, 250.00; Hypertension, 401.9
   Principal Procedure: None indicated by the documentation provided
   Secondary Procedures: None indicated by the documentation provided

2. **Principal Diagnosis:** Osteoarthritis, localized, bilateral of hips, 715.15
   Secondary Diagnoses: None indicated by the documentation provided
   Principal Procedure: Total hip replacement, 81.51
   Secondary Procedures: Hip bearing surface, ceramic-on-ceramic, 00.76

3. **Principal Diagnosis:** Pneumonococcal meningitis, 320.1
   Secondary Diagnoses: Pneumococcal pneumonia, 481; acute suppurative otitis media, 382.00
   Principal Procedure: Lumbar puncture, 03.31
   Secondary Procedures: None indicated by the documentation provided

4. **Principal Diagnosis:** Coronary atherosclerosis of native coronary arteries, 414.01
   Secondary Diagnosis: Stable angina, 413.9; Diabetes mellitus, type II, 250.00
   Principal Procedure: Aortocoronary bypass of three coronary arteries, 36.13
   Secondary Procedures: Extracorporeal circulation for open heart surgery, 39.61; Combined right and left heart catheterization, 37.23; Coronary arteriography using two catheters (Judkins technique), 88.56

5. **Principal Diagnosis:** Senile osteoporosis, 733.01
   Secondary Diagnoses: Aftercare for healing traumatic fracture of bone, V54.19
   Principal Procedure: Removal of implanted device from radius, 78.63 (removal was invasive: See note under code)
   Secondary Procedures: Open reduction without internal fixation, radius, 79.22; Bone graft to radius, 78.03

6. **Principal Diagnosis:** Dehydration, 276.51
   Secondary Diagnoses: Gastroenteritis, 558.9
   Principal Procedure: None indicated by the documentation provided
   Secondary Procedures: None indicated by the documentation provided

7. **Principal Diagnosis:** Hepatic coma/encephalopathy, 572.2
   Secondary Diagnoses: Alcoholic cirrhosis of liver, 571.2; Alcohol dependence, continuous use, 303.91
   Principal Procedure: None indicated by the documentation provided
   Secondary Procedures: None indicated by the documentation provided

8. **Principal Diagnosis:** Carotid artery occlusion, without cerebral infarction, 433.10

   Secondary Diagnoses: Amaurosis fugax, 362.34

   Principal Procedure: Unilateral carotid endarterectomy, 38.12

   Secondary Procedures: Procedure on single vessel, 00.40; Arteriography of cerebral arteries, 88.41

9. **Principal Diagnosis:** Acute duodenal ulcer with hemorrhage, 532.00

   Secondary Diagnoses: Hernia, hiatal (sliding), 553.3

   Principal Procedure: Endoscopic control of duodenal bleeding, 44.43

   Secondary Procedures: None indicated by the documentation provided

10. **Principal Diagnosis:** Poisoning, crack (other specified central nervous system stimulant), 970.8; Poisoning, cocaine (crack) undetermined intent, E980.4; Accident occurring at home, E849.0

    Secondary Diagnoses: Failure, respiratory failure, acute, 518.81; Failure, renal, acute, 584.9

    Principal Procedure: Endotracheal tube intubation, 96.04

    Secondary Procedures: Mechanical ventilation, less than 96 hours, 96.71

11. This exercise is an example of a patient admitted with multiple concurrent conditions that all received evaluation and treatment, with several of the diagnoses potentially meeting the definition of principal diagnosis. The physician was asked what was the most likely principal diagnosis based on the definition explained to him. His initial thought was that it was either the diarrhea, dehydration, or the angioneurotic edema. His final selection was the angioneurotic edema because it required more investigation and treatment than the other two conditions.

    Principal Diagnosis: Angioneurotic edema, 995.1

    Secondary Diagnoses: Cellulitis of face, 682,0; Cellulitis of orbits, 376.01; Diarrhea, 787.91; Dehydration 276.51; Carcinoma of the lung, 162.9; Carcinoma of the kidney, 189.0; Secondary malignant neoplasm of mediastinum, 197.1; Secondary malignant neoplasm of lymph nodes, intra-abdominal, 196.2; History of carcinoma of anus, V10.06; Staph aureus septicemia, 038.11; Hypertension, 401.9; Hyperthyroidism, 242,90; Anal ulcer, 569.41

    Principal Procedure: None indicated by the documentation provided

    Secondary Procedures: None indicated by the documentation provided

12. **Principal Diagnosis:** Infection, urinary tract, 599.0

    Secondary Diagnoses: Prostatitis, acute, 601.0; prostatitis, chronic, 601.1; Hypertension, 401.9; Hypertrophy, prostate, benign, 600.01; History, infection, urinary, V13.02

    Principal Procedure: None indicated by the documentation provided

    Secondary Procedures: None indicated by the documentation provided

13. **Principal Diagnosis:** Complication, due to device, arterial, renal dialysis, 996.73

    Secondary Diagnoses: Hypertension with renal failure, 403.91; Glomerulonephritis, chronic, 582.9; Disease, renal, end stage, 585.6

    Principal Procedure: Thrombectomy, arteriovenous shunt, 39.49

    Secondary Procedures: Catheterization, vein, for renal dialysis, 38.95; Hemodialysis, 39.95

14. **Principal Diagnosis:** Pneumonia, aspiration, 507.0

    Secondary Diagnoses: Failure, respiratory, acute, 518.81; Disease, lung, obstructive, with exacerbation (worsening), 491.21

    Principal Procedure: Therapy, oxygen, 93.96

    Secondary Procedures: None indicated by the documentation provided

15. **Principal Diagnosis:** Admission for, prophylactic organ removal, ovary, V50.42

    Secondary Diagnoses: Neoplasm, malignant, primary, ovary, 183.0; Admission for prophylactic organ removal, other (uterus, etc.), V50.49; History, family, malignant neoplasm, ovary, V16.41

    Principal Procedure: Hysterectomy, abdominal, laparoscopic, 68.41

    Secondary Procedures: Salpingo-oophorectomy, bilateral, laparoscopic, 65.63; Robotic assisted surgery, laparoscopic, 17.42

Chapter 4

Infections and Parasitic Diseases

1. **First-Listed Diagnosis:** Acute chlamydial cervicitis, 099.53

   Secondary Diagnoses: Cervicitis, 616.0

   First-Listed Procedure: None indicated by the documentation provided

   Secondary Procedures: None indicated by the documentation provided

2. **Principal Diagnosis:** AIDS, 042

   Secondary Diagnoses: Pneumonia, pneumocystis, 136.3; Candidiasis, mouth, 112.0

   Principal Procedure: None indicated by the documentation provided

   Secondary Procedures: None indicated by the documentation provided

3. **First-Listed Diagnosis:** Chronic viral hepatitis B, 070.32

   Secondary Diagnoses: Cirrhosis, 571.5; Dependence, heroin (in remission), 304.03; Drug, therapy, long term use, methadone, V58.69 (Liver failure is not coded because it is suspected, and suspected conditions are not coded for outpatients.)

   First-Listed Procedure: None indicated by the documentation provided

   Secondary Procedures: None indicated by the documentation provided

4. **Principal Diagnosis:**   Septicemia due to gram negative organism, 038.40

   Secondary Diagnoses: Severe sepsis (systemic inflammatory, response syndrome due to infectious process with organ dysfunction), 995.92; Acute respiratory failure, 518.81

   Principal Procedure: Insertion of endotracheal tube/intubation, 96.04

   Secondary Procedures: Mechanical ventilation, less than 96 hours, 96.71

5. **First-Listed Diagnosis:**   Erysipelas, 035

   Secondary Diagnoses: None indicated by the documentation provided.

   First-Listed Procedure: None indicated by the documentation provided

   Secondary Procedures: None indicated by the documentation provided

6. **First-Listed Diagnosis:**   Mumps, 072.9

   Secondary Diagnoses: None indicated by the documentation provided

   First-Listed Procedure: None indicated by the documentation provided

   Secondary Procedures: None indicated by the documentation provided

7. **First-Listed Diagnosis:**   Urethritis, gonococcal, acute, 098.0

   Secondary Diagnoses: Cystitis, gonococcal, acute, 098.11

   First-Listed Procedure: None indicated by the documentation provided

   Secondary Procedures: None indicated by the documentation provided

8. **First-Listed Diagnosis:**   Tuberculosis, pulmonary, 011.90

   Secondary Diagnoses: Hypertension, 401.9; Status post coronary angioplasty, V45.82

   First-Listed Procedure: None indicated by the documentation provided

   Secondary Procedures: None indicated by the documentation provided

9. **First-Listed Diagnosis:**   Atrophy, muscles, lower extremity, 728.2

   Secondary Diagnoses: Postpolio syndrome (Late effect of poliomyelitis), 138

   First-Listed Procedure: None indicated by the documentation provided

   Secondary Procedures: None indicated by the documentation provided

10. **Principal Diagnosis:**   Meningitis, aseptic, due to Coxsackie virus, 047.0

   Secondary Diagnoses: None indicated by the documentation provided

   Principal Procedure: Spinal puncture, 03.31

   Secondary Procedures: None indicated by the documentation provided

11. **Principal Diagnosis:**   Septicemia, gram-negative (Klebsiella), 038.49

   Secondary Diagnoses: Infection, urinary tract, 599.0; Dehydration, 276.51; Infection, Klebsiella, 041.3; Neoplasm, malignant, secondary, lymph, 196.3; History, personal, malignant neoplasm, breast, V10.3

   Principal Procedure: None indicated by the documentation provided

   Secondary Procedures: None indicated by the documentation provided

12. **First-Listed Diagnosis:** Varicella, with pneumonia, 052.1
    Secondary Diagnoses: Dehydration, 276.51; Ileus, 560.1; Otitis, media, 382.9
    First-Listed Procedure: None indicated by the documentation provided
    Secondary Procedures: None indicated by the documentation provided

13. **First-Listed Diagnosis:** Infection, acanthamoeba, 136.21
    Secondary Diagnoses: Keratitis, specified type, 370.8 (Use additional code note with code 136.21 in Tabular.)
    First-Listed Procedure: None indicated by the documentation provided
    Secondary Procedures: None indicated by the documentation provided

14. **First-Listed Diagnosis:** Hepatitis, viral, type C, chronic, 070.54
    Secondary Diagnoses: Hepatitis, autoimmune, 571.42
    First-Listed Procedure: None indicated by the documentation provided
    Secondary Procedures: None indicated by the documentation provided

15. **Principal Diagnosis:** Poisoning, food, due to Salmonella, with gastroenteritis, 003.0
    Secondary Diagnoses: Dehydration, 276.51
    Principal Procedure: None indicated by the documentation provided
    Secondary Procedures: None indicated by the documentation provided.

Chapter 5

Neoplasms

1. **Principal Diagnosis:** Primary malignant neoplasm of main bronchus, 162.2
   Secondary Diagnoses: Secondary malignant neoplasm of bone, 198.5; emphysema, 492.8
   Principal Procedure: Fiberoptic bronchoscopy with biopsy, 33.24
   Secondary Procedures: None indicated by the documentation provided

2. **Principal Diagnosis:** Admission (encounter) for chemotherapy, V58.11
   Secondary Diagnoses: Acute myeloid leukemia, 205.00
   Principal Procedure: Chemotherapy infusion/injection, 99.25
   Secondary Procedures: None indicated by the documentation provided

3. **Principal Diagnosis:** Dehydration, 276.51
   Secondary Diagnoses: Primary carcinoma of colon, 153.9; secondary carcinoma of liver, 197.7; Hospice care, V66.7
   Principal Procedure: None indicated by the documentation provided
   Secondary Procedures: None indicated by the documentation provided

4. **Principal Diagnosis:** Primary malignant neoplasm, pancreas, 157.0

    Secondary Diagnoses: Secondary malignant neoplasm, liver, 197.7; Dehydration, 276.51; Chronic kidney disease, stage 4, 585.4; Injury, superficial, face, 910.8; Injury, superficial, hand, 914.8; Encounter for palliative care (comfort care), V66.7

    Principal Procedure: None indicated by the documentation provided

    Secondary Procedures: None indicated by the documentation provided

5. **First-Listed Diagnosis:** Carcinoma in situ, cervix, 233.1

    Secondary Diagnosis: None indicated by the documentation provided

    First-Listed Procedure: Conization of the cervix, loop electrosurgical excision, 67.32

    Secondary Procedure: None indicated by the documentation provided

6. **First-Listed Diagnosis:** Malignant melanoma, 172.7

    Secondary Diagnoses: None indicated by the documentation provided

    First-Listed Procedure: Excision of lesion, skin, 86.3

    Secondary Procedures: None indicated by the documentation provided

7. **First-Listed Diagnosis:** Malignant melanoma, 172.7

    Secondary Diagnoses: History, family, malignant neoplasm, skin, V16.8

    First-Listed Procedure: Wide Excision of lesion, skin, 86.4

    Secondary Procedures: None indicated by the documentation provided

8. **Principal Diagnosis:** Secondary malignant neoplasm, ureteral, 198.1

    Secondary Diagnoses: Secondary malignant neoplasm, intra-abdominal, 198.89; Primary malignant neoplasm, stomach, 151.9; Other ureteric obstruction, 593.4

    Principal Procedure: Nephrostomy, 55.02

    Secondary Procedures: None indicated by the documentation provided

9. **First-Listed Diagnosis:** Secondary malignant neoplasm, bone, 198.5

    Secondary Diagnoses: Secondary malignant neoplasm, brain, 198.3; Primary malignant neoplasm, breast, 174.9

    First-Listed Procedure: Injection, therapeutic substance, 99.29

    Secondary Procedures: None indicated by the documentation provided

10. **Principal Diagnosis:** Malignant carcinoid tumor of appendix, 209.11

    Secondary Diagnoses: Carcinoid syndrome, 259.2

    Principal Procedure: Laparoscopic appendectomy, 47.01

    Secondary Procedures: None indicated by the documentation provided

11. **Principal Diagnosis:** Admission for chemotherapy, V58.11

    Secondary Diagnoses: Primary malignant neoplasm, ovary, 183.0; Secondary malignant neoplasm, unspecified site, 199.1

    Principal Procedure: Chemotherapy infusion, 99.25

    Secondary Procedures: None indicated by the documentation provided

12. **Principal Diagnosis:** Admission for radiotherapy, V58.0

    Secondary Diagnoses: Primary malignant neoplasm, testis, 186.9

    Principal Procedure: Radiation therapy, 92.29

    Secondary Procedures: None indicated by the documentation provided

13. **Principal Diagnosis:** Glioblastoma multiforme, parietal, 191.3

    Secondary Diagnoses: Secondary malignant neoplasm of lung, 197.0; Current smoker, 305.1; Pre-diabetes, 790.92

    Principal Procedure: Closed biopsy, via burr hole approach, brain, 01.13

    Secondary Procedures: Bronchoscopy with transbronchial lung biopsy, 33.27

14. **Principal Diagnosis:** Malignant primary carcinoma of endometrium, 182.0

    Secondary Diagnosis: Hypertension, 401.9; Anxiety disorder, 300.00; Hyperlipidemia, 272.4; Diabetes mellitus type II, 250.00; History of breast cancer, V10.3

    Principal Procedure: Radical abdominal hysterectomy, 68.69

    Secondary Procedures: Bilateral salpingo-oophorectomy, 65.61; Regional lymph node dissection 40.3

15. **First-Listed Diagnosis:** Neoplasm, malignant, primary, breast, 174.9

    Secondary Diagnoses: Drug, therapy, high risk medication, V58.69

    First-Listed Procedure: Infusion, intravenous, therapeutic substance, 99.29

    Secondary Procedures: None indicated by documentation provided

Chapter 6

Endocrine, Nutritional and Metabolic Diseases, and Immunity Disorders

1. **Principal Diagnosis:** Diabetes, type I, retinopathy, uncontrolled, 250.53

   Secondary Diagnoses: Diabetes, retinopathy, nonproliferative, mild, 364.04

   Principal Procedure: None indicated by the documentation provided

   Secondary Procedures: None indicated by the documentation provided

2. **First-Listed Diagnosis:** Diabetes, type II, nephropathy, not stated as uncontrolled, 250.40

   Secondary Diagnoses: Diabetes, nephropathy, 583.81

   First-Listed Procedure: None indicated by the documentation provided

   Secondary Procedures: None indicated by the documentation provided

3. **Principal Diagnosis:** Diabetic ketoacidosis, type I, uncontrolled, 250.11

   Secondary Diagnoses: Abscess tooth, 522.5

   Principal Procedure: None indicated by the documentation provided

   Secondary Procedures: None indicated by the documentation provided

4. **First-Listed Diagnosis:** Diabetes mellitus without mention of complication, type II, not stated as uncontrolled, 250.00

   Secondary Diagnoses: Long term (current) use of insulin, V58.67

   First-Listed Procedure: None indicated by the documentation provided

   Secondary Procedures: None indicated by the documentation provided

5. **First-Listed Diagnosis:** Primary hyperparathyroidism, 252.01

   Secondary Diagnoses: Benign neoplasm, parathyroid gland (Adenoma, see Neoplasm, benign), 227.1

   First-Listed Procedure: None indicated by the documentation provided

   Secondary Procedures: None indicated by the documentation provided

6. **First-Listed Diagnosis:** Hyperthyroidism, 242.90

   Secondary Diagnoses: Palpitation (heart), 785.1

   First-Listed Procedure: None indicated by the documentation provided

   Secondary Procedures: None indicated by the documentation provided

7. **Principal Diagnosis:** Diabetes mellitus, type I, uncontrolled, 250.03

   Secondary Diagnoses: None indicated by the documentation provided

   Principal Procedure: Insertion of insulin pump, 86.06

   Secondary Procedures: (Two procedures added) Catheterization, venous, 38.93; Injection, insulin, 99.17

8. **Principal Diagnosis:** Morbid obesity, 278.01

   Secondary Diagnoses: Hypertension, 401.9; Hyperlipidemia, 272.4; Insulin resistance, 277.7; Osteoarthritis of spine, 721.90; Osteoarthritis of multiple sites, 715.89; BMI (body mass index), 45–49.9, V85.42

   Principal Procedure: Roux-en-Y operation, gastroenterostomy, 44.39

   Secondary Procedures: None indicated by the documentation provided

9. **Principal Diagnosis:** Morbid obesity, 278.01

   Secondary Diagnoses: Hypertension, 401.9; Dyslipidemia, 272.4; Type II diabetes, 250.00; Osteoarthritis localized to knees, 715.36; Family history of metabolic disorders (obesity); BMI, 50.0–59.9 and over, V85.43

   Principal Procedure: Laparoscopic gastric restrictive procedure, 44.95

   Secondary Procedures: None indicated by the documentation provided

10. **First-Listed Diagnosis:** Familial hypercholesterolemia, 272.0

    Secondary Diagnoses: History of smoking, V15.82

    First-Listed Procedure: None indicated by the documentation provided

    Secondary Procedures: None indicated by the documentation provided

11. **Principal Diagnosis:** Diabetes mellitus, type II, uncontrolled, 250.02

    Secondary Diagnoses: Long term use of insulin, V58.67; Hypertension with chronic renal insufficiency, 403.90 and 585.9; Obesity, 278.00; Body mass index of 37, V85.37; Fracture, lateral malleolus, 824.2; Spondylolisthesis, acquired, ankle, 738.4; Slipping (injury), E885.9 (If documentation includes the location, a place of occurrence code—for example, home, E849.0—should be added.)

    Principal Procedure: Application of cast, ankle, 93.53

    Secondary Procedures: None indicated by the documentation provided

12. **Principal Diagnosis:** Hyperkalemia, 276.7

    Secondary Diagnoses: Hypertension with chronic renal insufficiency, 403.90 and 585.9; Gout, 274.9; Coronary artery disease, 414.00; Status post coronary artery bypass graft, V45.81; Hypercholesterolemia, 272.0; Benign prostatic hypertrophy, 600.00; Sickle cell trait, 282.5; Atrial fibrillation, 427.31; Diabetes, type II, uncontrolled, 250.02; Obesity, 278.00; Non-compliance with medical advice, V15.81

    Principal Procedure: None indicated by the documentation provided

    Secondary Procedures: None indicated by the documentation provided

13. **Principal Diagnosis:** Diabetes mellitus, type I, uncontrolled, 250.13

    Secondary Diagnoses: Diabetes mellitus, type I, uncontrolled, nephropathy, 250.43; Nephropathy due to diabetes, 583.81; Diabetes mellitus, type I, uncontrolled, ophthalmic, 250.53; Retinopathy, diabetic, nonproliferative, severe, 362.06; Infection, urinary tract, 599.0; Infection, E.coli, 041.4; History, infection, urinary, V13.02; History, noncompliance with medical treatment, V15.81; Alcoholism, 303.90

    Principal Procedure: None indicated by the documentation provided

    Secondary Procedures: None indicated by the documentation provided

14. **Principal Diagnosis:** Dehydration, 276.51

    Secondary Diagnoses: Hyperkalemia, 276.7; Pneumonia, 486; Gastroenteritis, 558.9; Diaper rash, 691.0

    Principal Procedure: None indicated by the documentation provided

    Secondary Procedures: None indicated by the documentation provided

15. **Principal Diagnosis:** Syndrome, Hunter's or Mucopolysaccharidosis type II, 277.5

    Secondary Diagnoses: None indicated by the documentation provided

    Principal Procedure: None indicated by the documentation provided

    Secondary Procedures: None indicated by the documentation provided

Chapter 7

Diseases of the Blood and Blood Forming Organs

1. **Principal Diagnosis:** Sickle-cell crisis, 282.62
    Secondary Diagnoses: Acute chest syndrome, 517.3
    Principal Procedure: None indicated by the documentation provided
    Secondary Procedures: None indicated by the documentation provided

2. **Principal Diagnosis:** Anemia in neoplastic disease, 285.22
    Secondary Diagnoses: Primary malignant neoplasm of pancreas, 157.9
    Principal Procedure: Blood transfusion, 99.03
    Secondary Procedures: None indicated by the documentation provided

3. **First-Listed Diagnosis:** Iron deficiency anemia, 280.9
    Secondary Diagnoses: None indicated by the documentation provided
    First-Listed Procedure: Bone marrow biopsy, 41.31
    Secondary Procedures: None indicated by the documentation provided

4. **First-Listed Diagnosis:** Nutritional anemia, 281.9
    Secondary Diagnoses: COPD, 496; Infarction, myocardial, past, 412
    First-Listed Procedure: None indicated by the documentation provided
    Secondary Procedures: None indicated by the documentation provided

5. **Principal Diagnosis:** Autoimmune hemolytic anemia, 283.0
    Secondary Diagnoses: Lupus, erythematosus, systemic, 710.0
    Principal Procedure: Splenectomy, 41.5
    Secondary Procedures: None indicated by the documentation provided

6. **First-Listed Diagnosis:** Anemia, blood loss, 280.0
    Secondary Diagnoses: Ulcer, stomach, with hemorrhage, 531.40
    First-Listed Procedure: None indicated by the documentation provided
    Secondary Procedures: None indicated by the documentation provided

7. **First-Listed Diagnosis:** Pernicious anemia, 281.0
    Secondary Diagnoses: Agammaglobulinemia, 279.00; Atrophic gastritis, chronic, 535.10
    First-Listed Procedure: None indicated by the documentation provided
    Secondary Procedures: None indicated by the documentation provided

8. **First-Listed Diagnosis:** Aplastic anemia, due to drugs, 284.89
    Secondary Diagnoses: Adverse effect, therapeutic use of chemotherapy, E933.1; Primary malignant neoplasm of ovary, 183.0
    First-Listed Procedure: None indicated by the documentation provided
    Secondary Procedures: None indicated by the documentation provided

9. **Principal Diagnosis:** Hemophilia, Type A, 286.0
    Secondary Diagnoses: Arthritis, due to or associated with, hemophilia (knees), 713.2
    Principal Procedure: Extracorporeal immunoadsorption, 99.76
    Secondary Procedures: None indicated by the documentation provided

10. **First-Listed Diagnosis:** Idiopathic thrombocytopenic purpura, 287.31
    Secondary Diagnoses: None indicated by the documentation provided
    First-Listed Procedure: None indicated by the documentation provided
    Secondary Procedures: None indicated by the documentation provided

11. **Principal Diagnosis:** Anemia, acute, blood loss, 285.1
    Secondary Diagnoses: Pressure ulcer, sacrum, 707.03; Pressure ulcer, hip, 707.04; Pressure ulcer stage III, 707.23; Fecal incontinence, 787.60; Spinal arthritis, 721.90; Chronic pain (back) 338.29; Diabetes mellitus, 250.00; Hypertension 401.9
    Principal Procedure: Blood transfusion, 99.03
    Secondary Procedures: None indicated by the documentation provided

12. **First-Listed Diagnosis:** Anemia, due to chemotherapy, 285.3
    Secondary Diagnoses: Neoplasm, malignant, secondary, bone, 198.5; Neoplasm, malignant, primary, breast, 174.9
    First-Listed Procedure: None indicated by the documentation provided
    Secondary Procedures: None indicated by the documentation provided

13. **First-Listed Diagnosis:** Anemia, in, chronic kidney disease, 285.21
    Secondary Diagnoses: Disease, kidney, chronic, requiring dialysis, 585.6
    First-Listed Procedure: None indicated by the documentation provided
    Secondary Procedures: None indicated by the documentation provided

14. **First-Listed Diagnosis:** Trait, sickle cell, 282.5
    Secondary Diagnoses: None indicated by the documentation provided
    First-Listed Procedure: None indicated by the documentation provided
    Secondary Procedures: None indicated by the documentation provided

15. **First-Listed Diagnosis:** Thalassemia, beta, major, 282.49
    Secondary Diagnoses: None indicated by the documentation provided
    First-Listed Procedure: Transfusion, packed (red) cells, 99.04
    Secondary Procedures: None indicated by the documentation provided

Chapter 8

Mental Disorders

1. **First-Listed Diagnosis:** Acute alcoholic intoxication in alcoholism, continuous, 303.01
   Secondary Diagnoses: Black eye, 921.0; Contusions, face, 920; Wound, open fingers, 883.0; Fight/brawl, E960.0 (If documentation includes place of occurrence, another E code could be used.)
   First-Listed Procedure: None indicated by the documentation provided
   Secondary Procedures: None indicated by the documentation provided

2. **First-Listed Diagnosis:** Anxiety depression, 300.4
   Secondary Diagnoses: Agoraphobia with panic disorder, 300.21
   First-Listed Procedure: None indicated by the documentation provided
   Secondary Procedures: None indicated by the documentation provided

3. **Principal Diagnosis:** Drug dependence, cocaine, continuous form, 304.21
   Secondary Diagnoses: None indicated by the documentation provided
   Principal Procedure: Detoxification therapy, drug, with rehabilitation, 94.66
   Secondary Procedures: None indicated by the documentation provided

4. **Principal Diagnosis:** Drug induced sleep disorder, hypersomnia, 292.85
   Secondary Diagnoses: Adverse effect, Lithium carbonate, E939.8; Bipolar disorder, Type II, most recent depressed state, 296.89
   Principal Procedure: Psychotherapy, supportive verbal, 94.38
   Secondary Procedures: None indicated by the documentation provided

5. **Principal Diagnosis:** Panic disorder without agoraphobia, 300.01
   Secondary Diagnoses: Chest pain, 786.50
   Principal Procedure: None indicated by the documentation provided
   Secondary Procedures: None indicated by the documentation provided

6. **First-Listed Diagnosis:** Somatization disorder, 300.81
   Secondary Diagnoses: Obsessional ruminations, 300.3
   First-Listed Procedure: None indicated by the documentation provided
   Secondary Procedures: None indicated by the documentation provided

7. **Principal Diagnosis:** Drug withdrawal, 292.0
   Secondary Diagnoses: Opioid type (heroin) dependence, 304.01
   Principal Procedure: Drug detoxification and rehabilitation, 94.66
   Secondary Procedures: None indicated by the documentation provided

8. **First-Listed Diagnosis:** Borderline personality disorder, 301.83
    Secondary Diagnoses: Cocaine dependence, in remission, 304.23
    First-Listed Procedure: None indicated by the documentation provided
    Secondary Procedures: None indicated by the documentation provided

9. **First-Listed Diagnosis:** Schizophrenia, paranoid type, chronic with acute exacerbation, 295.34
    Secondary Diagnoses: None indicated by the documentation provided
    First-Listed Procedure: None indicated by the documentation provided
    Secondary Procedures: None indicated by the documentation provided

10. **Principal Diagnosis:** Anorexia nervosa, 307.1
    Secondary Diagnoses: Electrolyte imbalance, 276.9
    Principal Procedure: None indicated by the documentation provided
    Secondary Procedures: None indicated by the documentation provided

11. **Principal Diagnosis:** Disorder, depressive, major, moderate, 296.22
    Secondary Diagnoses: Acute cervical strain, 847.0; Methadone/heroin dependence continuous, 304.01; Chronic pain syndrome, 338.4; Pneumonitis, 486; Late effect, sprain, 905.7; Suicide, attempted, hanging, E953.0
    Principal Procedure: None indicated by the documentation provided
    Secondary Procedures: None indicated by the documentation provided

12. **First-Listed Diagnosis:** Acute alcoholic intoxication in a patient with chronic alcoholism, 303.00
    Secondary Diagnoses: None indicated by the documentation provided
    First-Listed Procedure: None indicated by the documentation provided
    Secondary Procedures: None indicated by the documentation provided

13. **First-Listed Diagnosis:** Schizophrenia, schizopheniform, chronic, 295.42
    Secondary Diagnoses: Disorder, attention deficit with hyperactivity, 314.01; Disorder, conduct, socialized, aggressive, 312.23, Disabilities, learning, 315.9; Pyromania, 312.33; History, family, psychiatric disorder, V17.0
    First-Listed Procedure: Therapy, behavior 94.33
    Secondary Procedures: Therapy, family, 94.42; Therapy, group, 94.44; Therapy, psychiatric drug, 94.25

14. **Principal Diagnosis:** Withdrawal symptoms, drug, 292.0
    Secondary Diagnoses: Dependency, cannabis, continuous, 304.31; Dependency, cocaine, continuous, 304.21
    Principal Proocedure: Detoxification therapy, drug, 94.65
    Secondary Procedures: None indicated by the documentation provided

15. **Principal Diagnosis:** Disorder, posttraumatic stress, 309.81
    Secondary Diagnoses: Suicide ideation, V62.84
    Principal Procedure: Psychotherapy, 94.39
    Secondary Procedures: Therapy, behavior, 94.33; Therapy, psychiatric drug, 94.25

Chapter 9

Diseases of the Nervous System and Sense Organs

1. **First-Listed Diagnosis:** Alzheimer's disease, 331.0
   Secondary Diagnoses: Dementia due to Alzheimer's disease, with behavioral disturbance, 294.11
   First-Listed Procedure: None indicated by the documentation provided
   Secondary Procedures: None indicated by the documentation provided

2. **First-Listed Diagnosis:** Diabetes mellitus, type II, not stated as uncontrolled, with ophthalmic manifestations, 250.50
   Secondary Diagnoses: Moderate non-proliferative diabetic retinopathy, 362.05
   First-Listed Procedure: None indicated by the documentation provided
   Secondary Procedures: None indicated by the documentation provided

3. **First-Listed Diagnosis:** Glaucoma, suspect, 365.00
   Secondary Diagnoses: None indicated by the documentation provided
   First-Listed Procedure: None indicated by the documentation provided
   Secondary Procedures: None indicated by the documentation provided

4. **First-Listed Diagnosis:** Epilepsy, petit mal, 345.00
   Secondary Diagnoses: None indicated by the documentation provided
   First-Listed Procedure: None indicated by the documentation provided
   Secondary Procedures: None indicated by the documentation provided

5. **Principal Diagnosis:** Retinal detachment, recent, partial with single defect, 361.01 (see Index: Hole, retina, round with detachment)
   Secondary Diagnoses: Status post cataract extraction, V45.61
   Principal Procedure: Cryoretinopexy for reattachment of retina, 14.52
   Secondary Procedures: None indicated by the documentation provided

6. **First-Listed Diagnosis:** Pterygium, peripheral, progressive, 372.42
   Secondary Diagnoses: None indicated by the documentation provided
   First-Listed Procedure: Excision, pterygium, with corneal graft, 11.32
   Secondary Procedures: None indicated by the documentation provided

7. **Principal Diagnosis:** Strabismus, concomitant, convergent see Esotropia, monocular, 378.01
    Secondary Diagnoses: None indicated by the documentation provided
    Principal Procedure: Resection, muscle, extraocular, lateral rectus, 15.13
    Secondary Procedures: None indicated by the documentation provided

8. **Principal Diagnosis:** Meningitis, due to H. influenzae, 320.0
    Secondary Diagnoses: Otitis media, acute, suppurative, 382.00
    Principal Procedure: Lumbar puncture, 03.31
    Secondary Procedures: None indicated by the documentation provided

9. **Principal Diagnosis:** Whooping cough (pertussis), 033.9
    Secondary Diagnoses: Meningitis due to Whooping cough, 320.7
    Principal Procedure: None indicated by the documentation provided
    Secondary Procedures: None indicated by the documentation provided

10. **First-Listed Diagnosis:** Loss, hearing, sensorineural, 389.10 (More specific diagnosis needed to provide a more specific hearing loss code)
    Secondary Diagnoses: Tinnitus, subjective, 388.31
    First-Listed Procedure: None indicated by the documentation provided
    Secondary Procedures: None indicated by the documentation provided

11. **First-Listed Diagnosis:** Headache, post-traumatic, 339.20
    Secondary Diagnoses: Late, effect, injury, intracranial, 907.0; Late effect of, motor vehicle accident, E929.0
    First-Listed Procedure: None indicated by the documentation provided
    Secondary Procedures: None indicated by the documentation provided

12. **Principal Diagnosis:** Syndrome, carotid body or sinus, 337.01
    Secondary Diagnoses: None indicated by the documentation provided
    Principal Procedure: Implantation, electrodes, cardiac, atrium and ventricle, 37.72
    Secondary Procedures: Implantation, pacemaker, cardiac, dual chamber, 37.83

13. **Principal Diagnosis:** Stenosis, spinal, lumbar, 724.02
    Secondary Diagnoses: Durotomy, incidental, 349.31
    Principal Procedure: Laminectomy, decompression, 03.09
    Secondary Procedures: Repair, spinal (structures) dura, 03.59

14. **Principal Diagnosis:** Neuropathy, toxic, 357.7
    Secondary Diagnoses: Late, effect, toxic effect, nonmedicinal, 909.1, Late effect of, poisoning, E929.2
    Principal Procedure: None indicated by the documentation provided
    Secondary Procedures: None indicated by the documentation provided

15. **Principal Diagnosis:** Pain, acute, 338.19

    Secondary Diagnoses: Pain, chronic syndrome, 338.4; Pain, low back, 724.2; Pain, leg, 729.5; Late, effect, injury, nerve roots, 907.3; Late effect of, motor vehicle accident, E929.0

    Principal Procedure: Therapy, physical, 93.39

    Secondary Procedures: Therapy, occupational, 93.83

Chapter 10

Diseases of the Circulatory System

1. **Principal Diagnosis:** Acute myocardial infarction, inferior wall, initial episode, 410.21 (statement in scenario states the chest pain was determined to be result of an inferior wall myocardial infarction, and he was treated for it)

    Secondary Diagnoses: Arteriosclerosis, coronary, due to lipid-rich plaque, 414.3; Atrial fibrillation, 427.31

    Principal Procedure: Combined right and left heart catheterization, 37.23

    Secondary Procedures: Combined right and left heart angiocardiography, 88.54; Coronary arteriography (Judkins technique), 88.56

2. **Principal Diagnosis:** Coronary atherosclerosis, native coronary arteries, 414.01

    Secondary Diagnoses: Postoperative/iatrogenic pulmonary embolism, 415.11

    Principal Procedure: (Aorta) Coronary artery bypass of four or more coronary arteries, 36.14

    Secondary Procedures: Cardiopulmonary bypass/extracorporeal circulation, 39.61

3. **First-Listed Diagnosis:** Late effect, CVA, with hemiparesis of dominant side, 438.21

    Secondary Diagnoses: Late effect, CVA, with dysphasia, 438.12; Hypertension, benign, 401.1; Atrial fibrillation, 427.31

    First-Listed Procedure: None indicated by the documentation provided

    Secondary Procedures: None indicated by the documentation provided

4. **Principal Diagnosis:** Cerebral embolus with infarction, 434.11

    Secondary Diagnoses: Hemiparesis, affecting nondominant side, 342.92; Hypertension, unspecified, 401.9

    Principal Procedure: None indicated by the documentation provided

    Secondary Procedures: None indicated by the documentation provided

5. **First-Listed Diagnosis:** Cardiac arrest, 427.5

    Secondary Diagnoses: Cardiomegaly and hypertensive heart disease, 402.90 (Because this was an outpatient or ER visit and the doctor describes the myocardial infarction as "probably" due to acute myocardial infarction triggered by strenuous exertion, the MI is not coded because "probable" diagnoses are not coded on outpatients.)

    First-Listed Procedure: Cardiopulmonary resuscitation, 99.60

    Secondary Procedures: None indicated by the documentation provided

6. **First-Listed Diagnosis:** Hypertensive heart and kidney disease with heart failure and chronic kidney disease, 404.93

    Secondary Diagnoses: Congestive heart failure, 428.0; Chronic kidney disease, stage 2, 585.2; Diabetes mellitus, type II with neurological manifestations, 250.60; Polyneuropathy due to diabetes, 357.2

    First-Listed Procedure: None indicated by the documentation provided

    Secondary Procedures: None indicated by the documentation provided

7. **Principal Diagnosis:** Coronary atherosclerosis, native coronary artery, 414.01

    Secondary Diagnoses: Acute coronary syndrome, 411.1

    Principal Procedure: Insertion, coronary, nondrug eluting stent, 36.06

    Secondary Procedures: PTCA, 00.66; Procedure on single vessel, 00.40; Insertion of one stent, 00.45; Left heart catheterization, 37.22; Coronary arteriogram, 88.56; Infusion of platelet inhibitor, 99.20

8. **Principal Diagnosis:** Abdominal aneurysm without mention of rupture, 441.4

    Secondary Diagnoses: Essential hypertension, 401.9; Gouty arthritis, 274.0

    Principal Procedure: Endovascular implantation of graft, abdominal aorta, 39.71

    Secondary Procedures: Ultrasound of abdomen, 88.76

9. **Principal Diagnosis:** Deep vein thrombosis of iliac vessel, proximal lower extremity, 453.41

    Secondary Diagnoses: Congestive heart failure, 428.0

    Principal Procedure: Duplex venous ultrasonography, 88.77

    Secondary Procedures: None indicated by the documentation provided

10. **Principal Diagnosis:** Congestive heart failure, 428.0

    Secondary Diagnoses: Long term (current) use of anticoagulants, V58.61; History of venous thrombosis, V12.51

    Principal Procedure: Duplex venous ultrasonography, 88.77

    Secondary Procedures: None indicated by documentation provided (Intravenous drugs are not coded)

11. **Principal Diagnosis:** Chronic combined systolic and diastolic heart failure, 428.42

    Secondary Diagnoses: Chronic respiratory failure, 518.83; Hypertension, 401.9; Dependent on supplemental oxygen, V46.2; Fracture, radius, distal, 813.42; Urinary tract infection, 599.0; History of urinary tract infections, V13.02; Hospice care, V66.7; Fall from commode, E884.6; Accident occurred at home, E849.0

    Principal Procedure: Application, splint, wrist, 93.54

    Secondary Procedures: None indicated by documentation provided

12. **Principal Diagnosis:** Angina pectoris, 413.9

    Secondary Diagnoses: Cocaine dependence, 304.20; Alcohol abuse, 305.00; Tobacco use dependence, 305.1; Pneumonia 486; Bipolar I disorder, 296.7

    Principal Procedure: None indicated by documentation provided

    Secondary Procedures: None indicated by documentation provided

13. **First-Listed Diagnosis:** Failure, heart, diastolic, chronic, 428.32

    Secondary Diagnoses: Failure, heart, congestive, 428.0

    First-Listed Procedure: None indicated by documentation provided

    Secondary Procedures: None indicated by documentation provided

14. **Principal Diagnosis:** Failure, heart, congestive 428.0

    Secondary Diagnoses: Failure, heart, diastolic, acute on chronic, 428.33; Hypertension, 401.9; Diabetes mellitus, with neuropathy, type II, 250.60; Neuropathy, diabetic, 357.2

    Principal Procedure: None indicated by documentation provided

    Secondary Procedures: None indicated by documentation provided

15. **Principal Diagnosis:** Infarction, myocardial, ST elevation, anterolateral wall, 410.01

    Secondary Diagnoses: Arteriosclerosis, coronary, native artery, 414.01

    Principal Procedure: Angioplasty, coronary, percutaneous transluminal, 00.66

    Secondary Procedures: Insertion, stent, artery, coronary, non-drug eluting, 36.06; Procedure on three vessels, 00.42; Insertion of two vascular stents, 00.46

Chapter 11

Diseases of the Respiratory System

1. **Principal Diagnosis:** Acute exacerbation of chronic obstructive pulmonary disease, 491.21

   Secondary Diagnoses: History, smoking, V15.82 (The respiratory insufficiency is integral to COPD and not coded.)

   Principal Procedure: None indicated by the documentation provided

   Secondary Procedures: None indicated by the documentation provided

2. **Principal Diagnosis:** Aspiration pneumonia, 507.0

   Secondary Diagnoses: Pneumonia, bacterial, unspecified, 482.9

   Principal Procedure: None indicated by the documentation provided

   Secondary Procedures: None indicated by the documentation provided

3. **First-Listed Diagnosis:** Asthma, extrinsic, 493.00

   Secondary Diagnoses: Allergic rhinitis is not coded separately; see excludes note under category 477.0—allergic rhinitis with asthma (493.0)

   First-Listed Procedure: None indicated by the documentation provided

   Secondary Procedures: None indicated by the documentation provided

4. **Principal Diagnosis:** Hyperplasia of tonsils and adenoids, 474.10

   Secondary Diagnoses: None indicated by the documentation provided

   Principal Procedure: Tonsillectomy with adenoidectomy, 28.3

   Secondary Procedures: None indicated by the documentation provided

5. **Principal Diagnosis:** Pneumonia, unspecified, 486

   Secondary Diagnoses: Multiple myeloma, 203.00; Pancytopenia, 284.89; Adverse effect, therapeutic use of antineoplastic (chemotherapy) agents, E933.1; Depression, 311

   Principal Procedure: Blood transfusion, packed red cells, 99.04

   Secondary Procedures: None indicated by the documentation provided

6. **First-Listed Diagnosis:** Asthma, unspecified, 493.90

   Secondary Diagnoses: Long term (current) use of steroids, V58.65

   First-Listed Procedure: None indicated by the documentation provided

   Secondary Procedures: None indicated by the documentation provided

7. **First-Listed Diagnosis:** Pharyngitis, streptococcal, 034.0

   Secondary Diagnoses: Otitis, media, suppurative, acute, 382.00 ("Possible" early tonsillar abscess is not coded as this is an outpatient record.)

   First-Listed Procedure: None indicated by the documentation provided

   Secondary Procedures: None indicated by the documentation provided

8. **Principal Diagnosis:** Obstructive chronic bronchitis with acute bronchitis, 491.22
   Secondary Diagnoses: Hypertension, 401.9; Coronary artery disease, 414.00; Status post CABG, V45.81; Congestive heart failure, 428.0; Late effect, CVA, hemiparesis, nondominant side, 438.22
   Principal Procedure: None indicated by the documentation provided
   Secondary Procedures: None indicated by the documentation provided

9. **First-Listed Diagnosis:** Acute frontal sinusitis, 461.1
   Secondary Diagnoses: Acute maxillary sinusitis, 461.0
   First-Listed Procedure: None indicated by the documentation provided
   Secondary Procedures: None indicated by the documentation provided

10. **Principal Diagnosis:** Spontaneous pneumothorax, 512.8
    Secondary Diagnoses: Pleural effusion, 511.9; Emphysema, 492.8
    Principal Procedure: Insertion of chest tube, 34.04
    Secondary Procedures: None indicated by the documentation provided

11. **Principal Diagnosis:** Pleurisy, 511.0
    Secondary Diagnoses: Systemic lupus erythematosus, 710.0; SLE related nephritis, 583.81; Dehydration with hyponatremia, 276.1; Hypokalemia, 276.8; Azotemia, 790.6; Diarrhea, 787.91
    Principal Procedure: Insertion of chest tube, 34.04
    Secondary Procedures: None indicated by the documentation provided

12. **Principal Diagnosis:** Chronic obstructive lung disease with acute bronchitis, 491.22
    Secondary Diagnoses: Cor pulmonale, 416.9; Supplemental oxygen dependent, V46.2; Hospice care, V66.7
    Principal Procedure: None indicated by the documentation provided
    Secondary Procedures: None indicated by the documentation provided

13. **Principal Diagnosis:** Pneumonia, viral, 480.9
    Secondary Diagnoses: Dehydration, 276.51
    Principal Procedure: None indicated by documentation provided
    Secondary Procedures: None indicated by documentation provided

14. **Principal Diagnosis:** Pneumonia, pseudomonas, 482.1
    Secondary Diagnoses: Obstructive, asthma, with status asthmaticus, 493.21; Mass, lung, 786.6; Diabetes, steroid induced or secondary, 249.00; Failure, heart, congestive, 428.0; Failure, respiratory, acute, 518.81; Dependence, tobacco, 305.1; Palliative care, V66.7; Drug, therapy, long-term, steroid, V58.65
    Principal Procedure: None indicated by documentation provided
    Secondary Procedures: None indicated by documentation provided

15. **Principal Diagnosis:** Neoplasm, malignant, primary, lung, upper lobe, 162.3
    Secondary Diagnoses: Effusion, pleural, malignant, 511.81
    Principal Procedure: Thoracentesis, 34.91
    Secondary Procedures: None indicated by documentation provided

Chapter 12

Diseases of the Digestive System

1. **Principal Diagnosis:** Cholelithiasis with cholecystitis, chronic, 574.10

   Secondary Diagnoses: Laparoscopic procedure converted to open procedure, V64.41

   Principal Procedure: Cholecystectomy (open), 51.22 (Laparoscopy that was attempted is not coded)

   Secondary Procedures: None indicated by the documentation provided

2. **Principal Diagnosis:** Crohn's disease of small intestine, 555.0

   Secondary Diagnoses: Intestinal obstruction due to mural thickening, 560.89; Erythema nodosum, 695.2

   Principal Procedure: Partial resection of small intestine, 45.62

   Secondary Procedures: (No code for end-to-end anastomosis)

3. **Principal Diagnosis:** Inguinal hernia, 550.90

   Secondary Diagnoses: Precordial chest pain, 786.51; Procedure not carried out because of contraindication, V64.1; Hypertension, unspecified, 401.9; Chronic obstructive pulmonary disease, 496

   Principal Procedure: None indicated by the documentation provided

   Secondary Procedures: None indicated by the documentation provided

4. **Principal Diagnosis:** Acute gastritis with hemorrhage, 535.01

   Secondary Diagnoses: Chronic pyloric/stomach ulcer with hemorrhage, 531.40; Hiatal hernia, 553.3; Helicobacter pylori infection/organism, 041.86; Stomach polyp, 211.1; Colon polyp, 211.3; Diverticulosis of colon without hemorrhage, 562.10; Congestive heart failure, 428.0; Atrial fibrillation, 427.31

   Principal Procedure: Esophagogastroduodenoscopy (EGD) with closed biopsy, 45.16

   Secondary Procedures: Endoscopic destruction of colon polyp, 45.43, Endoscopic destruction of stomach polyp, 43.41

5. **Principal Diagnosis:** Gastroenteritis, 558.9

   Secondary Diagnoses: Dehydration, 276.51; Pneumonia, 486; Hiatal hernia, 553.3; Reflux esophagitis, 530.11

   Principal Procedure: None indicated by the documentation provided

   Secondary Procedures: None indicated by the documentation provided

6. **Principal Diagnosis:** Gastrojejunal ulcer with hemorrhage, 534.40

   Secondary Diagnoses: Hiatal hernia, 553.3; Reflux esophagitis, 530.11; Status post coronary artery bypass graft, V45.81; History deep vein thrombosis and pulmonary embolism, V12.51; Long term (current) use anticoagulant, V58.61; Congestive heart failure, 428.0; Arthritis, 716.90; Hyperlipidemia, 272.4

Principal Procedure: Esophagogastroduodenoscopy (EGD), 45.13
Secondary Procedures: Blood transfusion (plasma), 99.07;

7. **Principal Diagnosis:** Gastric varices, 456.8
Secondary Diagnoses: Hematemesis, 578.0; Chronic alcoholism, 303.90; Alcoholic liver cirrhosis, 571.2; Acute alcoholic hepatitis, 571.1; Esophageal varices without mention of bleeding, 456.21
Principal Procedure: TIPS (intra-abdominal venous shunt), 39.1
Secondary Procedures: None indicated by the documentation provided

8. **Principal Diagnosis:** Calculus of the gallbladder and bile duct with chronic cholecystitis, 574.71
Secondary Diagnoses: Acute pancreatitis, 577.0
Principal Procedure: Cholecystectomy, open, 51.22
Secondary Procedures: Exploration of common duct, 51.51

9. **Principal Diagnosis:** Acute pancreatitis, 577.0
Secondary Diagnoses: Pancreatitis, chronic, 577.1; Alcohol withdrawal, 291.81; chronic alcoholism, 303.90
Principal Procedure: None indicated by the documentation provided
Secondary Procedures: None indicated by the documentation provided

10. **Principal Diagnosis:** Dental caries into pulp, 521.03
Secondary Diagnoses: Chronic apical periodontitis, 522.6; Long-term (current) use of anticoagulants, V58.61; Monitoring for therapeutic drug, V58.83; Heart valve replacement, V43.3
Principal Procedure: Dental extractions, 23.19
Secondary Procedures: None indicated by the documentation provided

11. **Principal Diagnosis:** Acute ischemia of intestine, 557.0
Secondary Diagnoses: Acute respiratory failure, 518.81; Septicemia due to E. coli, 038.42; Sepsis, 995.91; Hypertension, 401.9; Hypothyroidism 244.9; Hospice care, V66.7
Principal Procedure: Exploratory laparotomy, 54.11
Secondary Procedures: None indicated by the documentation provided

12. **Principal Diagnosis:** Perforation of transverse colon, 569.83
Secondary Diagnoses: Intra-abdominal abscess, 567.22; Malfunctioning tracheostomy, 519.02; Chronic respiratory failure, 518.83; Ventilator dependent, V46.11; Polymyositis, 710.4; Dermatomyositis, 710.3; Septicemia due to E. coli, 038.42; Sepsis, 995.91
Principal Procedure: Transverse colectomy, 45.74
Secondary Procedures: Loop ileostomy, 46.01; Drainage of intra-abdominal abscess, 54.19; Revision of tracheostomy, 31.74

13. **First-Listed Diagnosis:** Reflux, gastroesophageal, 530.81

    Secondary Diagnoses: Hernia, hiatal, 553.3; Ulcer, duodenal, chronic 532.70 (Note: May also code 792.1 for tarry or abnormal stool color, as it was an indication for the visit, but no cause was identified and patient instructed to discontinue use of the over-the-counter medications that could have possibly been causing problem.)

    First-Listed Procedure: Esophagogastroduodenoscopy, 45.13

    Secondary Procedures: None indicated by documentation provided

14. **Principal Diagnosis:** Calculus, common bile duct – see Choledocholiathisis, 574.51

    Secondary Diagnoses: Ulcer, duodenal, chronic, 532.70

    Principal Procedure: Removal, calculus, bile duct, endoscopic, 51.88

    Secondary Procedures: Sphincterotomy, choledochal, endoscopic, 51.85

15. **Principal Diagnosis:** Cirrhosis, alcoholic, 571.2

    Secondary Diagnoses: Varices, esophageal, bleeding, in cirrhosis of liver, 456.20; Alcoholism, continuous, 303.91; Withdrawal, alcohol, 291.81; Thrombocytopenia 287.5

    Principal Procedure: Esophagogastroduodenoscopy, 45.13

    Secondary Procedures: Detoxification, alcohol, 94.62

Chapter 13

Diseases of the Genitourinary System

1. **Principal Diagnosis:** Urinary tract infection, 599.0

    Secondary Diagnoses: Bacterial infection, Proteus, 041.6; Hypertension, unspecified, 401.9; Coronary atherosclerosis of native vessels, 414.01; Status post PTCA, V45.82; Chronic obstructive pulmonary disease, 496; Personal history of urinary tract infections, V13.02

    Principal Procedure: None indicated by the documentation provided

    Secondary Procedures: None indicated by the documentation provided

2. **Principal Diagnosis:** Nodular prostate with urinary retention, 600.11

    Secondary Diagnoses: Primary malignant neoplasm of prostate, 185

    Principal Procedure: Transurethral resection of prostate, 60.29

    Secondary Procedures: None indicated by the documentation provided

3. **Principal Diagnosis:** Cystocele, paravaginal, 618.02

    Secondary Diagnoses: Urinary stress incontinence (female), 625.6; Diabetes mellitus, type II, not stated as uncontrolled, 250.00

    Principal Procedure: Repair of cystocele, 70.51

    Secondary Procedures: None indicated by the documentation provided

4. **Principal Diagnosis:** Acute renal failure, 584.9

   Secondary Diagnoses: Benign prostate hypertrophy with urinary obstruction, 600.01, Obstruction, urinary (use additional code note after 600.01 in Tabular), 599.69

   Principal Procedure: Insertion of indwelling urinary catheter, 57.94

   Secondary Procedures: Pyelogram, intravenous, 87.73

5. **Principal Diagnosis:** Acute pyelonephritis, 590.10

   Secondary Diagnoses: Acute renal failure, 584.9; Hypertension, unspecified, 401.9; History, calculi, urinary, V13.01

   Principal Procedure: Insertion of indwelling urinary catheter, 57.94

   Secondary Procedures: None indicated by the documentation provided

6. **Principal Diagnosis:** Chronic kidney disease, stage 3, 585.3

   Secondary Diagnoses: Hypertension, secondary, other, 405.99; Polycystic kidney disease, unspecified, 753.12

   Principal Procedure: None indicated by the documentation provided

   Secondary Procedures: None indicated by the documentation provided

7. **Principal Diagnosis:** Endometriosis of uterus, 617.0

   Secondary Diagnoses: Endometriosis of ovary, 617.1; Endometriosis of fallopian tube, 617.2; Endometriosis of pelvic peritoneum, 617.3; Carcinoma in situ, cervix, 233.1

   Principal Procedure: Vaginal hysterectomy, 68.59

   Secondary Procedures: Bilateral salpingo-oophorectomy, 65.61

8. **First-Listed Diagnosis:** Acute cystitis, 595.0

   Secondary Diagnoses: Escherichia coli (E. coli) infection, 041.4; Personal history of urinary tract infections, V13.02

   First-Listed Procedure: None indicated by documentation provided

   Secondary Procedures: None indicated by the documentation provided

9. **First-Listed Diagnosis:** Calculus of kidney, 592.0

   Secondary Diagnoses: (Renal colic is not coded as it is a symptom of the calculus.)

   First-Listed Procedure: None indicated by the documentation provided

   Secondary Procedures: None indicated by the documentation provided

10. **Principal Diagnosis:** Calculus of ureter, 592.1

    Secondary Diagnoses: None indicated by the documentation provided

    Principal Procedure: Lithotripsy (ESWL) of ureter, 98.51

    Secondary Procedures: None indicated by the documentation provided

11. **Principal Diagnosis:** Urinary tract infection, 599.0

    Secondary Diagnoses: Dehydration, 276.51; Malignant neoplasm of bladder, primary 188.9; Coronary artery disease, 414.00; Status post coronary artery bypass surgery, V45.81; Status post nephrostomy tubes in place; V44.6; Diabetes mellitus, type II, 250.00; Hypercholesterolemia, 272.0

    Principal Procedure: None indicated by the documentation provided

    Secondary Procedures: None indicated by the documentation provided

12. **Principal Diagnosis:** Menometorrhagia 626.2

    Secondary Diagnoses: Dysmenorrhea, 625.3; Uterine fibroid, 218.9; Acute blood loss anemia, 285.1; Bleeding tendencies, 286.9; Adverse effect of ibuprofen, E935.6; Intra-peritoneal adhesions, 568.0; Laceration of small bowel, 863.20 or Accidental puncture or laceration during a procedure 998.2; Post operative fever, 998.89; Post operative atelectasis, 997.39 and 518.0; Post operative hydronephrosis, 997.5 and 591; Hypoxemia, 799.02; Current smoker, 305.1

    Note: When a tear, such as a small tear of the intestine, is documented in the operative report, the surgeon should be queried as to whether the small tear was an incidental occurrence inherent in the surgical procedure or whether the tear should be considered by the physician to be a complication of the procedure. In an example such as this, the laceration of the small bowel could be coded two different ways. If the doctor describes it as a complication, code 998.2 is assigned. If the physician states it was an incidental occurrent inherent in the surgical procedure, code 863.20 is assigned. (*Coding Clinic,* Second Quarter, 2007, Third Quarter 1990.) One or the other code would be used.

    Principal Procedure: Total abdominal hysterectomy, 68.49

    Secondary Procedures: Bilateral salpingo-oophorectomy, 65.61; Lysis of adhesions, 54.59; Repair of small bowel 46.73; Insertion of ureteral stent, 59.8; Retrograde pyelogram, 87.74; Cystoscopy, 57.32 (coding optional)

13. **Principal Diagnosis:** Failure, renal, acute, 584.9

    Secondary Diagnoses: Dehydration, 276.51

    Principal Procedure: None indicated by documentation provided

    Secondary Procedures: None indicated by documentation provided

14. **Principal Diagnosis:** Incontinence, stress/urine stress (female) 625.6

    Secondary Diagnoses: Dependence, on, supplemental oxygen, V46.2; Disease, lung, obstructive, chronic, 496

    Principal Procedure: Operation, sling, urethra (sling) 59.4

    Secondary Procedures: None indicated by documentation provided

15. **Principal Diagnosis:** Bleeding, uterus, dysfunctional, 626.8
    Secondary Diagnoses: Sterilization, admission for, V25.2
    Principal Procedure: Ligation, fallopian tubes, by endoscopy, 66.29
    Secondary Procedures: Dilation and curettage, uterus, 69.09

Chapter 14

Complications of Pregnancy, Childbirth, and the Puerperium

1. **First-Listed Diagnosis:** Pregnancy, complicated by, abnormal glucose tolerance, 648.83
    Secondary Diagnoses: None indicated by the documentation provided
    First-Listed Procedure: None indicated by the documentation provided
    Secondary Procedures: None indicated by the documentation provided

2. **Principal Diagnosis:** Spontaneous abortion, without complications, 634.91
    Secondary Diagnoses: Hypertension, complicating pregnancy, transient, 642.33
    Principal Procedure: Dilatation and curettage, uterus, after abortion, 69.02
    Secondary Procedures: None indicated by the documentation provided

3. **Principal Diagnosis:** Delivery, complicated by, cephalopelvic disproportion, 653.41
    Secondary Diagnoses: Delivery, complicated by previous Cesarean section, 654.21; Outcome of delivery, single live born, V27.0
    Principal Procedure: Cesarean delivery, low cervical, 74.1
    Secondary Procedures: None indicated by the documentation provided

4. **Principal Diagnosis:** Elderly primigravida, delivered without complications, 659.51
    Secondary Diagnoses: Single live born infant, V27.0
    Principal Procedure: Manually assisted vaginal delivery, 73.59
    Secondary Procedures: None indicated by the documentation provided

5. **Principal Diagnosis:** Normal delivery, 650
    Secondary Diagnoses: Single live born infant, V27.0
    Principal Procedure: Induction of labor by artificial rupture of membranes, 73.01
    Secondary Procedures: None indicated by the documentation provided

6. **First-Listed Diagnosis:** Pregnancy, complicated by, drug dependence, 648.33
    Secondary Diagnoses: Cocaine dependence, unspecified, 304.20; Infection of genitourinary tract in pregnancy, 646.63; Urinary tract infection, 599.0
    First-Listed Procedure: None indicated by the documentation provided
    Secondary Procedures: None indicated by the documentation provided

7. **First-Listed Diagnosis:** Abscess of breast, pregnancy, postpartum, 675.14

   Secondary Diagnoses: None indicated by the documentation provided

   First-Listed Procedure: None indicated by the documentation provided

   Secondary Procedures: None indicated by the documentation provided

8. **Principal Diagnosis:** Other complications of pregnancy, cholelithiasis, 646.84

   Secondary Diagnoses: Calculus of gallbladder with acute cholecystitis, 574.00

   Principal Procedure: Laparoscopic cholecystectomy, 51.23

   Secondary Procedures: None indicated by the documentation provided

9. **Principal Diagnosis:** Legally induced abortion, excessive hemorrhage, admitted as incomplete, 635.11

   Secondary Diagnoses: Pregnancy, complicated by anemia, 648.23; Anemia, blood loss, 280.0

   Principal Procedure: D&C following abortion, 69.02

   Secondary Procedures: None indicated by the documentation provided

10. **Principal Diagnosis:** Missed abortion, 632

    Secondary Diagnoses: None indicated by the documentation provided

    Principal Procedure: D&C following abortion, 69.02

    Secondary Procedures: None indicated by the documentation provided

11. **Principal Diagnosis:** Pregnancy, delivered, placenta previa with hemorrhage, 641.11

    Secondary Diagnoses: Pregnancy, delivered, twin pregnancy, 651.01; Pregnancy, delivered, premature, 35 weeks, 644.21; Pregnancy, delivered, anemia, 648.21; Anemia, blood loss, 280.0; Outcome of delivery, twins, liveborn, V27.2

    Principal Procedure: Cesarean delivery, low cervical, 74.1

    Secondary Procedures: None indicated by documentation provided

12. **Principal Diagnosis:** Pregnancy, delivered, decreased fetal movements, 655.71

    Secondary Diagnoses: Pregnancy, delivered, with previous cesarean deliveries, 654.21; Pregnancy, delivered, with grand multiparity, 659.41; Pregnancy, delivered, with iron deficiency anemia, 648.21; Anemia, iron deficiency, 280.9; Pregnancy, delivered, with gestational hypertension, 642.31; Outcome of delivery, single, liveborn, V27.0

    Principal Procedure: Cesarean delivery, low cervical, 74.1

    Secondary Procedures: Tubal ligation, bilateral, ligation and crushing, 66.31

13. **Principal Diagnosis:** Pregnancy, management affected by, fetal heart rate or rhythm, delivered, 659.71

    Secondary Diagnoses: Pregnancy, complicated by anemia, delivered, 648.21; Anemia, microcytic, 280.9; Outcome of delivery, single liveborn, V27.0

    Principal Procedure: Cesarean, section, low cervical, 74.1

    Secondary Procedures: Rupture, membranes, artificial, 73.09; Monitoring, fetal, intrapartum, 75.34

14. **Principal Diagnosis:** Delivery, complicated, labor, premature, delivered, 644.21

    Secondary Diagnoses: Pregnancy, complicated by, cystocele, delivered, 654.41; Pregnancy, management affected by, elderly multigravida, delivered, 659.61; Sterilization, admission for, V25.2; Outcome of delivery, single liveborn, V27.0

    Principal Procedure: Delivery, manually assisted, 73.59

    Secondary Procedures: Monitoring, fetal, intrapartum, 75.34; Ligation, fallopian tube, with division, by endoscopy, 66.22

15. **Principal Diagnosis:** Pregnancy, complicated by, placenta, previa, delivered, 641.11

    Secondary Diagnoses: Delivery, cesarean for, (double) footling, delivered, 652.81; Hypertension, complicating, pregnancy, gestational, delivered, 642.31; Delivery, premature, delivered, 644.21; Delivery, complicated by previous cesarean delivery, delivered, 654.21; Pregnancy, complicated by, amnioitis, delivered, 658.41; Outcome of delivery, single, liveborn, V27.0

    Principal Procedure: Cesarean, section, low cervical 74.1

    Secondary Procedures: None indicated by documentation provided

Chapter 15

Diseases of the Skin and Subcutaneous Tissue

1. **Principal Diagnosis:** Pressure ulcer, buttock, 707.05

   Secondary Diagnoses: Pressure ulcer, stage III, 707.23; Chronic skin ulcer on heel, 707.14; Atherosclerosis, generalized, 440.9

   Principal Procedure: Debridement of muscle, 83.45

   Secondary Procedures: Excisional debridement of wound, 86.22

2. **First-Listed Diagnosis:** Pilonidal cyst with abscess, 685.0

   Secondary Diagnoses: None indicated by the documentation provided

   First-Listed Procedure: Incision of pilonidal cyst or sinus, 86.03

   Secondary Procedures: None indicated by the documentation provided

3. **First-Listed Diagnosis:** Contact dermatitis due to cosmetics, 692.81

   Secondary Diagnoses: Acne, cystic, 706.1

   First-Listed Procedure: None indicated by the documentation provided

   Secondary Procedures: None indicated by the documentation provided

4. **First-Listed Diagnosis:** Cellulitis of leg, 682.6

   Secondary Diagnoses: Open wound of leg, complicated (infection), 891.1

   First-Listed Procedure: None indicated by the documentation provided

   Secondary Procedures: None indicated by the documentation provided

5. **First-Listed Diagnosis:** Disseminated superficial actinic porokeratosis, 692.75
   Secondary Diagnoses: None indicated by the documentation provided
   First-Listed Procedure: Skin biopsy, 86.11
   Secondary Procedures: None indicated by the documentation provided

6. **First-Listed Diagnosis:** Primary hyperhidrosis, 705.21
   Secondary Diagnoses: None indicated by the documentation provided
   First-Listed Procedure: Injection, botulinum toxin (botulism antitoxin), 99.57
   Secondary Procedures: None indicated by the documentation provided

7. **First-Listed Diagnosis:** Contact dermatitis due to animal dander, 692.84
   Secondary Diagnoses: None indicated by the documentation provided
   First-Listed Procedure: None indicated by the documentation provided
   Secondary Procedures: None indicated by the documentation provided

8. **First-Listed Diagnosis:** Left-sided ulcerative colitis, 556.5
   Secondary Diagnoses: Erythema nodosum, 695.2
   First-Listed Procedure: None indicated by the documentation provided
   Secondary Procedures: None indicated by the documentation provided

9. **First-Listed Diagnosis:** Type I diabetes, not stated as uncontrolled, 250.81
   Secondary Diagnoses: Ulcer of heel of foot, 707.14
   First-Listed Procedure: None indicated by the documentation provided
   Secondary Procedures: None indicated by the documentation provided

10. **First-Listed Diagnosis:** Pityriasis rosea, 696.3
    Secondary Diagnoses: None indicated by the documentation provided
    First-Listed Procedure: None indicated by the documentation provided
    Secondary Procedures: None indicated by the documentation provided

11. **First-Listed Diagnosis:** Basal cell carcinoma of skin, scalp, 173.4
    Secondary Diagnoses: Actinic keratosis, 702.0
    First-Listed Procedure: Biopsy, skin, punch, 86.11
    Secondary Procedures: Excision, lesion, skin, 86.3

12. **Principal Diagnosis:** Abscess, skin, back, 682.2
    Secondary Diagnoses: MRSA infection organism, 041.12; Diabetes, type II, poorly controlled, 250.00; Hypertension, 401.9
    Principal Procedure: Incision and drainage, abscess, skin, 86.04
    Secondary Procedures: None indicated by documentation provided

13. **Principal Diagnosis:** Cellulitis, abdominal wall, 682.2
    Secondary Diagnoses: Bacteremia, 790.7; Infection, pseudomonas, 041.7; Stasis dermatitis, 454.1; Cellulitis, leg, 682.6; Cirrhosis, alcoholic, 571.2; Hypoalbuminemia, 273.8; Obesity, morbid, 278.01
    Principal Procedure: None indicated by documentation provided
    Secondary Procedures: None indicated by documentation provided

14. **Principal Diagnosis:** Syndrome, Stevens-Johnson, toxic epidermal necrolysis overlap, 695.14

    Secondary Diagnoses: Edema, eyelid, 374.82; Exfoliation, skin, due to erythematous condition, 20-29 percent, 695.52; Table of drugs and chemical, penicillin, therapeutic use E code (for adverse effect), E930.0

    Principal Procedure: None indicated by documentation provided

    Secondary Procedures: None indicated by documentation provided

15. **Principal Diagnosis:** Ulcer, pressure, coccyx, 707.03

    Secondary Diagnoses: Ulcer, pressure, stage IV, 707.24; Failure, heart, diastolic, chronic, 428.32; Arteriosclerosis, coronary artery, native vessel, 414.01; Occlusion, artery, coronary, chronic total, 414.2

    Principal Procedure: Debridement, bone, (coccyx, other), 77.69

    Secondary Procedures: None indicated by documentation provided

Chapter 16

Diseases of the Musculoskeletal System and Connective Tissue

1. **Principal Diagnosis:** Displacement of lumbar intervertebral disc without myelopathy, 722.10

   Secondary Diagnoses: Osteoarthritis, spine, 721.90

   Principal Procedure: Excision of intervertebral disc (Laminotomy was the approach), 80.51

   Secondary Procedures: None indicated by the documentation provided

2. **Principal Diagnosis:** Compression/pathological fracture of vertebrae, 733.13

   Secondary Diagnoses: Senile osteoporosis, 733.01

   Principal Procedure: Injection of anesthetic into spinal canal for analgesia, 03.91

   Secondary Procedures: None indicated by the documentation provided

3. **First-Listed Diagnosis:** Degenerative osteoarthritis, generalized, multiple site, 715.09

   Secondary Diagnoses: Osteoarthritis, lumbosacral spine, 721.3; Hypertension, unspecified, 401.9; Coronary atherosclerosis of autologous vein bypass graft, 414.02; Angina, 413.9

   First-Listed Procedure: None indicated by the documentation provided

   Secondary Procedures: None indicated by the documentation provided

4. **Principal Diagnosis:** Systemic lupus erythematosus, 710.0 (Admission for chemotherapy is not used as the patient does not have neoplastic disease)

   Secondary Diagnoses: Nephrotic syndrome due to SLE, 581.81; Anemia of chronic disease, 285.29; Inflammatory myopathy due to the SLE, 359.6; Swan-neck deformity of the fingers, acquired due to SLE, 736.22

   Principal Procedure: Chemotherapy, 99.25

   Secondary Procedures: None indicated by the documentation provided

5. **First-Listed Diagnosis:** Stress fracture of tibia, 733.93

   Secondary Diagnoses: Stress fracture of metatarsal, 733.94; Sprain, lumbosacral, 846.0; (If an E code is desired: Cumulative trauma from repetitive impact, E927.4)

   First-Listed Procedure: None indicated by the documentation provided

   Secondary Procedures: None indicated by the documentation provided

6. **Principal Diagnosis:** Acute osteomyelitis, fibula, 730.06

   Secondary Diagnoses: Staphylococcus infection, unspecified, 041.10

   Principal Procedure: Debridement of bone, proximal fibula, 77.67

   Secondary Procedures: Incision and drainage, bone, proximal fibula, 77.17

7. **Principal Diagnosis:** Mechanical complication of prosthetic joint, aseptic loosening, 996.41

   Secondary Diagnoses: Gouty arthritis, 274.0; Knee replacement status, V43.65

   Principal Procedure: Revision of knee replacement, total, 00.80

   Secondary Procedures: None indicated by the documentation provided

8. **Principal Diagnosis:** Articular bearing surface wear of prosthetic hip joint, 996.46

   Secondary Diagnoses: Hypertension, 401.9; Gastroesophageal reflux disease, 530.81

   Principal Procedure: Revision of hip replacement, acetabular liner and femoral head only, 00.73; V43.64, Hip replacement status

   Secondary Procedures: Hip bearing surface, Ceramic-on-ceramic, 00.76

9. **First-Listed Diagnosis:** Pain in joint, multiple sites, 719.49

   Secondary Diagnoses: Stiffness in joint, multiple sites, 719.59; Swelling of joint, multiple sites, 719.09; Fatigue, 780.79; Anorexia, 783.0 (Weight loss could be used if space permits for reporting, 783.21)

   First-Listed Procedure: None indicated by the documentation provided

   Secondary Procedures: None indicated by the documentation provided

10. **First-Listed Diagnosis:** Recurrent dislocation of joint, shoulder, 718.31

    Secondary Diagnoses: Arthritis, traumatic, shoulder, 716.11

    First-Listed Procedure: Closed reduction, shoulder dislocation, 79.71

    Secondary Procedures: None indicated by the documentation provided

11. **Principal Diagnosis:**   Rotator cuff tear, nontraumatic, 727.61

    Secondary Diagnoses: Tenosynovitis, shoulder, 726.10; Hypertension, 401.9

    Principal Procedure: Arthroscopic and mini-open approach for rotator cuff repair, 83.63

    Secondary Procedures: Arthroscopic synovectomy, shoulder, 80.71; Arthroscopy, shoulder, 80.21 (Coding of arthroscopy is optional.)

12. **Principal Diagnosis:**   Tear, old, medial meniscus, posterior horn, 717.2

    Secondary Diagnoses: Hypertensive heart disease, 402.90

    Principal Procedure: Arthroscopic partial medial meniscectomy, 80.6

    Secondary Procedures: Arthroscopy, knee, 80.26 (Coding of arthroscopy is optional.)

13. **Principal Diagnosis:**   Hallux, valgus, 735.0

    Secondary Diagnoses: Defect, ventricular septal, 745.4; Bronchitis, chronic, asthmatic, 493.20

    Principal Procedure: Bunionectomy, with soft tissue correction, 77.53

    Secondary Procedures: Echocardiography, 88.72; Therapy, respiratory, 93.99

14. **Principal Diagnosis:**   Pain, back, low, 724.2

    Secondary Diagnoses: Neoplasm, malignant, primary, breast, 174.9; Myelofibrosis, secondary, 289.83; Syndrome, myelodysplastic (low grade), 238.72; Table of drugs and chemical, antineoplastic agents, therapeutic use E code (adverse effect), E933.1

    Principal Procedure: Scan, radioisotope, bone, 92.14

    Secondary Procedures: Scan, CAT, bone, 88.38

15. **Principal Diagnosis:**   Sprain, knee, old, cruciate, anterior, 717.83

    Secondary Diagnoses: Sprain, knee, old, collateral, medial, 717.82; Tear, meniscus, medial, posterior horn, old, 717.2

    Principal Procedure: Repair, knee, triad, 81.43

    Secondary Procedures: None indicated by documentation provided

Chapter 17

Congenital Anomalies and Certain Conditions Originating in the Perinatal Period

1. **Principal Diagnosis:**   Mixed hearing loss, (bilateral) 389.22

   Secondary Diagnoses: Anomaly of ear with impairment of hearing, 744.00

   Principal Procedure: Implantation of cochlear implant, 20.96

   Secondary Procedures: Implantation of cochlear implant (second ear), 20.96

2. **Principal Diagnosis:** Biliary atresia, 751.61

   Secondary Diagnoses: Obstructive jaundice from congenital obstruction of bile duct (atresia), 774.5

   Principal Procedure: Roux-en-Y cholecystojejunostomy, 51.32

   Secondary Procedures: Intraoperative cholangiography, 87.53

3. **Principal Diagnosis:** Coarctation of aorta, 747.10 (If this was the same hospital and the same hospital stay as the infant's birth, a code from the V30 category would be assigned as principal diagnosis)

   Secondary Diagnoses: None indicated by the documentation provided

   Principal Procedure: Excision of vessel without graft, 38.64

   Secondary Procedures: Cardiopulmonary bypass (pump oxygenator), 39.61

4. **Principal Diagnosis:** Syndrome of infant of diabetic mother, 775.0

   Secondary Diagnoses: Observation for suspected condition, infectious, in a newborn, V29.0

   Principal Procedure: None indicated by the documentation provided

   Secondary Procedures: None indicated by the documentation provided

5. **Principal Diagnosis:** Stenosis of pulmonary (heart) valve, congenital, 746.02

   Secondary Diagnoses: Stenosis of pulmonary artery, congenital, 747.3; History of surgery on heart and great vessels, V15.1; History of congenital malformations, V13.69

   Principal Procedure: Replacement of pulmonary valve with tissue graft, 35.25

   Secondary Procedures: Repair of pulmonary artery with patch graft, 39.56; Cardiopulmonary bypass, 39.61; Intraoperative echocardiogram, 88.72

6. **Principal Diagnosis:** Meconium aspiration pneumonia, 770.12

   Secondary Diagnoses: Small for dates or gestational age, 764.08; For 39 weeks of gestation in an infant small for dates, 765.29

   Principal Procedure: None indicated by the documentation provided

   Secondary Procedures: None indicated by the documentation provided

7. **First-Listed Diagnosis:** Cleft palate with cleft lip, complete, bilateral, 749.23

   Secondary Diagnoses: Feeding difficulties/problems, child, 783.3

   First-Listed Procedure: None indicated by the documentation provided

   Secondary Procedures: None indicated by the documentation provided

8. **First-Listed Diagnosis:** Fetal growth retardation, birth weight 1600 grams, 764.96

   Secondary Diagnoses: Premature infant, birth weight 1600 grams, 765.16; Infant the result of a 36 week gestation, 765.28

   First-Listed Procedure: None indicated by the documentation provided

   Secondary Procedures: None indicated by the documentation provided

9. **First-Listed Diagnosis:** Crack baby, 760.75

   Secondary Diagnoses: Transitory tachypnea of a newborn, 770.6

   First-Listed Procedure: None indicated by the documentation provided

   Secondary Procedures: None indicated by the documentation provided

10. **First-Listed Diagnosis:** Feeding problems in newborn, 779.3

    Secondary Diagnoses: Cord around neck affecting the newborn, 762.5

    First-Listed Procedure: None indicated by the documentation provided

    Secondary Procedures: None indicated by the documentation provided

11. **First-Listed Diagnosis:** Newborn infant via cesarean delivery in hospital, V30.01

    Secondary Diagnoses: Newborn observation for infectious condition not found, V29.0; Premature infant, 1920 grams, 765.17; Premature infant at 32 completed weeks, 765.26

    First-Listed Procedure: None indicated by the documentation provided

    Secondary Procedures: None indicated by the documentation provided

12. **First-Listed Diagnosis:** Newborn infant via vaginal delivery in hospital, V30.00

    Secondary Diagnoses: Newborn observation for infectious condition not found, V29.0; Premature infant, 2035 grams, 765.18; Premature infant at 33 completed weeks, 765.27; Transient tachypnea of newborn, 770.6; Respiratory distress in newborn, 770.89; Hypermagnesemia in newborn, 775.5; Metabolic acidosis in newborn, 775.81; Hyperbilirubinemia in newborn, premature, 774.2

    First-Listed Procedure: None indicated by the documentation provided

    Secondary Procedures: None indicated by the documentation provided

13. **First-Listed Diagnosis:** Bicornuate uterus, 752.34 (New code 10-1-10; previously 752.3.)

    Secondary Diagnoses: None indicated by documentation provided

    First-Listed Procedure: None indicated by documentation provided

    Secondary Procedures: None indicated by documentation provided

14. **Principal Diagnosis:** Herpes, simplex, congenital, 771.2

    Secondary Diagnoses: Small, for dates, newborn, (weight 2040 grams), 764.08

    Principal Procedure: None indicated by documentation provided

    Secondary Procedures: None indicated by documentation provided

15. **Principal Diagnosis:** Premature, infant, (weight 1600 grams), 765.16

    Secondary Diagnoses: Newborn, gestation, 32 completed weeks, 765.26; Spina bifida, occulta, 756.17

    Principal Procedure: None indicated by documentation provided

    Secondary Procedures: None indicated by documentation provided

Chapter 18

Symptoms, Signs, and Ill-Defined Conditions

1. **First-Listed Diagnosis:** Change in bowel habits, 787.99
   Secondary Diagnoses: Family history of malignant neoplasm, colon, V16.0
   First-Listed Procedure: Colonoscopy, 45.23
   Secondary Procedures: None indicated by the documentation provided

2. **First-Listed Diagnosis:** Findings, abnormal, radiology, gastrointestinal, 793.4
   Secondary Diagnoses: Abdominal pain, generalized, 789.07; Fatigue, 780.79; Nausea, 787.02
   First-Listed Procedure: None indicated by the documentation provided
   Secondary Procedures: None indicated by the documentation provided

3. **Principal Diagnosis:** Lung mass, 786.6
   Secondary Diagnoses: Cough, 786.2; Chest pressure, 786.59; Bradycardia, 427.89; Procedure not carried out because of contraindication, V64.1
   Principal Procedure: Fiberoptic bronchoscopy, 33.22
   Secondary Procedures: None indicated by the documentation provided

4. **Principal Diagnosis:** Chest pain, atypical, 786.59
   Secondary Diagnoses: Angina pectoris, 413.9; Gastroesophageal reflux disease, 530.81
   Principal Procedure: Esophagogastroduodenoscopy, 45.13
   Secondary Procedures: Cardiovascular stress test, 89.41; Cardiovascular function study, 92.05

5. **First-Listed Diagnosis:** Numbness of legs, 782.0
   Secondary Diagnoses: Difficulty in walking, 719.7; Lack of coordination, 781.3; Tremors of hands, 781.0
   First-Listed Procedure: None indicated by the documentation provided
   Secondary Procedures: None indicated by the documentation provided

6. **First-Listed Diagnosis:** Mammographic microcalcifications, 793.81
   Secondary Diagnoses: Fibrocystic disease, breast, 610.1
   First-Listed Procedure: None indicated by the documentation provided
   Secondary Procedures: None indicated by the documentation provided

7. **First-Listed Diagnosis:** Cervical high risk human papillomavirus (HPV), DNA positive, 795.05
   Secondary Diagnoses: Warts, genital, 078.11
   First-Listed Procedure: None indicated by the documentation provided
   Secondary Procedures: None indicated by the documentation provided

8. **First-Listed Diagnosis:** Diarrhea, 787.91

   Secondary Diagnoses: Failure to thrive, child, 783.41

   First-Listed Procedure: None indicated by the documentation provided

   Secondary Procedures: None indicated by the documentation provided

9. **First-Listed Diagnosis:** Headache, 784.0

   Secondary Diagnoses: Fever, 780.60; Nausea with vomiting, 787.01; Meningismus, 781.6

   First-Listed Procedure: Lumbar puncture or spinal tap, 03.31

   Secondary Procedures: None indicated by the documentation provided

10. **Principal Diagnosis:** Abdominal pain, right upper quadrant, 789.01

    Secondary Diagnoses: Nausea and vomiting, 787.01; Findings, abnormal, ultrasound, abdomen, 793.6; Elevated blood pressure readings, 796.2

    Principal Procedure: Ultrasound of abdomen, 88.76

    Secondary Procedures: None indicated by the documentation provided

11. **Principal Diagnosis:** Dysphagia

    Secondary Diagnoses: Anxiety disorder, 300.00; Dehydration, 276.51

    Principal Procedure: Esophagogastroduodenoscopy, 45.13

    Secondary Procedures: None indicated by the documentation provided

12. **First-Listed Diagnosis:** Fever and chills, 780.60

    Secondary Diagnoses: None indicated by the documentation provided

    First-Listed Procedure: None indicated by the documentation provided

    Secondary Procedures: None indicated by the documentation provided

13. **First-Listed Diagnosis:** Findings, abnormal, stress test, 794.39

    Secondary Diagnoses: Elevation, blood pressure reading, 796.2

    First-Listed Procedure: None indicated by documentation provided

    Secondary Procedures: None indicated by documentation provided

14. **First-Listed Diagnosis:** Pain, jaw, 784.92 (New code 10-1-10, previously 526.9.)

    Secondary Diagnoses: Pain, shoulder, 719.41; Findings, abnormal, electrocardiogram, 794.31

    First-Listed Procedure: None indicated by documentation provided

    Secondary Procedures: None indicated by documentation provided

15. **First-Listed Diagnosis:** Colic, infantile, 789.7

    Secondary Diagnoses: None indicated by documentation provided

    First-Listed Procedure: None indicated by documentation provided

    Secondary Procedures: None indicated by documentation provided

Chapter 19

Injuries

1. **First-Listed Diagnosis:** Burn, third degree, chest, 942.32
   Secondary Diagnoses: Burn, second degree, upper arms, 943.23; Burn, extent of body surface, 25% body surface, 9% third degree, 948.20
   First-Listed Procedure: None indicated by the documentation provided
   Secondary Procedures: None indicated by the documentation provided

2. **Principal Diagnosis:** Dislocation, mandible, closed, 830.0
   Secondary Diagnoses: Wound, open, hand, 882.0
   Principal Procedure: Closed reduction of mandibular fracture, 76.75
   Secondary Procedures: Suture, skin, 86.59

3. **Principal Diagnosis:** Fracture, femur, lower end, supracondylar, closed, 821.23
   Secondary Diagnoses: Fracture, talus, closed, 825.21
   Principal Procedure: Open reduction with internal fixation, femur, 79.35
   Secondary Procedures: Open reduction with internal fixation, talus (tarsal bone), 79.37

4. **Principal Diagnosis:** Superior glenoid labrum lesion, 840.7
   Secondary Diagnoses: None indicated by the documentation provided
   Principal Procedure: Arthroplasty and repair of the shoulder, 81.83
   Secondary Procedures: None indicated by the documentation provided

5. **Principal Diagnosis:** Head injury with loss of consciousness from 31 to 59 minutes, 850.12
   Secondary Diagnoses: Open wound of face, without complication, multiple sites, 873.49; Abrasions of hands, 914.0; Contusion, abdominal wall, 922.2; Contusion,, lower leg, 924.10; Contusion, knee, 924.11
   Principal Procedure: Suture repair of facial/skin lacerations, 86.59
   Secondary Procedures: None indicated by the documentation provided

6. **First-Listed Diagnosis:** Injury to blood vessel, aorta, 902.0
   Secondary Diagnoses: Wound, open, abdominal wall, complicated, 879.3
   First-Listed Procedure: None indicated by the documentation provided
   Secondary Procedures: None indicated by the documentation provided

7. **Principal Diagnosis:** Crushing injury, foot, 928.20
   Secondary Diagnoses: Fracture, open, metatarsal bones, 825.35
   Principal Procedure: Open reduction with internal fixation, metatarsal bones, 79.37; Fasciotomy, 83.14
   Secondary Procedures: None indicated by the documentation provided

8. **Principal Diagnosis:** Foreign body, esophagus, 935.1

   Secondary Diagnoses: Esophagitis, reflux, 530.11

   Principal Procedure: Esophagogastroduodenoscopy, 45.13

   Secondary Procedures: Removal of foreign body, esophagus, intraluminal, 98.02

9. **Principal Diagnosis:** Fracture of vertebrae without mention of spinal cord injury, 805.4

   Secondary Diagnoses: None indicated by the documentation provided

   Principal Procedure: Repair of vertebral fracture (reduction of fracture), 03.53

   Secondary Procedures: Lumbar fusion, posterior technique, 81.08; Excision (harvesting) of bone for graft, 77.79

10. **First-Listed Diagnosis:** Open wound, with tendon involvement, wrist, 881.22

    Secondary Diagnoses: Injury, ulnar nerve, 955.2

    First-Listed Procedure: Suture repair of laceration, 86.59

    Secondary Procedures: None indicated by the documentation provided

11. **Principal Diagnosis:** Injury, internal, laceration, liver, major with open wound, 864.14

    Secondary Diagnoses: Injury, internal, laceration, jejunum with open wound, 863.39; Injury, internal, kidney, hematoma with open wound, 866.11; Lacerations/open wounds, skin, upper extremity and lower extremity, 884.0 and 894.0; Poisoning, alcohol, 980.0

    Principal Procedure: Repair, liver, laceration, 50.69

    Secondary Procedures: Repair, suture, jejunum, laceration, 46.73; Removal foreign body (glass) abdominal cavity, 54.92

12. **Principal Diagnosis:** Fracture, open, vault of skull (parietal) with cerebral contusion, without return to consciousness, 800.61

    Secondary Diagnoses: Fracture, open, vault of skull (parietal) with subdural hemorrhage without return to consciousness, 800.71; herniation of brain stem, 348.4; cerebral edema, 384.5

    Principal Procedure: Craniotomy, decompressive, 01.24

    Secondary Procedures: Duraplasty, 02.12; Insertion of intracranial pressure monitor catheter, 01.10; Insertion of endotracheal tube, 96.04; Mechanical ventilation less than 96 hours, 96.71; Bronchoscopy, flexible, fiberoptic, 33.22

13. **Principal Diagnosis:** Fracture, mandible, angle, 802.25

    Secondary Diagnoses: Fracture, tooth, 873.63; Wound, open, jaw, 873.44; Infection, urinary tract, 599.0; Injury, superficial, hand, abrasion, 914.0

    Principal Procedure: Reduction, fracture, mandible, open, 76.76

    Secondary Procedures: Repair, wound/laceration, skin, 86.59; Extraction, tooth, by forceps, 23.09

14. **Principal Diagnosis:** Fracture, tibia, upper end, 823.00

    Secondary Diagnoses: Hemophilia, A, 286.0; Human immunodeficiency virus, infection, V08; Status, knee joint prosthesis, V43.65 (External cause, Fall, E880.9; Accident, occurring at home, E849.0.)

    Principal Procedure: Reduction, fracture, tibia, closed, 79.06

    Secondary Procedures: None indicated by documentation provided

15. **Principal Diagnosis:** Fracture, trimalleolar, 824.6

    Secondary Diagnoses: Late, effect, cerebrovascular disease, hemiplegia, affecting non-dominant side (hemiplegia on left side for right handed patient) 438.22; Diabetes mellitus, type II, 250.00; Hypertension, 401.9; Ischemia, heart, 414.9; Infection, urinary tract, 599.0

    Principal Procedure: Reduction, fracture, ankle – leg (tibia/fibula), 79.06

    Secondary Procedures: None indicated by documentation provided

Chapter 20

Poisoning, Adverse Effects, and Complications

1. **First-Listed Diagnosis:** Poisoning, antidepressants, 969.0

    Secondary Diagnoses: Poisoning, lorazepam, 969.4; Poisoning, alcohol, 980.0; Depression, 311; Suicide intent by tranquilizers, E950.3; Suicide intent by other agents (alcohol), E950.9

    Note: Any of the poisoning codes may be listed first.

    First-Listed Procedure: None indicated by the documentation provided

    Secondary Procedures: None indicated by the documentation provided

2. **Principal Diagnosis:** Nausea with vomiting, 787.01

    Secondary Diagnoses: Fatigue, 780.79; Adverse effect/therapeutic use, digoxin, E942.1; Congestive heart failure, 428.0; Acute myocardial infarction, subsequent episode of care within 8 weeks, 410.92

    Principal Procedure: None indicated by the documentation provided

    Secondary Procedures: None indicated by the documentation provided

3. **Principal Diagnosis:** Postoperative wound infection, 998.59

    Secondary Diagnoses: Cellulitis, abdominal wall, 682.2; Infection, Staphylococcus aureus, methicillin resistant, 041.12; Diabetes mellitus, type II, not stated as uncontrolled, 250.00

    Principal Procedure: None indicated by the documentation provided

    Secondary Procedures: None indicated by the documentation provided

4. **Principal Diagnosis:** Epistaxis, 784.7

   Secondary Diagnoses: Adverse effects of drug, Coumadin, E934.2; Long-term (current) use of anticoagulant, V58.61; Atrial fibrillation, 427.31; Congestive heart failure, 428.0; Anemia, chronic blood loss, 280.0

   Principal Procedure: Packing, nose, anterior and posterior, 21.02

   Secondary Procedures: None indicated by the documentation provided

5. **First-Listed Diagnosis:** Drug allergy, 995.27

   Secondary Diagnoses: Otitis media, acute, 382.9

   First-Listed Procedure: None indicated by the documentation provided

   Secondary Procedures: None indicated by the documentation provided

6. **Principal Diagnosis:** Poisoning, cocaine, 970.81

   Secondary Diagnoses: Accidental poisoning, cocaine, E854.3; Cocaine dependence, 304.20; Hypertension, unspecified, 401.9

   Principal Procedure: None indicated by the documentation provided

   Secondary Procedures: None indicated by the documentation provided

7. **First-Listed Diagnosis:** Infection due to presence of cardiac device or complication, infection, due to device, cardiac, 996.61

   Secondary Diagnoses: Cellulitis, chest wall, 682.2; History, disease, infection, MRSA, V12.04

   First-Listed Procedure: None indicated by the documentation provided

   Secondary Procedures: None indicated by the documentation provided

8. **First-Listed Diagnosis:** Vertigo and light-headedness, 780.4

   Secondary Diagnoses: Adverse effects in therapeutic use, anti-hypertensive medications, E942.6; Hypertension, unspecified, 401.9

   First-Listed Procedure: None indicated by the documentation provided

   Secondary Procedures: None indicated by the documentation provided

9. **First-Listed Diagnosis:** Poisoning, antibiotics, 960.8

   Secondary Diagnoses: Accidental poisoning, antibiotics, E857; Diarrhea, 787.91; Urinary tract infection, 599.0; Infection, Escherichia coli, 041.4

   First-Listed Procedure: None indicated by the documentation provided

   Secondary Procedures: None indicated by the documentation provided

10. **Principal Diagnosis:** Infection due to central venous catheter, 999.31

    Secondary Diagnoses: Septicemia, Staphylococcal, methicillin susceptible, 038.11; Sepsis/SIRS without organ dysfunction, 995.91; Carcinoma of colon/large intestine, 153.9

    Principal Procedure: Removal, foreign body (VAD) from skin and subcutaneous tissue, 86.05

    Secondary Procedures: None indicated by the documentation provided

11. **Principal Diagnosis:** Complication of prosthesis: Aseptic loosening of knee replacement device, tibial component, 996.41

    Secondary Diagnoses: Parkinson's disease 332,0; Near total blindness both eyes, 369.04; Glaucoma, 365.9; Old MI, 412; Abnormal finding, cardiac function test, specifically stress test, 794.39; Replacement of knee joint, V43.65 (This code is probably redundant with principal diagnosis.); Osteoarthrosis, generalized, 715.09

    Principal Procedure: Revision, arthroplasty, knee, tibial component only, 00.81

    Secondary Procedures: None indicated by the documentation provided

12. **Principal Diagnosis:** Disruption of cesarean wound, 674.14 (See the excludes notes under 998.3.)

    Secondary Diagnoses: Pregnancy delivered with morbid obesity, 649.14; Morbid obesity, 278.01; Body mass index of 45.0, V85.42; Pregnancy delivered with cardiovascular disease, 648.64; Cardiomyopathy, 425.4

    Principal Procedure: None indicated by the documentation provided

    Secondary Procedures: None indicated by the documentation provided

13. **Principal Diagnosis:** Complication, transplant, kidney, 996.81

    Secondary Diagnoses: Malignant neoplasm, transplanted organ, 199.2; Lymphoma, (kidney-solid organ) 202.80; Disease, renal, end stage, 585.6

    Principal Procedure: Removal, kidney, transplanted, 55.53

    Secondary Procedures: Hemodialysis, 39.95

14. **Principal Diagnosis:** Complication, transplant, liver, 996.82

    Secondary Diagnoses: Disease, graft-versus-host, acute, 279.51; Rash, 782.1; Diarrhea, 787.91; Ascites, 789.59

    Principal Procedure: Biopsy, skin, 86.11

    Secondary Procedures: None indicated by documentation provided

15. **First-Listed Diagnosis:** Anaphylactic reaction, peanuts, 995.61

    Secondary Diagnoses: None indicated by documentation provided

    First-Listed Procedure: None indicated by documentation provided

    Secondary Procedures: None indicated by documentation provided

Chapter 21

Supplementary Classifications—E-Codes

Note: Students were to assign only E-code(s) to each scenario.

1. **E code(s):** Fight, E960.0; Accident occurring at a stadium, E849.4; Activity status, student, E000.8; Activity, spectator at sports event, E029.1

2. **E code(s):** Shooting, stated as intentional, E955.0; Accident occurring in a garage, private home, E849.0; Activity status, specified as unemployed, E000.8

3. **E code(s):** Collision, motor vehicle and another motor vehicle, E812.0; Accident occurring on a highway, E849.5; E000.0, Activity status, civilian work done for pay

4. **E code(s):** Fall from scaffolding, E881.1; Accident occurring at an industrial place, construction site, E849.3; Activity status, civilian work done for pay, E000.0; Activity, building and construction, E016.2

5. **E code(s):** Fall from ladder, E881.0; Accident occurring on home premises, E849.0; Activity status, specified as unemployed, E000.8; Activity, other household maintenance, E013.9

6. **E code(s):** Collision, motor vehicle on highway, with bridge abutment, driver, E815.0; Accident occurring on a highway, E849.5; Activity status, student, E000.8; Activity, electronic, device, handheld (phone), E011.1

7. **E code(s):** Accident, aircraft, at landing, E840.3; Accident occurring at a public building, airport, E849.6; Activity status, specified off work, E000.8

8. **E code(s):** Cut, cutting by broken glass, E920.8; Accident occurring on a beach resort, E849.4; Activity status, specified vacation/leisure, E000.8; Activity, walking E001.0

9. **E code(s):** Accident, diving, E883.0; Accident occurring in a swimming pool, private residence, E849.0; Activity status, student, E000.8; Activity, diving, E002.1

10. **E code(s):** Shooting, inflicted by other person, stated as homicidal, hand gun, E965.0; Accident occurring on a street, E849.5; Activity status, student, E000.8

11. **E code(s):** Fall from bed; E884.4, Accident occurring in a hospital, E849.7; Activity status, specified, retired, E000.8

12. **E code(s):** Assault, stab, body part, E966; Accident occurring in a parking lot, E849.8; Activity status, specified, unemployed worker E000.8

13. **E code(s):** Cataclysmic storm, tornado; E908.1; Struck accidentally by falling tree, E916; Accident occurring on at a private home, E849.0; Activity status, specified, off work/leisure, E000.8

14. **E code(s):** Assault, burning, burns, scalding, E968.3; Abuse of child, by boyfriend of mother, E967.0; Accident occurring at a private home, E849.0; Activity status, student, E000.8; Activity, personal bathing E013.0

15. **E code(s):** Heat (exhaustion), due to manmade conditions (blast furnace,) E900.1; Accident occurring in a steel mill, E849.3; E000.0, Activity status, civilian work done for pay

16. **E code(s):** Lifting, injury, E927.8; Accident occurring at a park (public) E849.4; E000.0 Activity status, civilian work done for pay; Activity status, landscaping, E016.1

17. **E code(s):** Fall, from, heelies, E885.1; Accident occurring in a parking lot, E849.8; Activity status, student, E000.8; Activity, running, E001.1

18. **E code(s):** Fall, from, collision, in sports, E886.0; Accident occurring at a place for recreation, E849.4; Activity status, leisure, E000.8; Activity, basketball E007.6

19. **E code(s):** Fall, off, skis, E885.3; Accident occurring at a resort, E849.4; Activity status, specified, vacation/leisure, E000.8; Activity, skiing, E003.2

20. **E code(s):** Hit by, motor vehicle, public street, E814.7 (pedestrian); E849.5, Accident occurring on a street; Activity status, student, E000.8; Activity, running E001.1

Chapter 22

Late Effects

1. **First-Listed Diagnosis:** Scar, 709.2
   Secondary Diagnoses: Late effect, burn, leg, 906.7; Late effect, accident, caused by fire, E929.4
   First-Listed Procedure: None indicated by the documentation provided
   Secondary Procedures: None indicated by the documentation provided

2. **First-Listed Diagnosis:** Cervicobrachial syndrome, 723.3
   Secondary Diagnoses: Late effect, injury, nerve roots, spinal, 907.3; Late effect, motor vehicle accident, E929.0
   First-Listed Procedure: None indicated by the documentation provided
   Secondary Procedures: None indicated by the documentation provided

3. **First-Listed Diagnosis:** Late effect, cerebrovascular disease, apraxia, 438.81
   Secondary Diagnoses: Late effect, cerebrovascular disease, aphasia, 438.11; Late effect, cerebrovascular disease, facial weakness, 438.83
   First-Listed Procedure: None indicated by the documentation provided
   Secondary Procedures: None indicated by the documentation provided

4. **First-Listed Diagnosis:** Muscular wasting, 728.2
   Secondary Diagnoses: Late effect, poliomyelitis (postpolio syndrome), 138
   First-Listed Procedure: None indicated by the documentation provided
   Secondary Procedures: None indicated by the documentation provided

5. **Principal Diagnosis:** Chronic Epstein-Barr infection, 780.79
   Secondary Diagnoses: Late effect, other infectious diseases, 139.8
   Principal Procedure: None indicated by the documentation provided
   Secondary Procedures: None indicated by the documentation provided

6. **First-Listed Diagnosis:** Arthropathy associated with other infectious and parasitic diseases, 711.89
   Secondary Diagnoses: Late effect, Lyme disease, infectious and parasitic disease, 139.8
   First-Listed Procedure: None indicated by the documentation provided
   Secondary Procedures: None indicated by the documentation provided

7. **Principal Diagnosis:** Late effects, cerebrovascular disease, paralytic syndrome, affecting bilateral, 438.53
   Secondary Diagnoses: Quadriplegia, specified as due to previous stroke, 344.09
   Principal Procedure: None indicated by the documentation provided
   Secondary Procedures: None indicated by the documentation provided

8. **Principal Diagnosis:** Transient ischemic attack, 435.9
   Secondary Diagnoses: Essential hypertension, unspecified, 401.9; Late effect, cerebrovascular disease, hemiparesis, nondominant side, 438.22; Diabetes mellitus, type II, with nephropathy, 250.41; Chronic kidney disease, stage II, 585.2
   Principal Procedure: None indicated by the documentation provided
   Secondary Procedures: None indicated by the documentation provided

9. **Principal Diagnosis:** Nonunion of fracture, 733.82
   Secondary Diagnoses: Late, effect, fracture of lower extremities, 905.4; Late, effect, accidental injury, fall, E929.3
   Principal Procedure: Open reduction of fracture with internal fixation, tibia, 79.36
   Secondary Procedures: Bone graft, tibia, 78.07; Excision of bone for graft, other, 77.79

10. **Principal Diagnosis:** Traumatic arthritis, hip, 716.15
    Secondary Diagnoses: Late, effect, fracture of neck of femur, 905.3; Late, effect, motor vehicle accident, E929.0
    Principal Procedure: Total hip replacement, 81.51
    Secondary Procedures: Hip replacement bearing surface, ceramic-on-ceramic, 00.76

11. **First-Listed Diagnosis:** Late, effect, cerebrovascular disease, specified type, 438.89

   Secondary Diagnoses: Disorder, seizure, 345.90

   First-Listed Procedure: None indicated by documentation provided

   Secondary Procedures: None indicated by documentation provided

12. **First-Listed Diagnosis:** Irritability, 799.22

   Secondary Diagnoses: Impulsiveness, 799.23; Late effect, injury, intracranial, 907.0

   Principal Procedure: None indicated by documentation provided

   Secondary Procedures: None indicated by documentation provided

13. **Principal Diagnosis:** Late effect, cerebrovascular disease, specified type, 438.89

   Secondary Diagnoses: Contracture, hand, 718.44; Contracture, wrist, 718.43; Hypertension, 401.9; Bronchitis, chronic, simple, 491.0

   Principal Procedure: Transfer, tendon, hand, 82.56

   Secondary Procedures: None indicated by documentation provided

14. **Principal Diagnosis:** Failure, respiratory, chronic, 518.83

   Secondary Diagnoses: Late, effect, poisoning, 909.0; Dependence, drug, 304.90; Dependence, on, respirator/ventilator, V46.11; Status, tracheostomy, V44.0

   Principal Procedure: Ventilation, mechanical, by tracheostomy, 96.72

   Secondary Procedures: None indicated by documentation provided

15. **Principal Diagnosis:** Malunion, fracture, 733.81

   Secondary Diagnoses: Late, effect, fracture, extremity, upper, 905.2; Arteriosclerosis, coronary, 414.00; Insufficiency, renal, chronic, 585.9; Diabetes mellitus, type II, 250.00

   Principal Procedure: Reduction, fracture, humerus, open, with internal fixation, 79.31

   Secondary Procedures: Graft, bone, humerus, 78.02; Excision, bone, for graft, iliac crest, 77.79

Chapter 23

Supplementary Classifications—V Codes

1. **Principal Diagnosis:** Newborn, single liveborn, born in hospital, cesarean delivery, V30.01

   Secondary Diagnoses: Extreme immaturity, birthweight 945 grams, 765.03; Weeks of gestation, 27 weeks, 765.24; Respiratory distress syndrome, 769

   Principal Procedure: None indicated by the documentation provided

   Secondary Procedures: None indicated by the documentation provided

2. **First-Listed Diagnosis:** Follow-up examination, combined treatment (surgery and chemotherapy), V67.6

   Secondary Diagnoses: History, malignant neoplasm, bladder, V10.51; Benign prostatic hypertrophy, 600.00

   First-Listed Procedure: Cystoscopy, 57.32

   Secondary Procedures: None indicated by the documentation provided

3. **First-Listed Diagnosis:** Admission/encounter for desired sterilization, V25.2

   Secondary Diagnoses: Multiparity, V61.5

   First-Listed Procedure: Laparoscopic ligation fallopian tube with Falope ring, 66.29

   Secondary Procedures: None indicated by the documentation provided

4. **Principal Diagnosis:** Single liveborn, born in hospital, without mention of cesarean delivery, V30.00

   Secondary Diagnoses: Observation and evaluation of newborns for suspected condition not found, metabolic, V29.3

   Principal Procedure: None indicated by the documentation provided

   Secondary Procedures: None indicated by the documentation provided

5. **First-Listed Diagnosis:** Aftercare following joint replacement, V54.81

   Secondary Diagnoses: Organ or tissue replacement, joint, hip, V43.64; Long-term (current) use of anticoagulants, V58.61; Encounter for physical therapy, V57.1; Abnormality of gait, 781.2

   First-Listed Procedure: Combined physical therapy, 93.38

   Secondary Procedures: None indicated by the documentation provided

6. **Principal Diagnosis:** Newborn, single liveborn with mate liveborn, born in hospital, cesarean delivery, V31.01

   Secondary Diagnoses: Preterm infant, birthweight 1800 grams, 765.17; Weeks of gestation, 34 weeks, 765.27; Neonatal jaundice related to preterm delivery, 774.2

   Principal Procedure: Phototherapy, 99.83

   Secondary Procedures: None indicated by the documentation provided

7. **Principal Diagnosis:** Observation for suspected condition, not found, motor vehicle accident, V71.4

   Secondary Diagnoses: None indicated by the documentation provided

   Principal Procedure: None indicated by the documentation provided

   Secondary Procedures: None indicated by the documentation provided

8. **First-Listed Diagnosis:** Pregnancy with history of hydatidiform mole, V23.1

   Secondary Diagnoses: Pregnancy, supervision for, previous infertility, V23.0

   First-Listed Procedure: None indicated by the documentation provided

   Secondary Procedures: None indicated by the documentation provided

9. **First-Listed Diagnosis:** Examination, well child care, routine visit, V20.2
   Secondary Diagnoses: None indicated by the documentation provided
   First-Listed Procedure: None indicated by the documentation provided
   Secondary Procedures: None indicated by the documentation provided

10. **Principal Diagnosis:** Donor, kidney, V59.4
    Secondary Diagnoses: Allergy, history, to, latex, V15.07
    Principal Procedure: Total nephrectomy, unilateral, 55.51
    Secondary Procedures: None indicated by the documentation provided

11. **First-Listed Diagnosis:** Change of dressings, nonsurgical, both hands, V58.30
    Secondary Diagnoses: Abrasions, fingers, without infection, 915.0
    First-Listed Procedure: None indicated by the documentation provided
    Secondary Procedures: None indicated by the documentation provided

12. **First-Listed Diagnosis:** Aftercare, fracture, traumatic, pelvic, V54.19
    Secondary Diagnoses: Diabetes mellitus, type II, 250.00; Hypertriglyceridemia, 272.1; Hypertension, 401.9
    First-Listed Procedure: None indicated by the documentation provided
    Secondary Procedures: None indicated by the documentation provided

13. **Principal Diagnosis:** Fitting, device, cardiac, specified (valve), V53.39
    Secondary Diagnoses: None indicated by documentation provided_
    Principal Procedure: Replacement, heart, valve, mitral, 35.24
    Secondary Procedures: None indicated by documentation provided

14. **First-Listed Diagnosis:** Observation, suspected, specified condition, V71.89
    Secondary Diagnoses: Exposure, to, hazardous chemicals, V87.2
    Principal Procedure: None indicated by documentation provided
    Secondary Procedures: None indicated by documentation provided

15. **First-Listed Diagnosis:** Admission, for, vaccination, prophylactic, respiratory syncytial virus, V04.82
    Secondary Diagnoses: Newborn, gestational age (at birth) 29-30 completed weeks, 765.25
    First-Listed Procedure: Injection, therapeutic agent, 99.29
    Secondary Procedures: None indicated by documentation provided